Working the Phones

Wildcat: Workers' Movements and Global Capitalism

Series Editors:
Peter Alexander (University of Johannesburg)
Immanuel Ness (City University of New York)
Tim Pringle (SOAS, University of London)
Malehoko Tshoaedi (University of Pretoria)

Workers' movements are a common and recurring feature in contemporary capitalism. The same militancy that inspired the mass labour movements of the twentieth century continues to define worker struggles that proliferate throughout the world today.

For more than a century labour unions have mobilised to represent the political-economic interests of workers by uncovering the abuses of capitalism, establishing wage standards, improving oppressive working conditions, and bargaining with employers and the state. Since the 1970s, organised labour has declined in size and influence as the global power and influence of capital has expanded dramatically. The world over, existing unions are in a condition of fracture and turbulence in response to neoliberalism, financialisation and the reappearance of rapacious forms of imperialism. New and modernised unions are adapting to conditions and creating class-conscious workers' movement rooted in militancy and solidarity. Ironically, while the power of organised labour contracts, working-class militancy and resistance persists and is growing in the Global South.

Wildcat publishes ambitious and innovative works on the history and political economy of workers' movements and is a forum for debate on pivotal movements and labour struggles. The series applies a broad definition of the labour movement to include workers in and out of unions, and seeks works that examine proletarianisation and class formation; mass production; gender, affective and reproductive labour; imperialism and workers; syndicalism and independent unions, and labour and Leftist social and political movements.

Also available:

Just Work?
Migrant Workers' Struggles Today
Edited by Aziz Choudry and Mondli Hlatshwayo

Southern Insurgency:
The Coming of the Global Working Class
Immanuel Ness

The Spirit of Marikana:
The Rise of Insurgent Trade Unionism in South Africa
Luke Sinwell with Siphiwe Mbatha

Working the Phones

Control and Resistance in Call Centres

Jamie Woodcock

PlutoPress
www.plutobooks.com

First published 2017 by Pluto Press
345 Archway Road, London N6 5AA

www.plutobooks.com

Copyright © Jamie Woodcock 2017

The right of Jamie Woodcock to be identified as the author of this work
has been asserted by him in accordance with the Copyright, Designs and
Patents Act 1988.

British Library Cataloguing in Publication Data
A catalogue record for this book is available from the British Library

ISBN   978 0 7453 9908 9   Hardback
ISBN   978 0 7453 9906 5   Paperback
ISBN   978 1 7868 0014 5   PDF eBook
ISBN   978 1 7868 0016 9   Kindle eBook
ISBN   978 1 7868 0015 2   EPUB eBook

This book is printed on paper suitable for recycling and made from fully
managed and sustained forest sources. Logging, pulping and manufacturing
processes are expected to conform to the environmental standards of the
country of origin.

Typeset by Stanford DTP Services, Northampton, England

Simultaneously printed in the United Kingdom and United States of America

CONTENTS

Acknowledgements   vi

1. Introduction   1
2. Working in the Call Centre   34
3. Management   60
4. Moments of Resistance   97
5. Precarious Organisation   118
6. Conclusion   148

Notes   165
References   184
Index   194

ACKNOWLEDGEMENTS

I would like to start by thanking my partner Maev, without whose support this book could never have been completed. I am grateful too for the support of my parents. My PhD supervisors Bev Skeggs and Alberto Toscano provided encouragement and insightful feedback throughout the project, as did my examiners Gregory Schwartz and Adam Hanieh. I would also like to thank Søren Goard for the discussions throughout the project and comments on the manuscript. The process of converting the PhD research into a book was greatly supported by David Shulman and the rest of the team at Pluto. Finally, I would like to thank all of the workers I met during the research.

Jamie Woodcock

1

INTRODUCTION

The Call Centre is a television series which highlights a number of key themes that will be discussed in this book.[1] The publicity for *The Call Centre* describes it as a 'fly-on-the wall documentary series following the ups and downs of Swansea call centre CEO Nev Wilshire and his staff of extraordinary characters'. The first episode introduces the call centre with the narrator describing how 'over 1 million people now work in UK call centres with an average age of just 26. They are the factories of our time. But here at the 3rd largest call centre in Swansea the only thing being made are the cold calls we dread'. The camera pans over a familiar scene: row upon row of desks with workers speaking through headsets, supervisors at the end of each row, and whiteboards scrawled with targets. In contrast, Martin Scorsese's film *The Wolf of Wall Street*[2] might not at first glance seem to have as much to say about call centres. However, the protagonist Jordan Belfort starts working on the phones, sells penny stocks from a call centre, and his own company even starts with telesales. In particular the film highlights the sales ethos that permeates high-volume sales call centres. The documentary and the film are, of course, clearly designed for entertainment, rather than being a critical inquiry into the conditions of work. However, they illustrate a number of issues that offer insight into the experience of work and tie into the construction of negative views of call centres.

The CEO of the company, Nev Wilshire, is introduced in the first episode of *The Call Centre*. The narrator explains how Nev 'has developed a unique approach to keeping his young workforce on their toes'. The camera cuts to Nev: a man in his fifties with receding hair, wearing a suit with a loosened tie. He says: 'What sums up my management style? Hmm . . .'. The camera cuts to a shot of Nev standing on a table shouting at a worker, then to Nev leading a training session. Nev shouts: 'Are you yawning at the back? Get down!'. He then proceeds to throw a board marker at the worker in question, which hits the wall above them. The camera cuts back to Nev describing his management style, concluding that his inspiration is 'probably Napoleon . . . a dictator', followed by a shot of Nev summarily sacking a worker. Nev returns to his analogy to explain that 'his troops loved him', while the camera moves to a shot of a worker saying 'he's awful, absolutely awful', and another of a worker pretending to hang herself with the cord from a headset.³ This kind of management approach is often seen in representations of call centres in popular culture. For example, in *The Wolf of Wall Street*, when Belfort starts working on the phones, his first interaction begins with a manager telling him, 'You are lower than pond scum. You got a problem with that?' Jordan is taken over to the rows of phones as the manager explains, 'Your job is connector which means that you will be dialling the phone over five hundred times a day, trying to connect me with wealthy business owners and until you pass your series seven, that is all you're going to fucking be doing. Sit! Sit!'.⁴

The 'frontier of control' in the call centre seems firmly in the hands of management.⁵ There is, unsurprisingly, no mention of trade unions or organised struggle in the call centre. Nev's self-confessed management style not only alludes to factory despotism, but even involves an approving reference to an actual historical despot. This pop-cultural glimpse into the experience of the call centre floor provides a dim view of the potential for class struggle, offering only an opportunity for amusement. The narrator summarises this at one point as the camera pans across the office: 'With a sales floor simmering with stress, sex, and success . . . there's never a dull day when you work at this Swansea call centre.' The camera moves back to show a bland industrial park, nondescript buildings with rows of parked cars. As the shot continues back to include roundabouts and grass verges, it is easy to think that this could be anywhere in the country.

The emotional dimension of working in a call centre is on display during a scene in which Nev meets a new batch of trainees. Nev, speaking to a room of new workers, explains that 'happy people sell, miserable bastards don't. Isn't that right?! Happy people sing don't they?! It lifts your spirits. You don't sing sat on your arse, you sing standing up to project your voice'. The projector lights up with a karaoke style display and Nev signals to start: 'Ok – Mr Brightside, the Killers, C sharp! Here we go – on your feet!'. The trainees look embarrassed – both in front of the camera and at the prospect of singing – while Nev pushes on: 'Now we go for this – no messing!'. And in a mixture of different tones, abilities and levels of commitment, the music starts playing and the whole room begin to sing:

> I'm coming out of my cage / And I've been doing just fine / Gotta gotta be down / Because I want it all / It started out with a kiss / How did it all end up like this? / It was only a kiss / It was only a kiss . . .[6]

This is the first indication of the specific challenges of the indeterminacy of labour power (the difficulty faced when buying workers' time: although a capitalist may have purchased a worker's labour power by employing them, gaining the maximum benefit from this is not straightforward) in relation to the labour process in the call centre. The embarrassed workers are being forced to sing karaoke because, as Nev puts it, 'it is a challenge to motivate seven hundred people'. Again Nev's despotic management style is illustrated as he claims: 'I would sack somebody for not singing – I have sacked somebody – two people – for not singing. We have a motto here: happy people sell.' Similarly, Belfort's first taste of Wall Street involves the motivational exhortation: 'Smile and dial. And don't pick up your fucking head until 1:00.'

Emotions are used to make money in sales call centres. The hard-sell approach is enthusiastically taken up in *The Wolf of Wall Street*. Belfort loses his job on Wall Street and starts at the 'Investors' Center', a small call centre located in an office along a suburban row of shops. The products on offer are penny stocks from companies that lack the capital to be listed on the stock market. Jordan discovers that they can be bought for six cents a share and asks, 'Who buys this crap?' The supervisor answers, laughing, 'Honestly, mostly shmucks. Postmen, there's always postmen. Plumbers, um, they see our ads in the back of *Hustler*, *Popular Mechanics*, and our ads actually say they can get rich quick.' On discovering that the commission is 50 per cent, as opposed to the 1 per cent that he was making on Wall Street, Belfort decides to go for the hard sell:

Hello John, how are you doing today? You mailed in my company a postcard a few weeks back requesting information on penny stocks that had huge upside potential with very little downside risk, does that ring a bell? Ok great. The reason for the call today John is, something just came across my desk John, it is perhaps the best thing I have seen in the last six months, if you have sixty seconds I'd like to share the idea with you, you got a minute? The name of the company is Aerotyne International, it is a cutting edge, high-tech firm out of the mid-west awaiting imminent patent approval on the next generation of radar detectors that have huge military and civilian applications. Now, right now John, the stock trades over the counter at ten cents a share, and by the way John our analysts estimate it could go a heck of a lot higher than that. Your profit on a mere six thousand dollar investment would be upwards of six thousand dollars . . . exactly, you could pay off your mortgage . . . John, one thing I can promise you, even in this market, is that I never ask my clients to judge me on my winners, I ask them to judge me on my losers, because I have so few. And in the case of Aerotyne, based on every technical factor out there, John, we are looking at a grand slam home run . . . Four thousand? That would be forty thousand shares, John. Let me lock in that trade right now and get back to you with my secretary with an exact confirmation, sound good, John? Great, hey, John, thank you for your vote of confidence and welcome to the Investors' Center. Bye-bye.[7]

Belfort wows the other workers by making this sale seemingly through the force of his own personality. All the aspects recommended by trainers at call centres are present: emphasis of key words, use of the customer's first name, questions to keep them engaged, gesticulating to improve delivery, persistence on closing the sale and instrumental use of emotions. Later in the film Belfort explains to workers before a shift:

So you listen to me and you listen well. Are you behind on your credit card bills? Good, pick up the phone and start dialling! Is your landlord ready to evict you? Good! Pick up the phone and start dialling! Does your girlfriend think you're a fucking worthless loser? Good! Pick up the phone and start dialling! I want you to deal with your problems by becoming rich![8]

This highlights the individualist subjectivity of sales, the responsibility of the worker to close the sale, and in doing so get rich and solve their own problems.

The Call Centre also focuses on a high volume sales operation. The narrator explains how 'Nev's sales team makes roughly one and half million unsolicited calls a year, with each agent making up to two hundred calls per day'. The camera focuses on one particular example, a phone call that will be familiar to many: 'Just a quick call, it's in regards to a refund you may be entitled to now for payment protection insurance . . .' As the narration continues to explain against a backdrop of unsuccessful calls, 'the most effective way to guard against the barrage of cold calls that many of us hate is to register with the telephone preference service'. However, Nev has a different view on this: 'Well, anyone has got the right to register with telephone preference services. And we would totally respect, but, er, why would they?' He continues, pointing out that 'they'd miss out on our wonderful range of money saving opportunities and products that can enhance their living and they'd miss out on speaking to chicken head'.[9] The worker in question – given the nickname 'chicken head' by Nev – explains his experience of rejection on the phone: 'I think it's quite funny when they hang up. I had an old lady once saying that [she] hope[s] I die and [she] hope[s] I get killed and that.' But despite the amusement of this worker, or Nev's insistence on the wonderful service the call centre offers, the regulators took a different view. After the programme was aired, the Information Commissioner's Office (ICO) fined the company £225,000 for more than 2,700 different complaints they had received. The director of the ICO pointed out that 'while the activities of Nev and his call centre employees have provided entertainment for many, they hide a bigger problem within the cold calling industry'.[10]

These examples illustrate a number of points: first, that the action of the worker – rather than the customer – is decisive in making a sale; second, that the drive for profit in some call centre operations breaches norms about social behaviour – and sometimes even the law; and third, that sales calls penetrate into the daily lives of many people. This is a theme that we will return to a number of times, a negative experience of a labour process – both for the worker and the customer – that does not provide a social benefit, and therefore complicates the struggle for control at work.

The other side of the over-observed call-centre worker is the customer who is calling or being called. Mark Fisher argues that 'the closest that most of us come to a direct experience of the centrelessness of capitalism is an encounter with the call centre'.[11] The gaze of managers, corporations and the state is one-way. Trying to find out information or resolve a problem requires plummeting into

the crazed Kafkaesque labyrinth of call centres, a world without memory, where cause and effect connect together in mysterious, unfathomable ways, where it is a miracle that anything happens, and you lose hope of ever passing back over to the other side, where things seem to function smoothly . . . the repeating of the same dreary details many times to poorly trained and badly informed operatives, the building rage that must remain impotent because it can have no legitimate object, since – as is very quickly clear to the caller – there is no-one who knows, and no-one who could do anything even if they could.[12]

Fisher draws on Franz Kafka's novel *The Castle* which details K's struggle to gain access to the bureaucratic authorities. In one passage Kafka describes K's encounter with the telephone system in the castle:

There is no specific telephone connection with the castle, no exchange that puts our calls through; when you call someone in the castle from here, it rings on all the telephones in the lowest departments there, or rather it would ring on all of them were it not for the fact, which I know for certain, that on nearly all of them the bell is switched off. Every so often, though, an overtired official feels the need for a little distraction – particularly in the evening or at night – switches the bell on, then we get an answer, except it's just a joke. And that's very understandable, after all. Who has any right to ring in about his private little troubles in the middle of the most important jobs, which are invariably being done in a tearing hurry.[13]

These prophetic lines seem to capture the experience of dealing with a modern call centre. The confusing and often frustrating experience is one more akin to engaging with a 'decentralized, market Stalinist bureaucracy' than 'a central authority'. The term 'Kafkaesque', often used to characterise totalitarianism, is resonant in this circumstance.[14]

At the call centre where I was an employee, the workers were able to understand this frustration in two ways. They felt the power of the management gaze constantly. The fear of a recorded conversation coming back to haunt a worker – or worse deny them of their monthly bonus – kept behaviour in check. The gaze was not fleeting as digital recording meant every encounter with a customer would be stored away, able to be recalled at a moment's notice. There was no way that all the calls could be listened into, but the presence of supervisors on the call-centre floor could be used to direct further attention onto particular recordings. In one instance I spoke with a group of workers about receiving unsolicited calls from call centres. All of us had been called from withheld numbers and told that we could be entitled to a Payment Protection Insurance refund. The conversation involved angry responses from workers about the intrusion of these phone calls: 'How did they get my number?', 'Why do they always ring at the worst time?', 'I always ask for my number to be taken off, but I still get called!'. The anger that the person feels 'can only be a matter of venting', as Fisher argues, 'it is aggression in a vacuum, directed at someone who is a fellow victim of the system but with whom there is no possibility of communality'.[15] Even inside the call centre, moments before starting a shift of calling people who mostly do not want to be bothered, it is difficult to feel sympathy or identification with the disembodied voice on the other end of the phone.

It is this context that makes call-centre work particularly worthy of investigation. It is held in low regard by many, both as a job and as a phenomenon encountered from the outside. As a form of employment it is gendered and considered unskilled, with poor conditions and low pay, while lacking formal union organisation.[16] This helps to explain the widespread rejection of work in call centres, something well understood by managers when trying to motivate workers before each shift. There is also the pressure of having to perform emotional labour to meet targets, while additionally being expected to genuinely enjoy the experience. The issue of performance is difficult for management as it is not clear how to identify the elusive qualities that make a successful sales call. At one point in *The Call Centre* a young Welsh woman explains that she has 'to put a phone voice on the way I speak', and dropping her Welsh accent she enunciates in a blander tone: 'Phone, Don't, Calling . . . so I change my voice completely when I go on the phones.' Yet, as the narrator points out, 'Sometimes even a posh voice isn't enough to bag a sale', and the woman is shown getting cut off on the phone a number of times.[17]

We see the workers finish the song during the training session: 'Open up my eager eyes/'cause I'm Mr Brightside.' A satisfied Nev justifies this approach by explaining that 'there are a lot of unhappy people and it's my duty to get their heads up – to get them a bit enthusiastic – to get things back in perspective'. Yet, as the narrator explains, his 'passion for keeping his workforce happy doesn't stop at their professional life, it extends into their private life too'. In an astonishing scene – and it is important to note that some of this might be a performance for the camera – Nev approaches a downtrodden looking worker. He explains to her that: 'Bottom line, you've been a miserable bastard for the past couple of days.' Her relationship has recently ended and she explains that she was cheated on and that her attitude at work is 'not my fault, but yes'. Nev explains to her how she's 'going to get your happy head on. You're going to accept the boot up the arse that I'm going to give you'. He proceeds to take her around the office, telling her: 'shoulders back, tuck your arse in, let's go!' As they walk through the office Nev shouts, 'Any single blokes here? I've got a desperate female . . . Any single blokes need a hug . . . want a date?' Yet the woman seems unable to protest, simply saying, 'I can't believe you're doing this'. The management of workers in this call centre extends from the labour process into their lives; not only in the call centre but also outside of work, as, bizarrely, Nev arranges a speed dating evening for his workers too.

The wage paid to a worker denies them the full and independent use of all their emotions and affective abilities during working hours. The notion of traditional labour is therefore extended, with the new demand to align affects with profit. As *The Wolf of Wall Street*'s Jordan Belfort reflects after his stint at the Investors' Center, 'I was selling garbage to garbage men and making money hand over fist'. Despite the low quality of the product, he uses his confidence and charisma to manipulate the emotions of potential buyers in particular ways to close the sales. Despite Belfort's overwhelming self-confidence, there is no single recipe for how workers can successfully perform these affective dimensions of the labour process. While the standardisation of scripting and the application of technology to the calling process follow in the footsteps of Taylorism, the affective dimension can create problems for management. Taylor and Bain identify the contradiction between the quantitative and qualitative dimensions of the labour process – in terms of the number of sales and the quality of the phone calls – that cannot be resolved, creating 'an assembly-line in the head' for the worker.[18]

The managerial problem of retention of call-centre workers is another important theme that we will return to throughout the book. Nev's company runs a recruitment drive with a local radio station to encourage interest. This leads to a unique process that sees Nev once again in his element. The camera cuts to a shot of Nev walking through the call centre with an applicant in tow. He barks out across the call-centre floor: 'Good looking Welsh girl coming through, can she have a job?' A number of workers respond by shouting 'Yeah!', with one leering over and saying, 'There's a seat right here for her'. The parade continues with Nev asking her, 'Do you fancy this team?' Nev introduces her to a team leader. He asks 'How old are you?', she responds 'eighteen', 'What's your name?', 'Charlotte'. He shakes her hand and replies 'My name is Steve, nice to meet you. Don't worry about him [Nev], he's just trying to, er, assess your confidence levels by walking you up and down'. This overtly sexist behaviour is met with a splutter of nervous laughter. Nev interjects, '. . . and to see if any of the boys fancy you'. As if to signal the lack of options for a worker in this position, the team leader awkwardly asks, 'Where's HR [Human Resources]?'.

There is no mention of a trade union or any hint of collective organisation in *The Call Centre*. Instead, HR is identified as the force restraining the management style of Nev. In his words, 'The HR department, they don't sometimes despair of me, they totally despair of me. They're trying to do their job, trying to cover my arse [laughter], bless their hearts'. The camera moves back to Charlotte, the job applicant. Nev asks her, 'Fancy working here? Bunch of nutters, ain't they?'. Charlotte responds that she would 'fit in', and Nev offers her the job. In another gem of managerial knowledge, Nev explains, 'As easy as that, you know, they go through all this interview process, when all they've got to do is walk up and down the sales floor asking if she can have a job'.

The camera then focuses on an awkward moment between Nev and Charlotte. 'You OK?', he asks, to which she responds, almost too quickly, 'Yeah, I'm fine'. In a moment reminiscent of *The Office*, Nev then tells her to leave, and starts loudly shouting 'Go on, get out!' The young woman looks caught in the headlights. 'This is torture', she mutters. Following this, Charlotte talks to the camera: 'Oh, what a character [laughter], that's all I can say really. Such a character. Yeah, he's a great guy. Seems pretty cool . . . unless it carries on.' The camera lingers for a few seconds, although it feels a lot longer, before moving on to more scenes of Nev repeating his behaviour.

The Call Centre and *The Wolf of Wall Street* are clearly intended as entertainment. They construct a perspective on call-centre work that is for popular consumption. In this process, however, they reveal certain structures of power. The workers in *The Call Centre* have little or no power in the workplace and outside of it are exploited as figures of amusement. The presentation of the call-centre floor is problematic; it displays not only the work performance but also performance for the TV cameras. It is a representation created to fit into the particular expectations of reality TV. There is no glimpse of resistance; hardly surprising, given it would be captured on camera. It is not clear what the day-to-day experience of working in the Swansea call centre is really like. However, the performances that the individuals choose to make are interesting. Nev appears proud of his management style, going on at length to explain and justify it. If this is the call centre that a manager and the producers want the outside world to see, one wonders about the footage that did not make the final cut.[19] It would have been interesting to have further insight into the motivations behind the production, It is a rare representation of call-centre work, a major form of work in the economy, stripped back and reduced to comedy performances. Meanwhile, *The Wolf of Wall Street* captures the top-seller type of dynamic that call centres try to promote: if you sell hard enough you will be successful. Nevertheless, they both illustrate a number of key points and provide the first glimpses of what we will later explore.

WHERE DID CALL CENTRES COME FROM?

Call Centers for Dummies claims to be 'a road map that can help you lead and manage a call centre.'[20] The authors 'make some assumptions' about who is reading the book and suggests that they might be 'a hotshot MBA tracking through your career, and you find yourself running a call center,'[21] which is perhaps ironic considering the title of the book. The authors themselves are quite vague about the history of call centres, writing, 'although we can't really tell you when the first call center opened, we imagine that call centers started around the time that the telephone became a common household device . . . the evolution of call centers just makes sense.'[22]

This common sense point about the development of call centres is useful; however, as with many phenomena, it is important to go beyond the conclusion that something happened because it 'just makes sense'. A logical starting point is the invention of the telephone. The telephone is one of a number of technologies – alongside the automobile, the television, the computer and so on – that have had a far-reaching social impact on modern society. Claude S. Fischer argues that the telephone 'captures most cleanly the magnification of social contact'.[23] However, as with other examples of modern technology, there is a danger of falling into technological determinism, particular in a context of advertising and media hype. Technology is not neutral and it emerges in particular social contexts. As Marx and Engels argued, 'it would be possible to write quite a history of inventions, made since 1830, for the sole purpose of supplying capital with weapons against the revolts of the working class'. However, they also argued that workers' struggle can be

> helped on by the improved means of communication that are created by modern industry, and that place the workers of different localities in contact with one another. It was just this contact that was needed to centralise the numerous local struggles, all of the same character, into one national struggle between classes. But every class struggle is a political struggle. And that union, to attain which the burghers of the Middle Ages, with their miserable highways, required centuries, the modern proletarian, thanks to railways, achieve in a few years.[24]

Railways would have seemed revolutionary at the time they were writing, and modernity is furnished with many more recent examples: broadband and wireless internet, instant messaging, social media and so on. There are innumerable possibilities in technology, yet many of them are not realised under capitalism. This is true not only of what kinds of technology are invented, but also of how technology is utilised. Or, to put it in more specific terms:

telephony, of course, has its serious frustrations. Aside from annoyances, such as sales people and abusive callers; aside from problems of service, pricing, and equity; and aside from the harassment some people feel from receiving too many calls – a key drawback of the home telephone is that very same expanded sociability. To have access to others means that they have access to you, like it or not. Increased sociability can be a mixed blessing.[25]

Call centres can clearly be seen as part of that mixed blessing. The introduction of the Automatic Call Distributor (ACD) by Rockwell International in the mid-1970s was 'one of the most significant advancements' in the story of their development. Before this, 'airlines and major retailers used *phone rooms* – the precursors of call centers'. The ACD made 'large, centralized call centers practical and efficient by providing a way to distribute large numbers of incoming phone calls evenly to a pool of call center staff'.[26] This allowed the further application of information networking technology, which Phil Taylor and Peter Bain argue has led to call centres becoming characterised by the 'integration' of telephone and computer technologies.[27] This involves a shift from individual workers manually dialling phone numbers to outgoing calls being automatically dialled and connected, with incoming calls queued and distributed, vastly increasing the volume of calls that can be handled. It is this integration of computers and telephones which opens up the potential for detailed supervision and data collection.

OPPORTUNITIES FOR CAPITAL

The introduction of new methods of communication like the telephone provides important opportunities for capitalists. The combination of telephones and computers in the call centre allows the reconfiguration of different labour processes into concentrated sites. These include customer services, technical support and information, and sales. It would be 'inexplicable' that call centres proliferated as an organisational form from the 1980s 'without reference to the broader political and economic environment of neo-liberalism, deregulation, restructuring and the financialisation of markets'. This process began in the 1980s with the move towards the dismantling of the state monopoly over telecommunications, marked in 1984 by the privatisation of British Telecom in the UK. This was 'indicative of a trend to de-regulation which accelerated in the 1990s'.[28] The continuation of this process into further public utilities in the 1980s saw increasing areas becoming subjected to the pressures of competition.[29] It is therefore necessary to understand that, as Ellis and Taylor argue:

> The explosive growth of the call centre is as much the product of political economic factors; the impact of the policies of deregulation and privatisation, restructuring at the levels of industry and/or firm, the intensification of economy-wide and sectoral competitive pressure, the growth of the 'new economy', and underpinning everything the compulsion to maximise profits and reduce costs.[30]

The 1986 Financial Services and Building Society Acts accelerated the changes taking place. This meant the 'inter-penetration of the hitherto discrete markets' of banking, insurance and financial services,[31] which led to an increasing level of competition between firms tied up with the continuing advancements of technology. From the 1990s onwards there was 'a rush to catch-up with these patently successful innovators and to capitalise on the demonstrable cost-cutting and profit-maximising opportunities offered by the call centre'. The 'emulation took place not just in financial services',[32] but across the economy in sectors like communication, retail, entertainment and travel. The finance and telecommunications sectors appeared to have produced a 'lean, efficient and profitable model of customer contact', and for companies under the pressure of competition in other sectors, its 'attractions seemed irresistible'.[33] From the mid-1990s the 'most dynamic area of growth in white-collar employment internationally has been in call centres'.[34]

The drive for profitability spurred companies to innovate new methods and technologies to create call centres in the form they are found in today. Those companies that first adopt new methods 'gain competitive advantage' through technological innovation and greater profits, although this diminishes as others imitate. This signals the beginning of a new phase of competition as the new 'work system' is used 'more intensively'. It is therefore useful to consider that 'the introduction of the call centre does not constitute an end point but part of a process that can not be abstracted from the dynamic of capitalist accumulation'.[35]

Call centres that make sales are vital in this process of capital accumulation. As Marx argues in *Capital*, 'commodities cannot themselves go to market and perform exchanges in their own right'.[36] The need for communication in this process is not limited to the production of commodities themselves – although of course it is deployed in various ways to expedite the productive process. The role of communication comes to the fore in the transportation and sale of commodities.

In addition to the sites and networks established for the production and distribution of commodities, there need to be ways of selling them to consumers in order to realise their value. As Marx argued, the process of exchange requires that money is exchanged for a commodity, but prior to the exchange 'that money, however, is in someone else's pocket. To allow it to be drawn out, the commodity produced by its owner's labour must above all be a use-value for the owner of the money'.[37] In order to overcome this simple problem there has been the growth of complex marketing industries and increasingly novel ways of convincing people to part with their money. Commodities can be sold directly to consumers or to some other capitalist venture which can then sell them on. There are a number of problems to be overcome in this process: the first is how to make the potential customer aware that the commodity exists, convince them that they want to purchase it, and finally exchange it for payment. This is the role that call centres increasingly play. It is 'no longer obligatory to situate the loci of servicing in close proximity to customers', so 'economies of scale can be realised through the concentration of functions that would otherwise be decentralised'.[38] This can drive down costs, whether the call centre becomes the only outlet for selling commodities, or in addition to other means.

SALES CALL CENTRES

Call centres have emerged across industries, rather than as an industry in itself. Miriam Glucksmann provides five different categories of call centres based on 'the nature of the transaction undertaken'. Of the five variations, the first three do not relate to the call centre that will be our focus: 1) call centres that provide information to callers; 2) call centres that generally relate to the provision and repair of utilities or services like car breakdown assistance; 3) call centres that act as emergency services and helplines.[39]

The two that are more relevant here are those that sell goods and products or those that sell services. First, the call centres that sell goods and products involve processes that are closely linked to the supply chain of an organisation. Preceding the phone call, or even triggered by it, is the production process involved in creating the commodity and storing it until sale, then the various advertising and marketing schemes. Following the call the commodity must be distributed and delivered to the customer. The actual good or product being sold varies but the call centre worker is required to complete a sale with the customer. The development of this type of call centre is a variation on the sales assistant in a shop, now not limited to a single shop or dependent on waiting for customers to visit. The process therefore involves not only taking the order, payment details and forwarding on the information for delivery, but also answering questions about the product and in some cases the deployment of sales techniques.[40] The expansion of telesales in turn has an effect on the overall structure of organisations. The logistical side of the operation increases in importance and complexity, as the goods are no longer bought in-store. The product catalogues, whether online or offline, also increase in importance, which has implications for advertising and marketing.[41]

The second category of call centres most relevant here is those that sell services. There are a number of different services that can be sold, from financial, banking, insurance, transport, hiring, holidays or even tickets for events. There is a similar connection with the supply chain to that in the previous example, with differences of provision versus production and delivery versus consumption. While the supply chain of services tends to be more complex than the production of commodities, the call-centre worker remains the point of contact trying to complete a sale with the customer. This type of call centre has become a particular target for outsourcing, so much so 'that a considerable proportion of call operators are employed by stand-alone outsourced companies rather than directly by the company whose services they are selling'.[42]

The role of call centres also needs to be considered from the specific perspective of capital. Within sales call centres there is a concentration and combination of various preceding labour processes. It is now possible to 'buy a computer from a company that doesn't have a retail store, for example, or do your banking from a company that doesn't have physical branches'.[43] This reduces the geographical problem of reaching customers to close a sale and greatly increases the number of potential customers that can be contacted. The material products still need to be delivered to customers, and the impact of the growth of call centres has had an effect on the organisation of distribution and logistics. Regardless of what commodity is being sold – whether vacuum cleaners, broadband subscriptions or insurance – the task of the call-centre worker is to convince the people they are calling to complete the purchase. If the call centre is in-house, the intention is to find new ways to reach customers and increase sales. It is a result of the pressure to increase profitability; a desperate search to realise even more value through exchange.

In sales call centres, particularly those engaged in cold calling, it is relatively easy to calculate the performance of each worker. The computer-enabled telephone system can log each sale and note how long is taken between calls. The extraction of surplus value in the labour process is far more straightforward than in the other types of call centre. This is significant as the worker in cold-calling sales faces sharper pressures and is susceptible to the more aggressive forms of surveillance and control. However, the innovations that are tested and developed in the sales call centres are likely to be adopted in other call centres too over time due to the general competitive pressures to reduce costs.

GLOBAL CALL CENTRES AND OUTSOURCING

The growth of call centres has been 'instrumental in the disappearance or decline of some occupations, it is also associated with the growth of others and with the emergence of entirely new ones'.[44] In particular, Glucksmann identifies the occupations of warehousing and distribution as particular targets that have undergone significant transformations. There are also global implications for the divisions of labour involved in the development of call centres.

The phenomenon of outsourcing or off-shoring is often associated with call centres. In part this is because it is immediately visible – or perhaps it would be more appropriate to say audible – in popular culture and in most people's day-to-day lives. There is the common stereotype of British call centres being outsourced to India, or in Western countries similar shifts to preferred cheaper locations.[45] However, in addition to the physical relocation of call-centre operations, 'firms routinely reroute calls from UK to Indian centres when UK operators are busy, at night or weekends, or when overtime rates apply at home'.[46] This process is not only 'organizational' but also 'spatial' as call centres can be relocated to different parts of the world. This involves 'industrial and organizational divisions of labour' which 'enmesh with global divisions of uneven development'.[47] The trend of relocating call centres to India 'should be regarded as an extension, however dramatic, of the spatial dynamic that is inherent in the call centre project'.[48]

The sector 'looks quite similar across countries in terms of its markets, service offerings, and organisational features'. The most notable trend is that 'call centres have experienced phenomenal growth in virtually every country around the world'.[49] The idea that call centres are the 'new factories' is misleading in terms of their spatial distribution, because the spread of call centres is 'different from that found in manufacturing . . . while call centres are geographically mobile, their spread is quite uneven, shaped particularly by language and culture'.[50] The international relationships are less varied than those involved with the production of commodities and the linguistic demand highlights the continuing importance of imperialism. Therefore, despite the fact call centres are often viewed 'as a paradigmatic case of the globalisation of service work', the report found that the 'workplaces take on the character of their own countries and regions, based on distinct laws, customs, institutions, and norms. The "globalisation" of call centre activities has a remarkably national face'.[51]

The call centres that are organised internationally along linguistic lines (which themselves trace the history of imperialism) involve additional pressures. As Kiran Mirchandani has argued in a study of Indian call-centre workers, this form of transnational customer service work involves further complexities in terms of identity and race. The workers have to perform to their Western clients, engaging in 'authenticity work', in addition to the affective performances required from workers in the UK.[52]

Holman et al. attempt to understand job quality in call centres across the world. They measured job quality with two dimensions: 'the extent of discretion at work' and 'the intensity of performance monitoring'. These both relate to the questions of control at work, the first about the level of autonomy that the worker retains in the labour process, and the second is to do with the level of managerial control. In call centres the prevalence of scripting and computerised surveillance means that many jobs are susceptible to low scores in both dimensions. To develop the analysis across different countries job discretion was divided into: 'low to very low', 'moderate' and 'high to very high', while monitoring was divided into 'low' (less than monthly), 'moderate' (monthly to once a week), and 'high' (more than once a week to daily).[53] On this basis it is possible to compare job quality internationally. The report found when considering the two variables only 2 per cent of workers had very high-quality jobs. There were 12 per cent of workers in high to very high-quality jobs. The largest proportion was 67 per cent of workers in low to very low-quality jobs, while 36 per cent worked in very low-quality jobs.[54] What this shows is that a large proportion of workers face poor conditions at work, yet there are small groups of workers that have a very different experience of call-centre work.

IN THE UK

Many of these features are reproduced in the UK context. The ubiquitous use of surveillance technology has resulted in similarities across different countries in the way that the labour process is supervised and controlled. When trying to examine the UK in particular, it is difficult to ascertain overall figures. Call centres have been integrated into a wide variety of different industries, so the total number of workers can become obscured as they become aggregated into other categories. For example, the Office for National Statistics labour force survey has at least five different categories that could directly include call-centre workers, a number of categories that particular kinds of call-centre work could fall into, and also an additional category for 'not elsewhere classified'.[55] This problem has been noted by Miriam Glucksmann who cites how 'official occupation classifications' are 'too aggregated', but also 'exacerbated by such rapid change that categories are likely to be out of date or unable to keep pace with reality'.[56] A total figure can be found with research conducted by the trade union UNISON which claims that there are as many as one million workers employed in 5,000 call centres in the UK.[57] Despite problems of accuracy, this means that call-centre work has grown to become a significant portion of overall employment in the UK.

It is possible to gain some general insights into the conditions of call-centre work in the UK. In 2012 the wage for an entry-level call advisor in the lowest quartile is £13,200 per year (it should be noted that part-time workers would of course earn less annually). Team leaders – the first tier of supervisors – can earn up to £28,000 per year and team managers – the second tier of supervisors – can earn up to £34,000. Earnings can increase up to £78,000 per year for senior call-centre managers.[58] Therefore the wage differential means that a senior call-centre manager can earn six times the basic wage of one full-time equivalent, whilst supervisors earn between two and two-and-a-half times. The pay differential increases vastly in the South East, with an entry-level agent/advisor earning £12,000 per year, while an Operations

Manager can earn up to £102,500, over eight-and-a-half times as much.[59] There is widespread use of rewards for individual performance, with 90 per cent of companies reporting that they operated a bonus scheme. The use of bonuses was most likely in the private sector, with bonuses in the public services and not-for-profit organisations being comparatively 'rare'.[60]

The issue of casualisation is signalled by the problems of worker retention. Although it was reported as 'not a problem' by 68.5 per cent of companies, falling to 60 per cent in London, suggesting that 'the current economic climate could be playing a part here as high levels of unemployment could factor into call centre employees' decision to stay in their roles'.[61] The average staff turnover was 19 per cent, with ranges from 0 to 68 per cent, but this excludes agency staff. In London specifically, the average rose to 28 per cent. Even with the removal of the temporary agency staff in some cases the permanent staff turnover could reach very high levels. In an insightful moment the report details some of the responses that companies have introduced to deal with retention. The most common was 'better internal career development opportunities', but additionally others cited 'team involvement in department', 'less stressful environment', 'revised absence management', and 'recruit[ing] suitable people'. The list of responses indicates a number of grievances that could trigger workers leaving a call centre. In particular the question of absence management is important as it is tied to that of turnover: going absent without permission is leaving the job temporarily; 55 per cent of companies reported that absence is a 'moderate concern', 16 per cent 'said they thought absence is a major concern', with only 29 per cent stating that it is 'not a problem'.[62] In another interesting admission the companies reported thirty-four different responses to try and deal with absence problems. The rejection of work therefore appears to be a common phenomenon in call centres and is a theme that we will return to throughout the book.

The authors of *Call Centers for Dummies* admit that 'not everyone thinks that call center changes and evolution are positive'.[63] They locate this in part due to 'the impact of call centers on everyone's daily lives, and partly because some call centers had bad management and used bad business practices'. The workers in call centres are completely absent from their analysis; instead they focus on how call centres 'have raised the ire of consumers and caught the attention of legislators', something they blame on 'overly aggressive business practices'. This is quite a revealing phrase, suggesting that if managers had relied on regular forms of aggressive business practices, call centres would be seen in a more positive light. The prevalence of these practices in the UK was highlighted in an undercover exposé at GoGen (a charity fundraising call centre) which found that workers were 'told to be "brutal" and "ferocious" and that no one has an excuse not to give, even the poor or elderly'.[64]

A WORKERS' INQUIRY

This book involves an inquiry into an actual call-centre workplace and the experience of work. There has been a long history of different attempts to study workplaces, involving the 'primary material of academic researchers, first-hand accounts marshalled by journalists and autobiographical testimonies of workers themselves'.[65] From the 1970s there were a number of critical studies that sought to understand the workplace.[66] However, more recently – and particularly in academia – it has become far less popular to study work itself. This is somewhat baffling as work remains one of our main activities and therefore the questions of how, why, when and with whom we work are crucial for understanding society. What follows is a brief discussion of the methodological tradition that this book draws upon for the workplace study that follows, focusing on the different moments of workers' inquiries.[67]

Origins of a method

The theoretical inspiration for this project begins with the work of Karl Marx in *Capital*, in particular the chapter on the working day. It documents the conditions of workers in factories in the nineteenth century, and focuses on 'the establishment of a norm for the working day presents itself as a struggle over the limits of that day, a struggle between collective capital, i.e. the class of capitalists, and collective labour, i.e. the working class'.[68] Marx 'would not have been able to write this Chapter without the abundant information' supplied by the bourgeois factory inspectors.[69] This is evident in Marx's comments, like 'the "ruthless" factory inspector Leonard Horner was again on the spot' and that 'his services to the English working class will never be forgotten'.[70] The inspectors highlighted the process of exploitation in which the working day is extended by capitalists through a variety of means; however, their starting point was to treat workers in the same way that the quality of soil was important for agriculture. The use of these reports allowed Marx insights into the conditions of workers, but without drawing on their experiences directly, and is therefore more of a non-worker workers' inquiry.

What we find in Marx is the starting point for an inquiry, but one which also includes important further considerations. However, it is necessary to draw attention to what Michael Lebowitz has called the 'silence of *Capital*'.[71] This silence exists because *Capital* is fundamentally an attempt to explain the 'logic of capital but not the logic of wage-labour'. The subject of *Capital*, as the name perhaps implies, is capital – rather than workers. In order to re-emphasise the role of the worker in this argument it is necessary to focus on an 'examination of workers' actual struggles: their content, how they have developed, and where they are headed'.[72] We therefore have to move beyond *Capital*, and in effect, speak to the silences.

A direction for this is signalled in Marx's own call for a workers' inquiry published in a newspaper in France in 1880. Although it achieved some circulation at the time, it remained relatively unknown for fifty years. In the introduction to the survey Marx outlines the aim of the inquiry:

We hope to meet in this work with the support of all workers in town and country who understand that they alone can describe with full knowledge the misfortunes from which they suffer, and that only they, and not saviors sent by Providence, can energetically apply the healing remedies for the social ills to which they are a prey.[73]

This introduction clearly spells out the aim of the inquiry: understanding the exploitation of workers from their own perspective. Marx continues to argue that those conducting such surveys 'must wish for an exact and positive knowledge of the conditions in which the working class – the class to whom the future belongs – works and moves'. For Marx the postal survey was also intended as a method to make contact with workers. He states that 'it is not essential to reply to every question', and emphasises that 'the name and address should be given so that if necessary we can send communication'.[74] Workers are not being considered as passive subjects to be researched; instead they are being positioned as the only people who can describe their own conditions, and as the only ones who can transform them. This attempt to uncover the actual experience of workers and their struggles was a novel step. There are similarities with radical re-readings of history from below,[75] subaltern studies,[76] or the tracing of the history of women's oppression.[77] These insights provide examples of other ways in which the silences – whether of the oppressed, exploited or both – can be spoken to, drawing much-needed attention to their self-activity.

While there are no records of the result of Marx's survey, it remains an important first step. It is difficult to build any forms of organisation without an adequate knowledge of the conditions of those affected, thus knowledge production is already implicit in building workers' organisation. What is novel about this outline for a workers' inquiry is that it is laid out in a formal manner. As Asad Haider and Salar Mohandesi argue, Marx 'established a fundamental epistemological challenge' with the short introduction to the inquiry. What is less clear is the nature of the 'relationship between the workers' knowledge of their exploitation, and the scientific analysis of the "laws of motion" of capitalist society' found in *Capital*.[78] The workers' inquiry received little attention for almost seventy years after Marx first posed this 'challenge'.

The revival of interest

Within the Trotskyist movement there emerged attempts to grapple with the impact of Taylorism, the emergence of Fordism and the now somewhat archaic debate on Stalinist Russia. These alternative positions led to splits from the Fourth International between 1948 and 1951 and the creation of three new independent groups. The first group was the Johnson-Forest Tendency in the USA, taking the pen names of C. L. R. James and Raya Dunayevskaya. The second was the Chaulieu-Montal Tendency in France, with the pen names of Cornelius Castoriadis and Claude Lefort, that became *Socialisme ou Barbarie*. The third was the International Socialists in Britain – which did not solidify into a group until later on – led by a Palestinian Jew called Ygael Gluckstein, also known as Tony Cliff. The groups maintained regular contact with each other, with Castoriadis and Dunayevskaya working together into the 1960s.[79]

The new analysis of the Johnson-Forest Tendency was an attempt to reclaim Marxism, not just from a potentially one-sided reading of *Capital*, but also from what they saw as the distortions of Stalinism.[80] This 'grew out of studies and contacts with factory workers' and 'was the hallmark of the political tendency'.[81] This perspective can be found for example in *The American Worker*, which aimed to document the conditions and experience of rank-and-file workers in an American car factory.[82] It is a two-part study: the first part is a workers' inquiry written by Paul Romano, who worked in the car factory; the second part contains the theoretical analysis, written under a pen name by Grace Lee Boggs. Romano worked in a car plant during the research for the study and describes how he had spent most of his life in various industries of mass production amongst many other workers. Romano was very much an insider, arguing that, in terms of the workers, 'their feelings, anxieties, exhilaration, boredom, exhaustion, anger, have all been mine to one extent or another'.[83] Grace Lee Boggs argues that the strength of Romano's account lies in fact that 'never for a single moment' does it allow the reader to 'forget that the contradictions in the process of production make life an agony of toil for the worker, be his payment high or low'.

The method set out in *The American Worker* became a format for a political intervention. There were further inquiries: *Indignant Heart: A Black Worker's Journal*,[84] focusing on the journey of a black worker from the American south to militancy in car factories, and *A Women's Place*,[85] on housework, reproductive labour and women's struggle. There were also examples like *Punching Out*[86] and *Union Committeemen and Wildcat Strikes*,[87] which detailed the struggles of workers against both their management and the union bureaucracy. These inquiries documented the experience of workers and the oppressed in a particular form. As Haider and Mohandesi point out, this development opened up Marx's call for an inquiry to allow 'workers to raise their own unique voice, express themselves in their own language' rather than responding to formulaic, closed questionnaires.[88] The group 'relied heavily on what Dunayevskaya terms the "full fountain pen" method of writing'. This method 'involved having members of the group interview workers and then allowing these workers to edit their comments for publication'.[89] (This does complicate the original intentions as the 'openness of the narrative form exaggerates a tendency to slip from measured generalization to untenable overgeneralization'.) The importance of the contribution made by the Johnson-Forest Tendency is the insistence of focusing on the self-activity of workers. Although the narrative approach has limitations for the generalisation of particular findings, it provides a compelling attempt to speak to the silences of *Capital*.

The second group, *Socialisme ou Barbarie*, also broke away from the Fourth International, proposing that Russia had become a form of 'bureaucratic capitalism'.[90] They took inspiration from *The American Worker* and reprinted it in the first issue of *Socialisme ou Barbarie*.[91] Like those in the Johnson-Forest Tendency, they were interested in understanding how the 'new structure of the labour process' was leaving 'its mark on the daily life and the conscious-ness of the workers' in order to understand 'the consequences . . . for the self-organization of the workers'.[92] Their inquiries were built upon using factory-based newspapers which aimed to solicit testimonies from workers in order to analyse and publish them as political interventions. Claude Lefort raised the problem of 'who had the right to interpret these accounts?'.[93] The conclusion was that the members of *Socialisme ou Barbarie* could take on this role if it would allow workers to reflect further on their own experiences. They conducted investigations into the factories in France, for example Georges Vivier's 'Life in the Factory'.[94] This work was continued by Daniel Mothé and Henri Simon, following in the footsteps of Paul Romano in the Johnson-Forest Tendency. The General Motors car factory is replaced with the Renault Bilancourt factory for Mothé and an insurance company for Simon.[95]

This allowed the organisation to focus on the actual experience of workers in France and construct a perspective from the bottom up, despite the limitations that 'this "view from below" was male and factory centred'.[96] The project was 'rooted in a vision of the worker and of worker experience that is derived from reading and interpreting "proletarian-documentary literature"'. The group encountered a serious difficulty in basing their approach on these writings, as 'workers simply did not write'.[97] Although there were some successes with the method, the group fell apart in 1958.[98] At the time, *Socialisme ou Barbarie* received little attention outside the French-speaking world; this changed after the outburst of student and worker struggle in 1968. The remaining copies of the journal 'became a hot-selling item'[99] and it had an influence on 'important figures of the "workers' autonomy" wing of the Italian New Left in the 1960s and 1970s'.[100]

Italian workerism

The most direct inspiration for the current project is found, however, in the example of workerism in Italy. Its break with orthodoxy, although unrelated to Stalinist Russia, has nevertheless been described as 'a veritable "Copernican revolution" against the Marxism derived from the Third International'.[101] Marx's workers' inquiry was rediscovered and republished in the journal *Quaderni Rossi* in 1965.[102] *The American Worker* was translated into Italian,[103] alongside Daniel Mothé's writings from *Socialisme ou Barbarie*, and 'the Italians were influenced by and drew on this Franco-American experience of the direct examination of workers' struggles'.[104] The context of this new approach was an attempt to understand Taylorism and the new forms of supervision and control in the factories of Italy. It required the development of new analytical tools and a radical re-reading of Marx. These tools were used to search for resistance against the new forms of capitalist organisation in the factories. The ideas of workers' autonomy developed through these journals informed the methodological approaches that followed.

The first concerted attempt at a workers' inquiry took place at the FIAT car factory in Turin. There had been a series of industrial conflicts in the car industry at the end of the 1950s, 'with the glaring exception of FIAT'.[105] Therefore the choice of the firm represented the opportunity to test the theory that it would be possible to uncover the processes that were taking place at FIAT and understand the potential for future conflict in the factory. (There are similarities here with how call centres are generally perceived as workplaces without conflict.) Within the journal there was a particularly important debate on the difference between inquiry and co-research. A distinction was drawn between the inquiry 'from above' and inquiry 'from below'. Vittorio Rieser argued that 'co-ricerca', or co-research,

> is a fundamental method, but it requires being in a condition where you are pursuing enquiry with workers that you are organizing or workers that are already organized and therefore in either case strictly related to political work. As a small group we were not in the position to do this and neither were the unions that were able to organize workers in FIAT.[106]

In the case described by Rieser it was therefore necessary to use traditional research methods. It is described as being abstract because the conditions for pursuing co-research were not present. However, 'if the conditions are there, this is clearly the best method'. Traditional research methods can be used to 'acquire knowledge of the situation', and that includes the use of 'quantitative questionnaires (of which data must nevertheless always be approached with a critical eye)'.

This debate opened up the question of how to approach the use of sociological tools, but the 'search for a meeting point between Marxism and sociology' encountered a series of difficulties.[107] Marxism contains within it a political suspicion of certain forms of sociology, whereas sociology contains a suspicion of politics – especially in terms of a political conception of the working class. This creates an instability when combining the two, which can be seen in the tension between the continued use of sociological tools in the inquiries and the search for other ways to inject the political component into the project. The hostility towards sociology is evident in the example of Alquati's attempt at an inquiry at the Olivetti factory. Although initially the militants who were members of Italian Socialist Party were prepared to participate, the rest of the workers were 'more cautious' because of the 'contributions made by previous left sociologists to the intensifications of labour', and were not prepared to take part.[108]

This highlights the risk of uncritically using methods developed in industrial sociology. It is worth considering that management use (at least partly) similar techniques to gain a better understanding of the processes of production. As Frederick Taylor explained, 'managers assume . . . the burden of gathering together all of the traditional knowledge which in the past has been possessed by the workmen and then the classifying, tabulating, and reducing this knowledge to rules, laws, and formulae'.[109] As Braverman has argued, these kind of investigations – starting with Taylor's own project at the Midvale Steel company – not only laid the groundwork for the intense supervision of modern production, but also involved 'a theory which is nothing less than the explicit verbalization of the capitalist mode of production'.[110] Sociological tools can therefore also be used in a process of knowledge theft that intends to find new methods of exploitation and control. The politics of knowledge plays an important role in the understanding of how to use sociological tools in a workers' inquiry.

The kind of partisan knowledge that the workers' inquiry has the potential to produce begins from a very specific starting point. The approach starts with an understanding of a unique working-class perspective linked to a political position rather than the experience of work. In doing so it forms a political epistemology which differs from the sociological conception. This is asserted by Tronti in his claim to 'ferocious *unilaterality*', and that this 'class science was to be no less partial than that of capital; what it alone could offer, however, was the possibility of destroying the thraldom of labour once and for all.'[111] This new form of inquiry held important differences to that of the Johnson-Forest Tendency or *Socialisme ou Barbarie*, aiming to uncover the composition of the working class to understand how struggle will develop. The political component has been summarised by Alquati in a straightforward way: 'political militants have always done *conricerca*. We would go in front of the factory and speak with workers: there cannot be organization otherwise.'[112]

The basis of the workers' inquiry is therefore rooted in the movement of the working class. The inquiry forms the basis for an understanding of the new contexts in which the workplace is organised and requires an investigation of the current conditions upon which new forms of organisation can be built. As Marx argues in *Capital*, the 'worker emerges from the process of production looking different from when he entered it'. Starting as a seller of their own labour power, the workers come to the conclusion that they 'have to put their head together . . . as a class' so 'they can be prevented from selling themselves and their families into slavery and death by voluntary contract with capital'.[113] For Tronti this is '*a political leap*', and 'it is the leap that the passage through production provokes in what we can call the *composition of the working class* or even the *composition of the class of workers*'.[114]

For an inquiry today

The introduction of the concept of class composition represents an important step forward for the workers' inquiry. The starting point is Mario Tronti's claim that 'we have to invert the problem'; instead of starting with capital, 'change direction, and start from the beginning – and the beginning is working-class struggle'.[115] This is an attempt to overcome the silences of *Capital* discussed earlier. By beginning with labour rather than capital, the analysis seeks to understand how capital attempts to 'incorporate the working class within itself as simply labour power', while the 'working class affirms itself as an independent class-for-itself only through struggles which rupture capital's self-reproduction'.[116]

The composition of the working class, or of groups of workers, is therefore an important focus for an inquiry. The class composition can be broken down into two interrelated components: the technical and political composition. Technical composition refers to the 'analysis of the labor processes, of the technology, not in sociological terms but rather as sanctions of the relations of force between classes'.[117] An inquiry can therefore seek to understand this by examining the labour process and the particular organisation of the workplace. Francois Matheron argues that 'it makes sense' to focus on this 'in order to understand what "class struggle" means: there has never been more Marxist "evidence"'. The political composition of the working class is related to, but not determined by, the technical composition. The working class 'is not content with reacting to the dominion of capital, it is continually immersed in the process of political recomposition, and capital is obliged to respond with a continual restructuration of the labor process'. Therefore, the political composition involves the specific forms and relations of struggles as they change over time. Again, Matheron argues that 'it makes sense' to interrogate the 'political recomposition, the cycle of struggles'.[118]

The attempt undertaken here builds on the approach of Kolinko's *Hotlines*, an inquiry into German call centres.[119] The project aimed to 'understand the class reality at this point, be part of the conflicts and intervene'. It involved a group of militants engaging in discussions, working in a call centre, and collectively writing up the experience over a period of three years. The inquiry itself was divided into different stages. The first stage was called the 'pre-inquiry'. This involved research the workplace: academic and news articles, information from trade unions. These would then be used in theoretical discussions amongst the group aiming to collectively develop 'theoretical knowledge' which could be compared with 'our everyday life experience at the call centre'. So far we have presented part of this 'pre-inquiry', discussing call centres from two different approaches. The next stage for Kolinko was conducting interviews, both with the militants and other workers in the call centre to develop further insights. The interviews were intended as the opening stage of a discussion about the possibilities of struggle. A further aim was to encourage other militants to take part in further workers' inquiries so that experiences could be shared. In what follows, the inquiry involved working in a call centre alongside other workers, which is also supplemented with an interview.

The contribution of the Italian Workerists to the method of workers' inquiry is substantial. They developed the ideas put forward by Marx, the Johnson-Forest Tendency and *Socialisme ou Barbarie*. The method moved on from the questionnaire and the worker narratives towards a method for the co-production of knowledge and organisation. The nuances of inquiry 'from above' and 'from below' allow the construction of a research project that can begin with certain traditional methods, while aiming to go beyond the simple outside/insider division. It is important to stress that the workers' inquiry was not seen solely as academic method; instead it formed an important component of a political project. It is from this methodological tradition (if it is possible to call it that) that the rest of the book follows.

This book, then, is an inquiry into the conditions of call centre work in the UK. Call centres have become emblematic of the shift towards a post-industrial service economy and the growth of a neoliberal orthodoxy with widespread programmes of 'deregulation, privatization, and withdrawal of the state from many areas of social provision'.[120] This transformation of work has not been accompanied by a new wave of worker self-organisation or the development of successful trade union initiatives. It is in this economic environment – and one that is very favourable to capital – that call centres have flourished. However, on the other hand, the rise of call centres also represents the desperation of capital. This relentless drive to sell is a reflection of the struggle for companies to remain profitable, which often involves shifting the burden of selling onto workers who rely on commission.

The application of technology to the labour process and intensive performance-monitoring techniques paint a general picture of post-industrial work that 'become not Daniel Bell's dream, but Harry Braverman's nightmare'.[121] The figure of the call-centre worker is often presented as isolated, lacking agency and faced with precarious conditions. As Enda Brophy has succinctly summarised, 'working in a call centre tends to include a well-established mix of low wages, high stress, precarious employment, rigid management, draining emotional labour and pervasive electronic surveillance'.[122] If the call centre is conceived of as a site of struggle, the lack of workplace organisation or trade unionism has left the 'frontier of control' firmly in the hands of management.[123] However, wherever power is exercised there is the potential for resistance.

We will seek throughout the book to uncover this resistance and the possibilities for organisation. What follows is a study of the experiences of actually working in a high-volume sales call centre, drawing on a detailed ethnography and a narrative account. The conclusion that emerges from this, we argue, is that workers do resist in call centres in various ways. Throughout the research a number of call centres were considered, while the ethnography focuses on one in particular. The research was conducted undercover, as no call-centre manager would allow a critical researcher in. Given the challenges of researching the conditions of work today, the call centre itself is kept anonymous. While it is not possible to generalise directly from one, all of the three shared common features.

The argument developed here connects the study of the call centre with the understanding of how work has been transformed by neoliberalism and the intensification of the capital/labour relation. In this bleak context the capacity for workplace resistance can seem diminished. In the context of the call centre, the novel technological and managerial methods could be seen as overpowering structural forces that crush the agency of workers into submission. Yet, as Marx argued, people 'make their own history, but they do not make it as they please'. We will therefore reverse the polarity of the arguments about call centres as un-organisable, refocusing the analytical lens on the activity of workers themselves. The challenge is to identify the acts of resistance and tentative first steps towards new organisational forms that can emerge in the course of struggle. The obstacles that precarious workers face are articulated and we consider the kinds of tactics and strategies necessary to overcome them.

2

WORKING IN THE CALL CENTRE

'Smile down the phone, the customer can hear it!'

FINDING A JOB

I chose the site for my worker's inquiry the way most people now find casual employment: by responding to internet advertisements. I spent the day trawling job-listing sites, which in London are filled with generic postings for call-centre work. The adverts contained few details other than pay and hours, and a number of them led to pre-interview screenings. The advert for the job that I eventually got directed applicants to ring a voicemail number with a recording that instructed them to leave a message with their name, number and why they would be good at the job. This was the first attempt to screen applicants, as those who could not leave a convincing voicemail would be unlikely to be hired. I wrote down the details, practised a few times and then left my own rehearsed message. I received a call the following day and was invited to come in after the weekend for an interview.

It became clearer at the interview what kind of call centre I would be working in. In the introduction it was explained that the company sold insurance, or rather arranged repackaged products from insurance companies and sold them on to customers. The interview itself involved the applicants sitting around a large table with one recruiter. The group then had to take part in a series of ice-breaker-type games to learn each other's names, followed by team-building exercises. One involved building a tower out of straws, something which at first glance does not seem a key skill to be used in a call centre. The next part involved each applicant having an individual interview, with fairly straightforward questions about previous experience and skills. The trainer briefly channelled *The Wolf of Wall Street*, asking me how I would sell their pen, although they did mention that if successful we would be selling from a script. This was followed by questions about how we deal with the fact that 'it is a really boring job' and the warning that we would frequently get rejected while making calls. I received a call a few hours later that day to say that I had got the job.

The journey to work on the first day involved two trips on the Tube, changing at Bank. This route, from one neighbourhood to another with a brief stop near the City, traced some of the larger changes that have taken place across London. The first part involved getting caught in the flow of suits travelling into the financial centre, while the second was noticeably quieter. After leaving the Tube station it was a short walk to the call centre. It was housed in the husk of an old industrial building, flanked with a combination of new-build flats, chicken shops and estate agents. It was not entirely clear what the original purpose of the building was, but it had now been carved up between different office-type workplaces. The entrance was a nondescript door – I missed it on my first two walks around the outside of the building – which had a small notice in the window. It was surrounded with post-industrial detritus: plastic bags, bits of paper and bright yellow-and-red takeaway chicken boxes.

Once I arrived at the call centre, the first few minutes were spent filling in a variety of different forms. The contract included a clause stating that the 'terms and conditions of employment are not subject to the provisions of any collective agreement'. There was no option to complain about the inclusion of this phrase and presumably refusing to sign the contract would have meant not getting the job. While begrudgingly filling out the forms I overheard other workers joking about a pay rise, but then settled on the agreement that all they wanted was the heating fixed. They laughed, before they all went back to work.

At the beginning of the training the operation of the company was explained in more detail. In effect, they acted as an insurance broker, arranging various policies from different insurance companies and then selling them over the phone. This involved handling sales, customer service and claims, but not paying out the policy. The basic premise was marketing a free insurance offer with a low pay-out, and then attempting to up-sell additional paid options. The trainer explained that workers would begin in the 'academy' and once they had met their targets they would 'graduate', with plenty of training provided after the initial week. The trainer pointed at that 'because this is an insurance job it will look really good on your CV'. Which meant that if you were a student, 'after you graduate you could go on to a top company'. These remarks were an explicit recognition that most people would not be working at the company as a career; for most it would be a temporary and precarious stint.

While these introductory talks were going on, I noticed that expressions of the obligatory company values were plastered on the walls: 'focused, dynamic, pro-active, and committed'. Although these four terms appeared throughout the office in various fonts, they did not seem to mean anything in practice. The trainer pointed up at them and said, 'We want a culture with these! This is not like other places where they are stuck up on the walls – I mean they are stuck on the walls here too – but we also have them run through everything we do!' Bizarrely this extended to demanding that workers dressed in a smart/casual uniform in the call centre. Considering none of the customers would ever see a call-centre worker, the stipulation to wear black trousers and smart shoes appeared punitive and not clearly related to any of the four values.

The nature of the product being sold in the call centre meant that it previously came under the jurisdiction of the Financial Services Authority (FSA). The trainer stressed that learning all the FSA regulations 'could take months, so we are only going to focus on what you need to know'. The FSA is an independent organisation that regulates all UK financial services. It has four main aims: maintaining confidence in the UK financial system, contributing to the protection and enhancement of the stability of the UK financial system, securing the right degree of protection for consumers and contributing to reducing financial crime.

These lofty aims led to a series of jokes about the financial crisis and a surprising level of cynicism from some of the trainees.

The implications of the FSA regulation were summarised in the acronym TCF. Treating Customers Fairly (TCF) applied to script adherence, selling only on a non-advised basis (not providing financial advice to customers) and how to handle complaints. The impact of the 2008 financial crisis precipitated the splitting of the FSA into two new component parts – the Prudential Regulation Authority (PRA) and Financial Conduct Authority (FCA), the second dealing with brokers like the call centre. The trainer explained how the regulations would now be 'involved from the very start'. Previously they would 'come at the end with a stick and say "you haven't done this or that"' but now 'we are regulation and compliance orientated'. This change is indicative of the general media-led interpretation that the financial crisis was caused by a lack of regulation rather than by deeper systemic causes.

TCF was defined as a high-level principle in the FSA framework. Although 'It would avoid a lot of problems if we would be fair,' the trainer argued, 'this is a lot more than that'. It was taken to mean that calls should be clear and easy to understand, the right product should meet expectations, customers should not be taken advantage of and have access to resources, and the company should 'put things right after human error'. However, the trainer pointed out that it is not about being nice to customers, or all businesses offering identical services, nor should it be about the customer having no responsibilities. The common phrase 'the customer is always right' was rejected as a 'lie', and calls were recorded to prove that a customer had agreed to purchase a particular product. It was unexpected to hear that the computerised surveillance would also be used to enforce sales contracts with customers, in addition to the well-documented role in controlling workers. The trainer stressed that 'you will hear TCF a lot in this company'. However, I never heard a mention of it again after the training.

My initial training began with a probationary period called 'The Academy'. This phase was divided into three levels, each with sales objectives that had to be achieved before promotion to the next level. The pay was also based on the three levels: a basic pay rate of £7 per hour (which was just above the minimum wage but less than the London living wage), a 'Galácticos' bonus of £9 per hour, and 'Super Galácticos' bonus of £11 per hour. In addition to the bonus pay there would be a commission of £3 per sale on most insurance products. It was not immediately clear how to reach the bonus pay levels. They were assigned on the basis of a certain level of sales per hour (which could change), of having no more than one call failure to meet the company requirements in a month, and at the discretion of the managers. After having seen a poster listing that month's Galácticos and Super Galácticos (only six and four respectively), I asked why so few workers achieved it, given that the trainer had stressed how achievable the targets would be. The trainer nervously attempted to claim that the poster only listed the new people to meet the targets. However, another trainee pointed out that a previous month's poster was still up in the office and it listed the same names, thereby disproving the answer. The trainer became evasive and suggested that maybe it was in fact only the top sellers before swiftly moving on, ushering the workers into the break room.

I was surprised to hear that we would be making a live phone call later that same day. We read through the scripts, practised reading them out to each other and listened to further advice from the trainer. The next step was to move out to the call-centre floor and find a spare computer. I logged on, picked up the headset, and began going through the initial steps to start calling. Once confirmed, the automatic call dialler began dialling outbound calls. I felt my mouth go dry as I remembered that I would have to try to sell insurance to the people answering the phone. I felt relieved as the first call rang through to an answerphone, and I briefly spent some time adjusting the headset while the next call started. It took quite a few attempts to reach an actual person, and I experienced this same cycle of nerves and relief as each call rang through. Eventually I got to try out the script, fumbling the first few lines as someone explained they were not interested. The trainer, somewhat pleased with my attempt, let me return to the break room.

The training ended with a review of a series of logistical details. The shifts had to be requested a month in advance; however, you would only find out which shifts you had been assigned on the Friday night before the week in question, giving only a couple of days' notice to the worker. It was then explained that having a mobile phone on the call-centre floor was a disciplinary offense as the customer data is sensitive – and that it would also be a distraction. Each worker received a padlock and was assigned a locker in the break room. The final announcement of the day was that we would only be paid for half of the training, receiving the second half once we had 'graduated', and encouraging the trainees to come back the next day. This was the first of many signals that the company was worried about the high turnover of staff.

THE VIEW FROM THE CALL-CENTRE FLOOR

After entering through the front door, the call centre was accessed along a corridor and down a flight of stairs. Once in the basement, the room opened up into rows of desks. There were approximately one hundred in total, each equipped with an ageing desktop computer and a telephone with a headset. The outbound sales teams had one half of the office, and the other half was reserved for customer services, quality control and space for giving feedback. There were meeting rooms off the main office and a small kitchen with a break area and lockers. The IT and marketing teams were located in a separate room. The environment itself was loud and busy, with numerous conversations blending into each other amongst the noise. Although there was the potential for natural light, the small windows located along the top of walls were covered with dusty blinds, so instead fluorescent strip lighting beamed down from the ceiling.

The main part of the office was decorated with posters, some of them professing the values of the company. Others advertised special bonuses, including incentives offered for the recruitment of friends (awarded only if those friends stayed in the job for a minimum amount of time). There were a number of whiteboards scattered around the office, with workers' names and sales targets. The hand-drawn circles served to indicate how many sales each worker had to aim for, with one filled in after each sale. On top of this there were two large flat-screen televisions, one indicating sales and the other for customer services. The customer-service screen cycled between displaying what each person is currently doing and the number and type of inbound calls outstanding and successfully answered. The sales screen displayed the total number of sales and then sales by team on one side, while the other side prominently displayed the top individual seller followed by each worker ranked by the number of sales.

The start of each shift at the call centre begins in the break room. The supervisors lead a 'buzz session', which is essentially an opportunity for the company to remind workers of the different rules, stress the importance of quality, and then attempt to encourage some kind of enthusiasm for the upcoming shift. The content of these sessions varied, but most involved playing some sort of game. These range from competitions testing product knowledge (perhaps not the most exciting) to word games – for example, each person in turn shouting out the name of a country, following alphabetical order with no repetition, eliminating those who fail to do so until only the winner remains. Although being made to play children's games was somewhat demeaning, it did offer the benefit of stretching out the time before we had to be on the call-centre floor. Some workers tried to extend these sessions by asking lots of questions and pretending they needed more help than they actually did.

No matter how long the buzz session was extended, inevitably we would have to start making phone calls. Although the process is structured by the script, there are still complex demands on workers. As the trainer argued, 'it is not just what you say', but workers must also think about their 'pace, tone, conversation style, listening skills'. This was particularly important when using a standardised script, as the trainers insisted that your own personality should come across during the call. Apparently the Managing Director's favourite catchphrase was that 'people buy people'; he believed that the best sellers used similar techniques over and over again. If new workers had trouble with this, the trainer had some illuminating advice: 'Just use a bright and enthusiastic tone . . . and if you can't, three words: Put. It. On!'

All phone calls were structured by a script on the computer screen. This comprised five different hyperlinked sections, some with multiple pages. The trainer pointed out: 'We need people to make the sales; otherwise we would just use an automated system.' Workers were encouraged to build rapport with the customer, to learn additional details which can then be used as a basis for improvisation later on in the script. This improvisation was primarily expected during the description of the features of the insurance, a process called 'features-to-benefits'. For example, one of the five main benefits was that the customer is entitled to a rebate at the age of seventy if they have not claimed. The worker was expected to go further than simply reading out the computer-generated figure. This involved using hypothetical connecting phrases like 'which means that you could . . .' while being careful not to actually advise. This involves a demand to improvise a benefit for the feature, hopefully using some of the additional information gathered in the earlier rapport-building. The trainer described this as 'painting a picture', which is apparently the way to make sales.

Jokes were also a fundamental part of elaboration on the script. At two points on the script, workers are encouraged to try joking with the customer. The first is during the confirmation of details. There are two eligibility questions where the customer is asked to confirm 'that you spend seven out of 12 months a year in the UK?' and 'that this is where you pay your taxes?' These questions respectively open the door to two jokes: 'So no long holidays planned this year then?' and 'No escaping that, is there?' (On a couple of occasions I tried adding to the second question 'unless you are Vodafone',[1] but this was quickly discouraged by the supervisors.) The second point where joking is encouraged is later in the script, during the communication of the exclusion 'that you won't be covered for death as a result of . . . participation in any illegal acts', to which almost every worker adds, with feigned laughter, 'so if you were planning to rob a bank we wouldn't be able to pay out!' While this is presumably a new joke for the customer, the workers will get to enjoy it over and over again throughout the day.

The first full shift that I worked ended with no sales. I managed to pitch the product in full three times, and reached the Direct Debit payment page of the script. On the first occasion the customer objected, 'Isn't this just the free offer? Why do I need to pay anything?' The second got very defensive when asked for the bank details: 'Why would I give you those when I haven't seen anything in writing?' The third said they did not have their bank details with them. I asked whether it was on their card – 'No, I've lost my card'; their chequebook – 'Don't have one'; online banking – 'Don't use it'. At no point did they say they were not interested in the insurance, which meant that I had to keep pitching. These would become common objections that I had to handle over and over again.

The process for dealing with objections is called 'Clarify and Reassure' or 'C&R'. It is not scripted on the computer program but remains semi-scripted nonetheless. In a similar manner to the features-to-benefits, the C&R process is laid out on sheets of paper and handed out by supervisors. These sheets are used as guides but allow a certain level of freedom in how to handle objections. A 'compliant sale' can only contain three attempts as stipulated by regulations, and they therefore focus on probing the customer to gain more information about the objection to successfully overcome it. During breaks, trainees often discussed these problems with closing sales. Time off the phone became an opportunity to vent about how difficult the phone calls were, and to swap advice about how to finish a sale – at least during the initial phase of employment. In one discussion we all agreed that none of us would ever give out our own details to buy insurance over the phone.

The supervisors began coaching during the first shift. In addition to this, every call, whether a successful sale or not, was digitally recorded and stored for playback. Each sales call and a random selection of non-sales calls would be listened to and graded by the quality-control team. They would be graded as either green (passing quality standards), green D/N (passed but development needed) or red (failing to meet standards and therefore no commission). The supervisors would regularly listen into calls, and analyse how workers could be more successful in future. During weekly '1-2-1' (one-to-one) meetings, supervisors would grade performance and provide instructions on how workers could improve. While the supervisors stressed that these were for training purposes, they produced printouts of the computer data which could also play a disciplinary role. Each week I was given a grading and a series of instructions about how to improve. These were always quite vague but in general involved remarks about being more 'assertive', 'give 110 per cent to every call', or even, parroting the rant by Blake (Alec Baldwin) in the film *Glengarry Glen Ross*, 'Remember your ABCs – Always Be Closing!'[2] The '1-2-1' feedback was always supplemented with the advice: 'Remember, every "no" is one step closer to a "yes!"', a tautological refrain about the logic of making sales.

There was a constant pressure to make sales on the call-centre floor. It began to feel like a contemporary version of Robert Linhart's experience on the Citroën assembly line in 1970s France. As 'someone from the establishment' (he was a former professor of economics) going into the factory, Linhart worried that he was not 'going to be able to cope'. His unsuccessful attempts led him to ask 'what will happen tomorrow if I still can't do that soldering? Will they throw me out? How ridiculous! A day and a half on the job . . . and then fired for being incapable!'[3] In the call centre, the television screen on the wall taunted workers with sales figures, acting as a constant reminder of how each individual worker compares to others. I found it nerve-wracking as I struggled to get sales while watching the more established, near-Stakhanovite workers constantly adding more sales. However, after a month or so I began to regularly make sales, not quite enough to 'graduate', but enough not to suffer Linhart's fearful outcome.

In a typical shift I would make approximately three to four hundred phone calls. The majority of these calls would go through to answerphone, especially during the part of the shift taking place during normal working hours. The calls that did connect often finished abruptly with the customer requesting a call back at a more convenient time, which is then scheduled with a drop-down menu and submitted back into the system. It is possible to leave notes for calls so that the next worker has some context; however, most people either left short notes that were unhelpful or none at all. The history for each customer can be displayed, which often shows that calls that go through to answerphone have been called repeatedly over a period of a month. This means that the majority of the shift is spent waiting to connect to a customer. While this may seem easier than constantly talking to customers, it is far from relaxing. The next attempt to pitch the product could always be only five seconds away, so the moments of respite are brief and the pressure is constant.

Any opportunities to take a break were jumped upon by workers. It was commonplace to see attempts to stretch out any time off the phone or try to alleviate boredom somehow while calling. There were a variety of different games played on the call-centre floor. These mainly involved making the most out of the small intervals when it was not required to speak to customers. However, one of the most popular games was finding a set of unusual words or a phrase that workers would have to fit into a call with a customer. Often this verged on the ridiculous and some of the phrases would require quite a creative approach to include in a call, for example 'spaghetti' or 'giraffe'. These collective acts of workers were separate from the attempted gamification of work that supervisors pushed during buzz sessions and throughout the shift.

ON THE PHONES

The need to escape the boredom of the phone calls was often exacerbated by the unpleasantness of particular interactions with customers. Although it would be possible to recount a series of these there are three examples that stand out most strongly and illustrate the difficulty of making sales calls.

The first example is from the first successful sale that I made in the call centre. I spoke to a woman with a thick regional accent on a bad quality phone line. She initially seemed interested in purchasing the insurance policy but was unsure of what level of cover she would need. Each time a customer requests a change to the lump sum on the insurance policy it is necessary to go back over all of the figures and ensure that they are making a decision based on the correct details. The customer changed her mind about the lump sum three times during the phone call before deciding that she wanted a joint policy with her partner, and wanted to know how that would affect each of the lump sums. This meant that the breakdown of the figures and the full details of the policy had to be repeated on six separate occasions. Unsurprisingly, the customer got confused and it required extensive C&R objection handling to continue the call. After almost an hour I managed to close the sale, which had required a number of call-backs after the phone line dropped. The fact that it was a sale meant that the call would definitely be listened to afterward, making the experience even more stressful, on top of the constant attention it required throughout.

The second example is from an unsuccessful call. The customer began by confirming details for renewal of the free insurance offer and it appeared to be a fairly typical call. One of the rapport-building opportunities follows the question about number of dependents. If customers do have any it is encouraged to ask them about their children, how old they are and so on. This is to collect information to strengthen the pitch for life insurance later on. For example, if they have young children, asking what would happen to them if they died, although hopefully phrased in a subtler manner. After asking the question about dependents, and probing to ask if the number was the same (thinking naively that maybe it had increased since a previous call when it had been recorded), the customer burst into tears on the phone and asked for the number to be changed as their young child had recently died of leukaemia. The customer was clearly distraught; however, the rules in the call centre state that it is only possible to end a sales call if the customer explicitly requests so. I attempted to achieve this by saying, 'I'm terribly sorry to hear that, would you like to continue with the call?' I was hoping that this would end the encounter; however, the nearest supervisor had started listening into my call and was now ordering me to continue to pitch the product. Without the withdrawal of the permission I had to keep reading the script with the customer becoming more and more upset. After a minute or so – which felt like much longer – the customer started shouting about how insensitive this was. I broke from the script, much to the disgust of the supervisor, and apologised profusely before ending the call. I was taken aside by the supervisor and given a telling off: 'You know, sometimes there are calls like this, but you do need to pitch the product to every customer!'.

The third example is similar if perhaps more sinister. The customer stated that they were in a rush while providing the details for the renewal of the free insurance offer. I promised to be as quick as possible, completing the information section of the form, before attempting to pitch the paid insurance product. The customer interrupted and explained that they were in a rush because they needed to get to hospital for dialysis, and pointed out that kidney problems would prevent them from getting life insurance. In a flash the supervisor was standing beside my desk, having picked up on what was happening on the call. The supervisor began mouthing that 'this person is sick! We offer guaranteed acceptance! This is your next sale!' and a smile spread across his face. I began to explain to the customer that the company could still offer the insurance policy as there would be no questions about health status. The customer responded by detailing exactly the seriousness of the illness and that a claim on the life insurance would definitely need to made soon. Under pressure from the supervisor, I continued to pitch the product, despite the customer becoming upset and eventually hanging up the phone. Again I was taken aside by the supervisor and verbally reprimanded for not being persistent enough to close the sale.

These kinds of phone calls are particularly difficult. Treatment of people, regardless of their situation, as potential sales that need to be closed is an uncomfortable experience. The retort of the supervisor was that successful sales are made by people who are 'resilient' or 'don't get put off by hearing no', as if the responsibility for the sale lies entirely with the call-centre worker, regardless of whether or not the person on the end of the phone actually wants or needs the product.

However, there are also sometimes encounters on the phone that are quite enjoyable. A funny or talkative customer – or even just a customer that says 'thank you' – can really brighten up a shift. These are few and far between, though, as the labour process demands instrumental sales pitches and not compassionate interactions. The use of empathy is reserved for understanding which sales techniques might work, rather than for genuinely relating to the person on the other end of the phone.

There are two examples from my experience of unusual phone calls that do not fit into the pattern described above. The first example was speaking to someone who was employed as a full-time trade union official. He explained that he was only interested in the free offer, but rather than ending the call asked whether I was a member of a union or not. In a strange moment of connection between a union bureaucrat and non-unionised worker, he started explaining the benefits of joining a union and how to go about doing it. I pointed out in a flat tone, 'Just to remind you, all calls are recorded and may be listened to to ensure accuracy or for training purposes, is that okay?'. At this point it dawned on him that perhaps talking about joining a union might endanger my job, so we had an amusingly coded discussion in which he wished me the best of luck. The second example was a call made to a customer whose first name was Stalin. The call itself was unremarkable, but it was the closest that theories of state capitalism came to being relevant in the workplace.[4]

The way that calls are distributed among workers is based on what are called 'leads', which are distinguished by the method used to gain the contact details. The leads varied in quality and affected the kind of customers spoken to. They were distributed to workers based on the worker's perceived ability to convert them into sales. The oldest leads are therefore used to train workers, whereas the best leads – those that are newest or include customers more likely to buy – are reserved for those who have proven themselves as able sellers. Therefore, being able to prove that you can sell on the worst leads allows access to higher-quality leads. Most leads were gained from offering free insurance, but the company had branched out into competition offers to collect more potential customer details. The most common of these was the chance to win £200 of grocery vouchers. Unsurprisingly, many of the people who answered these calls had forgotten about its connection to insurance and only wanted to be entered into the prize draw. This meant that it would be necessary to point out that 'on the form you filled out, it did say that a representative from [company name] will call about other benefits we are offering'. The vast majority of these calls ended abruptly with the customer refusing to continue. Those calls that did go ahead began with the stipulation: 'Don't try and sell me anything!' However, the company policy was that workers had to pitch the product regardless, which often ended in a confrontation with the customer.

The first page of the script changes depending on which lead the computer is supplying to the worker during a call. For example, if selling on the competition type it would include an introduction about having entered. This means that, while waiting for the call to connect, this preview is available. I came to dread the competition leads as it was very difficult to make a sale on these calls. When these leads became active there were lots of complaints from workers across the call-centre floor. Occasionally the supervisors would agree to mix the competition leads with better-quality ones, as part of their job was to organise the flow of leads to the sales teams. In one case I had been complaining about the quality of the grocery vouchers and then made a sale on the first different kind of lead I was given, which, while not necessarily reflective of that difference in lead type, was certainly satisfying.

The computer system's task of organising multiple leads with a large volume of workers simultaneously making calls inevitably ran into problems. If the pool of leads became depleted, the computer screen would display an error message and automatically check for new ones after two minutes or on request. The differentiation of teams meant that not every worker would run out of leads at the same time and it was not always possible for the supervisors to keep track of this. This created a situation where it would be possible to pretend that you were still receiving leads so long as other workers on your team also kept quiet. This disruption required a collective misbehaviour which, most of the time, workers were prepared to engage in. The computer system would also sporadically stop working altogether. During the week there was an IT department on the premises to carry out repairs, but at weekends this was not an option. The supervisors never let workers leave early when the phone system was inoperative, as there were always training or buzz session games that could be used to fill the time.

COMPUTERISED TAYLORISM

Control is ever-present in the call centre. From the constant presence of supervisors and the recording of phone calls to the automated electronic logs, methods of control and surveillance are many. The effect of this control on the labour process can be understood through an examination of Taylorist management principles. This includes the computerised supervision, which is perhaps analogous to the technician in a white coat with a stopwatch, but also recalls Harry Braverman's argument that behind the technician 'lies a theory which is nothing less than the explicit verbalization of the capitalist mode of production'.[5] The theory involves three principles: the first is 'the gathering and development of knowledge of the labour process', the second is 'the concentration of this knowledge as the exclusive province of management' and the third is the '*use of this monopoly over knowledge to control each step of the labor process and its mode of execution*'.[6]

The third principle stems from the organisation of tasks by management. For Frederick Taylor, the 'task specifies not only what is to be done, but how it is to be done and the exact time allowed for doing it'.[7] The process of reading from a script and then asking for set amounts of money during the phone call is a clear example of the *separation of conception from execution*. The necessity of closely following the script was reiterated continuously throughout the training and first shifts. One of the supervisors suggested that if you stick to the script, 'all the work is done for you!'. The *conception*, in terms of the preparation of the script, is entirely removed from their execution on the call-centre floor. Very little was said about how the scripts were developed, other than that the company spends a lot of time writing them. Braverman anticipates this process when he argues that mental labour, after being separated from manual labour, 'is then itself subdivided rigorously according to the same rule'. The purpose of this division is 'to cheapen the worker by decreasing his training and enlarging his output'.[8]

The use of a computer system linked to the phones allows for a significant degree of management control. Workers have to sign onto the computer system in order to make phone calls. The computer system logs the exact time that the worker starts their shift. There is an unpaid hour break between the two half-shifts, and two fifteen-minute breaks half-way through each half-shift. The computer system logs the start and end time of the break; if the break exceeds the limit, the system notifies a manager. During phone calls, the computer surveillance system will display three states: 'Previewing/Dialling' for the time when the automatic dialling system is ringing through the list of numbers; 'Connected', when the worker is talking to someone on the phone; and 'Wrapping', which provides an opportunity to record the outcome of the phone call and take any relevant notes. This is described as 'non-productive' time, only to be used when needed, never exceeding five seconds.

The labour process in the call centre can therefore be understood as a kind of computerised development of Taylorist management principles. Phil Taylor and Peter Bain argue that the 'driving force' behind the growth of call centres – whether as the 'rationalisation of back office functions or as entirely new creations' – results from the 'pursuit of competitive advantage'.[9] Call centres therefore come under pressure to minimise costs and maximise profits, which means that those running the call centres are 'under constant competitive pressure to extract more value from their employees', which 'from the point of view of capital' is a 'far from straightforward project'.[10]

The difficulty stems from the contradiction between the quantitative and qualitative objectives of the labour process. This became apparent during training: the constant focus on the quality of the phone calls as the most important aspect of the job sat uneasily alongside the strict quantitative targets for the number of phone calls per shift. Taylor and Bain argue that 'even in the most quality driven call centre' – and the call centre I worked in claimed to put a great importance on quality, particularly given its regulation by the Financial Conduct Authority – 'it is difficult to escape the conclusion that the labour process is intrinsically demanding, repetitive and, frequently, stressful'.[11]

This tension between quantity and quality in the call centre structures the relationship between worker and manager. The integration of the telephone and computer systems in the call centre provides the opportunity for 'extreme levels of surveillance, monitoring and speed-up',[12] which nevertheless creates another contradiction in the workplace. The 'intensive surveillance can be counterproductive', as it is 'costly in terms of workforce motivation and commitment'. However, 'abandonment' of surveillance is not possible, as these methods are 'integral to the operation of the call centre'.[13] These two related contradictions have a strong effect on the experience of call-centre workers, creating what Taylor and Bain describe as 'a situation in which the operator has "an assembly-line in the head", always feeling pressure and constantly aware that the completion of one task is immediately followed by another'.[14] The stress, often the result of this pressure to ensure that quantitative objectives are reached, reduces the ability of workers to achieve the qualitative objectives, which include what Taylor and Bain describe as the demand to 'smile down the phone'.[15]

This recalls the demand for flight attendants to maintain a perpetual smile, discussed by Arlie Hochschild in her account of emotional labour. She defined this kind of labour as 'requiring one to induce or suppress feeling in order to sustain the outward countenance that produces the proper state of mind in others'.[16] The method by which this can be achieved over the phone rather than in person is different. Taylor and Bain argue that the 'appropriate telephone manners and behaviours' alongside the previously mentioned need to 'smile down the phone' can be included within Hochschild's definition of 'outward countenance'.[17] The demand to 'smile down the phone' can be further illustrated by returning to *The Call Centre* documentary, discussed in Chapter 1.[18] When manager Nev explains that 'happy people sell, miserable bastards don't', his main interest (it is safe to assume) is not the happiness of the workforce as an end in itself. In the environment of a high-volume sales call centre there is constant pressure to reach targets. Nev wants workers to be 'happy' to make more sales.

In a stressful environment the demand to be 'happy' becomes increasingly difficult. It is not a question of the actual emotional state of the worker, but rather that they need to perform 'happy' emotions over the phone to close sales. This instrumentalisation of emotion occurs within certain bounds: short, pressurised encounters over the phone with the aim of closing sales.

AFFECTIVE LABOUR

The demand for call-centre workers to engage in labour with an emotional content has important implications. The aim of the labour process is to communicate with customers and attempt to convince them to purchase insurance, an immaterial commodity. This kind of immaterial work was is discussed by Franco 'Bifo' Berardi, drawing on the philosophy of Spinoza, as putting the 'soul' to work. The 'soul' is considered 'in a materialistic way' as 'the vital breath that converts biological matter into an animated body'. While 'industrial exploitation' dealt with 'bodies, muscles and arms . . . those bodies would not have any value if they weren't animated, mobile, intelligent, reactive'. The rise of post-Fordism, on the other hand, 'takes the mind, language and creativity as its primary tools for the production of value'.[19]

Although there remains a manual component to the labour process in the call centre – the demand to be at the desk for a set amount of time, the physical interaction with the computer and the headset, the verbalisation of communication at a particular pitch, tone and speed – the key element is mental labour. The attempt to make sales involves the 'investment in desire . . . at work, since social production has started to incorporate more and more sections of mental activity and of symbolic, communicative and affective action'. The affective aspect of this is particularly important. The labour process is 'not undertaken in view of the physical transformations of matter but communication, the creation of mental states, of feelings, and imagination'.[20]

Affective labour is difficult to supervise and control. The application of Taylorism to the assembly line provided more easily quantifiable inputs and outputs. There is no one way to make a successful sales call, something that was clear throughout the training with the emphasis on the importance of personality. The targets that supervisors are trying to achieve are complicated by the contradiction between quantitative and qualitative objectives. The control that supervisors exert over workers have a number of adverse effects, in particular the way the stress of quantitative targets reduces the overall quality of calls and vice versa. As Berardi argues, communication as work could, 'from a certain point of view . . . be seen as an enrichment of experience'. However, as the experience from a high-volume sales call centre illustrates, 'it is also (and this is generally the rule) an impoverishment, since communication loses its character of gratuitous, pleasurable and erotic contact, becoming an economic necessity, a joyless friction'.[21]

The results of the labour process in the call centres are intangible from the perspective of the worker. There is little engagement with the company or the insurance product itself. This lack of information leads to a distinct disconnection from what the phone call is actually about. The interchangeable nature of the job role in the call centre meant that it would have been possible to sell all kinds of different products, so long as there was access to the relevant script. In a study of stress in call centres in particular, Kerry Lewig and Maureen Dollard have outlined the importance of 'emotional dissonance'.[22] This is the psychological experience of the differences between the actual feelings of the call-centre worker and the emotions that they are performing. Modelled on cognitive dissonance, in which two contradictory ideas are held simultaneously, this concept refers to emotions and explains the feelings of guilt and stress workers experience as they try to convince customers to buy insurance while maintaining a positive, enthusiastic demeanour on the phone. They warn that 'emotional dissonance may ultimately lead to lowered self-esteem, depression, cynicism, and alienation from work'.

The affective package that workers are required to perform during the labour process is demanding. The experience was exhausting and emotionally draining. From my own experience of working eight-hour afternoon/evening shifts – unfortunately also complemented with a morning of reading and writing about call centres – the labour process was exhausting. In particular it made social phone calls something to avoid, as I became unable to break out of the routinised pattern of sales calls; in-person conversations became difficult too. Arriving home by about 10pm my food preparation fell into a pattern of baked beans on toast, followed by slouching on the sofa watching television.

This process of emotional dissonance is a specific alienating effect derived from the form of affective labour that is required in the call centre. This has some similarities with the process of industrial production, which 'mortifies' the 'body' and 'ruins' the 'mind' of the worker.[23] Affective labour clearly has different effects to those described by Marx in *Capital*, when he describes the 'division of labour characteristic of manufacture, under which each man is bound hand to foot for life to a single specialized operation'.[24] Marx continues to argue that in this process the worker becomes 'a living appendage of the machine'. Despite the differences between physical and mental effects, as Bertell Ollman reiterates, 'the worker's mind, too, has been ruined by the nature of his task and the conditions in which he does it'.[25]

The affective worker is different from the manual worker on the assembly line in a number of important ways. Marx describes, in a section of *Grundrisse* that has become known as the *fragment on the machines*, that:

Nature builds no machines, no locomotives, railways, electric telegraphs, self-acting mules etc. These are products of human industry; natural material transformed into organs of the human will over nature, or of human participation in nature. They are *organs of the human brain, created by human hand*; the power of knowledge, objectified. The development of fixed capital indicates to what degree general social knowledge has become a *direct force of production*, and to what degree, hence, the conditions of the process of social life itself have come under the control of the general intellect and been transformed in accordance with it. To what degree the powers of social production have been produced, only in the form of knowledge, but also as immediate organs of social practice, of the real life process.[26]

The notion of the 'general intellect' is important for understanding the role of machinery and capital in production. The increasing levels of capital-intensive machinery holds the potential to reduce the quantity of labour required in production, as automation has the potential to reduce how much work people need to do. However, the experience of most workers has not been a reduction in the length of the working day and more free time, but, in fact, quite the opposite. It entails a shift in which 'intellectual labor is no longer a social function separated from general labor, but it becomes a transversal function within the entire social process'.[27] As Christian Marazzi argues, 'communication – and its productive organization as information flow – has become as important as electricity once was in the age of mechanical production'.[28]

It is therefore possible to identify a shift from the exploitation of the *bodies* of workers during the Fordist mode of production to exploiting the *minds* of workers in increasingly larger numbers. These shifts towards the exploitation of mental labour – whether communicative, emotional or affective – forms part of the attempt to increase profitability in contemporary capitalism. Unlike under Fordism, 'it will no longer be possible to produce large quantities of standardized goods, not to accumulate inventories thinking that they will eventually sell at some future, non entirely predictable moment'. What takes its place is 'the need to produce limited amounts of differentiated goods', targeted 'according to the changing "taste" of consumers that we will need to know as well as possible in order to better reach them, while at the same time trying to find the best ways to realize gains in productivity'.[29] The increased pressure to realise the surplus value embedded in commodities has created new and innovative ways to reach customers and convince them to buy. This has also combined with the introduction of the profit motive further into new areas and subsequently commodifying goods and services that were previously produced or consumed in different ways. The result is an increased emphasis on affective and emotional labour, the drive to convince consumers stemming from the impulse to realise profit in ever more moments.

This is not to minimise the importance of productive physical labour in contemporary capitalism. Without the labour that went into reproducing labour-power, producing commodities for sale, or those for use by capital – for example, computers, telephones and networks – the affective work in call centres would not be possible. This involves a move from the formal to the real subsumption of workers to capital. Formal subsumption involves capital monopolising the means of production – the ownership of workplaces and the things inside them, for example – and compelling people to work for a wage. This shift to real subsumption 'means instead that the workers' lifetimes have been captured by the capital flow, and the souls have been pervaded by techno-linguistic chains'. This entails the 'introduction of pervasive technologies, the computerization of productive processes and of social communication [that] enact a molecular domination upon the collective nervous network'.[30]

Within mental labour it is possible to distinguish between *'brain workers'* and *'chain workers'*. Whereas *'brain workers'* are harnessed for their 'communication, invention and creation', the *'chain workers'* are those 'people who sit at their terminals in front of a screen, repeating every day the same operation a thousand times', and 'relate to their labor in a way similar to industrial workers'.[31] The call-centre worker – or *'chain worker'* – is therefore an appendage to a new kind of machine. Not the assembly line with its physical demands, but a complex network of telecommunications technology and, in this case, immaterial financial instruments – not particular movements repeated over and over, but a repetition of a performance aiming to convince people in new and innovative ways to part with their money.

This kind of experience – albeit for industrial workers – is discussed as a form of alienation in the early writings of Marx.[32] The concept of alienation is introduced as a way to understand the 'devastating effect of capitalist production on human beings, on their physical and mental states and on the social processes of which they are a part'.[33] As Marx explains:

The worker becomes poorer the more wealth he produces, the more wealth he produces, the more his production increased in power and extent. The worker becomes an ever cheaper commodity the more commodities he produces. The *devaluation* of the human world grows in direct proportion to the *increase in value* of the world of things. Labor produces not only commodities; it produces itself and the worker as a *commodity* – and this at the same rate at which it produces commodities in general . . . The worker is related to the *product of labour* as to an *alien* object. For it is clear that, according to this premise, the more the worker exerts himself in his work, the more powerful the alien, objective world becomes which he brings into being over against himself, the poorer he and his inner world become, and the less they belong to him.[34]

This is the underpinning of the classical Marxist notion of alienation. The conception of alienation is 'idealist in so far as it presupposes human authenticity, an essence that has been lost, negated, taken away, suspended'. The implication of this is that 'communism is thought by the young Marx as the restoration of an authentically human essence that was negated by the relation of capitalist production'.[35]

The tradition of Italian Workerism (see Chapter 1) puts forward a different perspective to this idealistic notion of alienation. It does not 'anticipate any restoration of humanity, does not proclaim any human universality, and bases its understanding of humanity on class conflict'.[36] In an influential text Mario Tronti argues:

The working class confronts its own labor as capital, as a hostile force, as an enemy – this is the point of departure not only for the antagonism, but for the organization of the antagonism. If the alienation of the worker has any meaning, it is a highly revolutionary one. The organization of alienation: This is the only possible direction in which the party can lead the spontaneity of the class. The goal remains that of refusal, at a higher level: It becomes active and collective, a political refusal on a mass scale, organized and planned. Hence the immediate task of working-class organization is to overcome passivity.[37]

This understanding of alienation as estrangement is not based on the loss of some kind of human essence. Instead it is a 'condition of estrangement from the mode of production and its rules, as refusal of work'. It is therefore, as Berardi puts it, to be 'seen as the condition of those who rebel assuming their partial humanity as a point of strength, a premise of a higher social form, of a higher form of humanity, and not as the condition of those who are forced to renounce their essential humanity'.[38]

This philosophical perspective demands that '*it is necessary to assume the standpoint of the refusal to work*, in order to understand the dynamics both of productive transformation and of political revolt'.[39] This refusal can be clearly seen in the high staff turnover in call centres. One response to this has been the 'growing preference for part-time permanent staff' as they are 'seen as able to deliver optimal performance for the entire duration of a shift'. All of the positions open at the call centre were part-time, with minimum weekly requirements and options to work longer if wanted. This flexibility correlates with 'the desirability of shift patterns which correspond to the peaks of customer demand', rather than the scheduling needs of the worker.[40] There were a number of non-financial incentives used in addition to the bonus structure at the call centre to encourage workers. The main incentive was the option of leaving early from a shift if a worker had reached their targets; an insightful strategy, since the best reward was to no longer be at work. It was fairly common to hit targets and leave early, especially in the final half hour of the shift, when supervisors would shout out 'get a sale and go!'.

The manipulation of the work schedule returns to the key problem of the capitalist enterprise, which bosses have grappled with since the inception of capitalism itself: how to extract the maximum amount of surplus value from workers during their time on the job. In this regard, the theories of Taylorism are 'an answer to the specific problem of how best to control alienated labour – that is to say, labour power that is bought and sold'.[41] The measurement of the length of the working day is a basic attempt to ensure that workers fulfil the sale of their labour power to the capitalist. By allowing workers to leave early once they had met their sales targets, management provided an incentive to intensify labour in the time workers spent on the job. This is an implicit recognition of the estrangement of workers from the labour process. After the application of Taylorism, which involves 'an acceleration of the rhythm of work, achieved by the elimination of the workday's "pores" (that is of "dead" production time)'.[42] The reward that works best for workers is a sanctioned realisation of their desire to refuse to work, celebrated even if they are only allowed to leave ten minutes early. However, this reward became so widespread in the call centre that management calculated that only 79 per cent of paid time was spent on the phone, and introduced a rule that no worker could leave earlier than that final half hour.

The prevalence of technological methods of control in the call centre does not solve all of management's problems. The methods for collecting statistics and recordings of phone calls still require human input to interpret and act upon them. This is evident in the number of supervisors employed in the call centre. Management requires this human component, since 'no electronic system can summon an agent to a coaching session, nor highlight the deficiencies of their dialogue with the customer'. It is therefore possible to say that call centres 'rely on a combination of technologically driven measurements and human supervisors'.[43] The use of scripts for telephone calls is 'an attempt to structure the very speech of workers into a series of predictable, regulated and routinised queries and responses'. Scripts are a logical extension of Taylorism, as 'they represent a qualitative transformation in the degree to which management attempts to exert control over the white-collar labour process'. It is this which Taylor and Bain argue 'represents an unprecedented level of *attempted* control which must be considered a novel departure'.[44]

3

MANAGEMENT

In the documentary *The Call Centre*,[1] as we saw in Chapter 1, Nev Wilshire embodies the figure of management. The first episode detailed Nev enforcing his managerial authority in various ways. While Nev shouts and even throws a pen at a worker, the narrator explains that he 'has developed a unique approach to keeping his young workforce on their toes'. Nev then discusses his management style, declaring his inspiration is 'probably Napoleon . . . a dictator'. This choice of inspiration also gives a new meaning to the term factory despotism, regardless of whether Nev is playing up to the cameras or not. While I saw nothing quite like this during my time working, it is indicative of the aggressive managerial style common in call centres.

In the discussion that follows, the role of management in the call centre will be interrogated. This will focus on the use of technological methods of supervision and control, but also on the role of supervisors themselves on the call-centre floor. The workplace itself was not formally organised and this meant that many of the technologies and practices have been implemented without collective resistance. However, as the examples of the 'undercover boss' and the interview with a call centre activist show, management still faces major challenges in controlling and motivating workers.

THE UNDERCOVER BOSS

It was clear from the start of my stint in the call centre that supervision was important for management. Yet before I made even a single call I encountered an unexpected management tactic. During the training there was an attendee who was noticeably out of place. He was much older than the other trainees, and wore a smart suit with a big watch and expensive shoes. It became clear in the course of the training that he was a consultant employed by the company, although this was not mentioned at first. He had been employed to try and 'streamline' the inbound side of the call centre. The outbound operations of the same call centre were taken as a model for improvement, so he would go through the training, work the phones and speak to employees. While he could draw on his thirty years of experience in the insurance industry – he had even developed some of the products they sold – he had never actually worked in a call centre. The undercover aspect fell apart during the training as he confessed his role to the group, despite the effect this could have on his own research. It seemed he did this to distance himself from the other young low-paid workers. As this discussion will show, our discovery of the consultant was more than an amusing anomaly. While his presence in the call centre is interesting in itself, it also provides a useful starting point for interrogating the role of supervision.

During the training an imaginary model reminiscent of those found in an economics textbook was used to explain the concept of insurance. It proposed that we imagine there are five farmers. Each one has a cow that costs £100. The farmers choose to insure their cows, each paying £25 to an insurance company. According to the model this allows the compensation of one cow per year with a healthy surplus of £25. At this point I asked, instead of paying money to the company, what was stopping the farmers pooling the money and choosing what to do with the surplus themselves? The trainer hesitated, giving the opportunity for the consultant to speak once again. He argued that this was not possible without the insurer's capital. I replied that an insurance cooperative would allow the farmers to build their own reserves, otherwise it would just be expropriated as profit by the company. The consultant stated: 'Well, it just wouldn't be possible' and 'That's just how it works'.

The consultant appeared as the personification of capital during the training session. His experience of working in insurance was combined with a basic managerial logic found in books like *Call Centers for Dummies*.[2] Yet he lacked any understanding of what working in a call centre actually involved. His undercover project was like those undertaken in the reality TV shows *Undercover Boss*[3] and *Back to the Floor*.[4] Both of these demonstrate how it is possible for workplace research methods to become appropriated by capital. *Back to the Floor* followed company bosses as they spend time working at the other end of the company. They work at the coal face – and quite literally in one episode. The aim is to understand how the company works in reality and the attitudes of the workers it employs. Hugh Dehn, the producer of the series, explains that 'virtually all of the bosses now positively advocate the system'.[5]

In extolling the virtues of the system Dehn focuses on the example of Butlin's holiday camps. On a return visit to Butlin's a few months after filming there, he finds the boss has repeated the process independently. As part of a £130 million improvement project, he spent three days working in the Butlin's call centre. Feeding back to the other members of the executive board, he states: 'I have been in there, and I was up to my neck in guano. It has got to be the furnace of the centre. It was absolutely bloody hell in there'.[6] This is not a sympathetic attempt to understand the stress of customer services. Rather than trying to improve the conditions in the call centre, the boss lays the blame at the lack of proper 'computer support systems, and only two telephone lines'. This is because 'the longer it took' to resolve phone calls, 'the angrier the customers became'. So the boss is able to find an instrumental use for his experience on the floor. The problem is the result of technical impediments to speeding up the labour process. At no point is there a consideration of the effects of increasing the pace of work. Following the presentation, the executives can be confident that customer services have undergone a quantitative, if not qualitative, improvement.

The reality-TV show *Undercover Boss* developed the format further. It follows 'high flying executives tak[ing] extraordinary steps to ensure their companies are fighting fit by going undercover in their own businesses'.[7] The episodes generally involve a series of common elements. The undercover boss is disguised with a new haircut, perhaps a hat, and maybe even a false moustache. There

is surprise at how difficult the work is and shock at the ineffi-
ciencies found. The workers often have difficult life stories and
suffer under adverse conditions. While some of the workers have
new ideas for improving production, these all go unheard. In each
programme there is a failure of communication with the top of the
company. Armed with these new insights the boss returns to the
head office to reflect on the experience, a selection of workers is
summoned and the boss reveals his true identity. After the shock
cutaways, they discuss the problems in the company. This usually
involves implementing new systems based on worker suggestions,
training courses and sometimes promotions. A series of rewards
are then handed out to workers who impressed the boss. As Toby
Miller has argued, like many other reality-TV shows, it is 'suffused
with deregulatory nostra of individual responsibility, avarice,
possessive individualism, hyper-competitiveness, and commodification'.[8] Blame is laid on individuals and problems (both in the
company and society) could be solved if they just tried that little
bit harder. However, there is recognition that the boss could not
have gained new knowledge without going undercover. There is
no attempt – and of course this is hardly a surprise – to understand
the antagonisms of the workplace.

Undercover Boss is an example of how an inquiry into a workplace
is not a neutral undertaking. The method is not the sole preserve of
those seeking to understand workers' struggle. Instead it can form
part of a project to increase exploitation and weaken resistance.
Indeed, there are many instances in which management has
used similar techniques to understand production. For example,
Frederick Taylor developed his scientific theory of management
this way. He took 'the step, extraordinary for anyone of his class,
of starting a craft apprenticeship in a firm whose owners were
social acquaintances of his parents'.[9] While working his way up
at the Midvale Steel Company he carried out a vast number of
experiments. This led Taylor to argue that 'managers assume . . .
the burden of gathering together all of the traditional knowledge
which in the past has been possessed by the workmen and then
of classifying, tabulating, and reducing this knowledge to rules,
laws, and formulae'.[10] But this was an inquiry carried out from the
perspective of capital, so the knowledge was to have a purpose. The

motivation was to discover new methods to overcome what Taylor believed was the 'universal prevalence and in fact inevitability of "soldiering"' on the part of workers. This is the deliberate attempt by workers to slow the speed of production.[11] This 'soldiering' will discussed further in the following chapter as one moment of resistance. For now, it is worth considering how it has concerned management since Taylor.

TECHNOLOGIES OF CONTROL

The antagonism in the workplace means that the *Undercover Boss* approach can only go so far. Once a greater knowledge has been gained – or stolen – it has to be acted upon. The development of control in call centres has been intimately bound up with new technology. At present it is articulated in two interrelated ways: through technology and by supervisors. The latter will be returned to later, but for now the former requires attention. The first call centres would seem quite anachronistic by comparison to those of today: workers huddled over phonebooks, dialling numbers, holding the telephone handset, all the while scribbling notes on paper to log their own calls. The introduction of new technology was, of course, a process rather than a single event. During my shifts in the call centre it was not possible to see how previous struggles had shaped their introduction. So I decided to interview Michael, a call-centre activist.[12] He had worked at a range of different call centres over an extended period of time. In the interview, Michael explained what it was like to work in a call centre as new technological methods of surveillance and control were introduced.

The example that Michael spoke about most was a typical high-volume sales call centre. The conditions were poor with all workers on zero-hour contracts. In a similar vein to what I presented in the previous chapter, he described his first experiences in a call centre:

> the first time that I had worked in an environment where the work was non-stop and regimented . . . You know it's almost the

pressure to hit targets, do you know what I mean? There never seemed to be a couple of hours without worrying about whether you were up on them. The targets for those would be just so high and also the targets in terms of the amount of calls that you need to make are so high, those were really, really draining.

The workplace had the characteristics common for sales jobs: a regimented labour process driven by quantitative targets. Michael explained that the now ubiquitous computer surveillance was not present at first. Breaks were not counted to the second, unless there was a particularly attentive supervisor with a watch. There was a degree of autonomy, 'as long as workers hit their targets, you pretty much got left alone'. But this relative freedom did not last. When the plans for new technology were announced 'people definitely saw that this was going to make the job tougher'. On this point Michael stressed that this 'is not to say that there wasn't kind of harsh controls and stuff before'. He continued to explain that 'there was a really wretched atmosphere in call centres from campaign managers [the supervisors], horrible kind of atmosphere, threats and all sorts of things like that going on'. Michael explained that supervisors were 'constantly listing things that people couldn't do ... There were all sorts of rules'. For example, 'hanging coats on the back of your chair was banned, little things like that'. These were things that did not affect the productivity of workers directly. This suggests the rules were more about power. Again, for example, Michael said he had 'seen people being chased into toilets because they have their phones on them and stuff like that!'. Importantly he stressed that 'all these things you can do with or without the computers'. Thus the new technological methods build upon an already existing aggressive style of management. The introduction of these technologies represented a solidifying of the supervisors' power. In doing so, it allowed for a much more effective imple-mentation of management control.

The technological innovations centre on the linking of the telephone to a computer. This allowed a three-way strengthening of management. The first was the speed-up of the labour process. The automatic call distributor heralded the beginning of the modern call centre. It took the process of connecting calls away from the control of the operator. This allowed the queuing of incoming calls and the automatic dialling of outgoing calls. The control of phone-call pacing was taken away from the worker, maximising the amount of calls made in a shift. The second is that computerisation allows the automated collection of huge quantities of data. The meshing of telephones with computers means that software can collect and collate data about each worker's performance. This goes even further with the complete integration of VoIP (Voice over Internet Protocol) technology. These quantitative variables are often context-free. They appear as something that cannot be debated, instead becoming the evidence base for rewards or discipline. The third is related to this data collection, but has a particular importance. Digital records of all phone calls are easily made and can be kept with marginal storage costs. Management saves each sales call in an archive, as the call itself acts as a verbal contract for the sale between the customer and company. This meant every single phone call I ever made could be played back at a moment's notice.

This practice makes possible an unprecedented level of surveillance. Every call encounter is preserved for eternity, every mistake might be punishable in the future. It is like the ability to recall every commodity produced on an assembly line, then retrospectively judge the quality of its production and apportion blame for errors to workers accordingly. The three examples discussed just above highlight the way managerial control is programmed into technology. To return to Braverman's insights from the previous chapter, control is seen as secondary to efficiency. The separation of conception from execution is driven by the imperative of efficiency. For example, the scripting of the phone call. Except, as Michael Burawoy argues, 'Braverman presents another view, based on the Babbage principle, according to which control is inseparable from the pursuit of efficiency'.[13] Babbage argued that 'one great advantage which we may derive from machinery . . . is from the check which it affords against the inattention, the idleness, or the dishonesty of human agents'.[14] It represents a novel way to combat the 'soldiering' of workers. The language used by Babbage is also reminiscent of Taylor's frustration. Thus the speed up in the call is not the only gain, it simultaneously introduced new methods of control.

Technological innovation could be treated as just the result of competition between capitalists. Yet this risks missing a nuanced understanding of how capital becomes built into machinery. Designers, like engineers, consider how a machine will be used. Thus 'the labor configuration to operate it' is considered by both and shapes the design itself. After all, the machine is 'made to be operated' and that operation involves costs. Other than the costs of the machine, 'the hourly costs of labor' become part of the 'calculation involved in machine design'. A design that allows operation to be broken down into parts becomes cheaper. It is then sought after by engineers and managers who 'have so internalized this value that it appears to them to have the force of natural law or scientific necessity'.[15] New technology is not neutral from the very start. It can be understood further in terms of management's objectives, the most obvious of which is to increase the volumes of calls handled by each worker. The automatic call dialler is one way to do this. Consider Braverman's explanation of how 'machinery offers management the opportunity to do by wholly mechanical means that which it had previously attempted to do by organizational and disciplinary means'. Taking the control of dialling away from workers allows the pace to be dictated centrally. These 'technical possibilities are of just as great interest to management as the fact that the machine multiplies the productivity of labor'.[16]

SUPERVISION

As explained in the discussion of the conversation with Michael above, the introduction of technology followed already developed supervisory practices. The supervisors play a crucial role on the call-centre floor, but one that can be overlooked by focusing on the technological methods. For example, Foucault's writing is often cited in discussions of call centres, but these mainly focus on his account of the Panopticon. While we will return to that later, Foucault's work on discipline is also useful for our understanding of supervision. Foucault discusses factory discipline at length. He understood that it 'was a question of distributing individuals in a space which one might isolate them and map them; but also articulating this distribution on a production machinery that had its own requirements'.[17] In factory work the implications of this are clear: separating workers based on the division of labour and increasing the speed of the assembly line. The spatial arrangements of the call centre are somewhat different. Each desk with its computer and headset has the same qualities as the other. It should not matter where workers sit, yet the call centre in which I was working had distinct sections. The row by the exit was for the top sellers, the opposite side for the newest trainees, and there were degrees of ability between. Each section had different supervisors with different roles. There were those training the newcomers and those encouraging the top sellers. The supervisors continued the practice of 'walking up and down the central isle of the workshop' – or along the call centre rows – to 'carry out a supervision that was both general and individual' of the performance of particular workers and the overall performance of the teams.[18]

The role of the supervisor has two interrelated parts. The first is the discipline of time – ensuring that workers arrive on time, checking breaks, booking shifts and preventing workers from leaving early. The second returns to the problem of the indeterminacy of labour. To 'assure the quality of the time used: constant supervision, the pressure of supervisors, the elimination of anything that might disturb or distract; it is a question of constituting a totally useful time'.[19] In the call centre this involves both the use of technology and human supervision. The innovations in technology automatically reduced the gaps between calls to the bare minimum. The challenge for management was then to devise new methods to further discipline time. This is because the 'time measured and paid must also be a time without impurities or defects; a time of good quality, throughout which the body is constantly applied to its exercise'.[20] Thus the supervisor in the call centre is crucial for the day-to-day management of workers. Although the top manager would occasionally come onto the floor, it was never clear what he was actually doing. He had not – as far as I am aware – ever worked in a call centre himself. The only real contact with him was at the company's social events or at the monthly award ceremony. He would deliver a dry PowerPoint presentation about the company's performance, with slide after slide of vague graphs. In practice, the supervisors acted as the agents of management.

There were four main supervisors in the call centre, two for the Academy trainees, and two to supervise the day and evening teams. They all had experience of working in call centres, whether this one or another. Each of the supervisors had quite different styles and personalities. Working out how to negotiate with them could have a significant impact on the experience of the shift. If a supervisor looked favourably on a worker the experience of work could be modulated. The supervisors could intensify the labour process in various ways. They decided who stayed after training as well as the probation deadlines with human resources. Thus building and maintaining a relationship with the supervisors had a noticeable impact, both upon the time actually spent working, but also the potential length of employment. It is also another demand on the emotional labour of workers – how to best interact with each supervisor to make the experience of work slightly easier.

The supervisor's pay was slightly higher than workers due to the possibility of significant monthly bonuses. These were awarded based on the performance of the teams they supervised, measured both by sales figures and the avoidance of 'red calls' (errors that contravened company or regulatory policy). These bonuses were large enough that failure to attain them would significantly affect their income and potentially their lifestyle. Mostly this did not cause problems in relations between supervisors and operators, with supervisors giving general advice and common warnings. However, towards the end of the month this would change. As the number of red calls approached the 10 per cent threshold (after which bonuses would be cancelled) they became noticeably agitated. The buzz sessions became more intense and the supervisors' behaviour increasingly aggressive. They would pick on individual workers for their mistakes and chastise them in front of the group. On one occasion we were herded into a training room and our supervisor ranted at us for over an hour about the importance of quality. This was partly to vent frustration, and partly to keep the trainees off the phones altogether. This practice definitely reduced the chances of further mistakes being made.

The supervisors struggled to achieve the managerial objectives. For example, at the end of one month in particular, the supervisors were desperate to keep their bonuses. One supervisor resorted to waving a picture of his baby son around. He claimed that if the team did not reach the sales target the baby 'would go hungry next month'. It is not clear whether the baby's food would be the first or last thing he cut from the budget. Yet this emotional blackmail does show how much he wanted the bonus, and the extent to which he was prepared to go in order to get it. Although this was perhaps a poor attempt, it is illustrative of a number of points. Firstly, despite the supervisors' quasi-managerial role, there was not much difference between their material conditions and those of more low-level workers. Secondly, getting workers to achieve targets was not straightforward. There was no one thing that supervisors could do to ensure this, meaning that they would rely on discipline and manipulation. Thirdly, the bonuses affected the supervisors' behaviour; they would even devise strategies that undermined the profitability of the call centre to safeguard their bonuses.

To illustrate the latter point, the monthly targets had a notable effect on the provision of training. In the last few days of the month the amount of training would increase dramatically. A large part of a shift could be spent in a separate room going over sales techniques or other kinds of training. In some instances the trainees would spend part of the shift just playing buzz-session games away from the call-centre floor. This ensured that the workers who were most likely to make bad calls were kept off the phones and constituted a last-ditch attempt by supervisors to maintain their averages. They would act in their own economic interest – even if that involved disrupting the labour process – to achieve their own goals. Unsurprisingly, there were no complaints from workers at getting these extra breaks.

The manipulative behaviour of the supervisors raises questions of power. The workforce was predominantly young and the majority of workers were women, approximately 80 per cent on a typical shift. In contrast, half the supervisors were men, along with almost all the senior management. Within this context it is perhaps no surprise to find there was a culture of sexism in the call centre. Many conversations included sexual content that was reminiscent of what appeared in the *Call Centre* documentary. Misogynistic and sexist comments were commonplace. Coming from a university setting – in which sexism is more likely to be the subject of a discussion than the content – I was not expecting to find this. This is not to imply that the university is free from sexism, but that there it operates in a much more covert manner. In the call centre it took an open form.

The relationship between supervisors and workers could in this context become overtly sexist. One of the male supervisors would often make sexist comments about women while they were working. These were mainly ignored by others in the call centre, to the point that they became normalised. Alongside his running commentary, he would walk around offering massages to young women. There were often complaints about him during the breaks and I followed up on one of these. The worker explained how she had told the supervisor not to touch her, nor did she want to 'banter'. After this he ignored her completely, both in this behaviour and his supervisory role. He stopped harassing her and offering sales advice. She said that she preferred this option as she could now just get on with her work and then leave. This kind of confrontation was not typical. The other workers I spoke to detailed how they would try to manipulate him in return. The aim of this was to get him to relax his supervision and even bend the rules to their benefit. There was a general sense of resignation that nothing could be done about his harassment – it was just to be expected.

The supervisors' power extended beyond the individual shift. Through control of the shift scheduling they could also change when workers had to come in. This had a big impact, particularly for those with other personal commitments, studies or second jobs. Any holiday allocation, which was unpaid, also had to be approved by supervisors. Failure to work the scheduled hours per week (in effect, taking unauthorised holiday) could result in dismissal. The supervisors could also determine when a worker had to be on the phones or what time they could leave a shift. In addition, supervisors could fire workers on the spot with little or no justification, partly due to peculiarities of the contract, and partly due to workers' lack of knowledge about employment rights. Thus it is unsurprising that supervisors used and abused their power over workers. The lack of contestation over the 'frontier of control' left workers feeling powerless[21] and strengthened the concentration of power in the hands of the supervisors. The example of the female worker who objected to sexual harassment ('massage') illustrates how organised refusal was difficult. Using the term 'banter' to cover objectionable comments was used to defuse tensions in favour of the supervisor and legitimate inappropriate behaviour; it should not be taken seriously, and the actions became trivialised as a 'joke'. If the complaint was pursued the blame would then lie with the person's failure to 'get the joke' or to 'play along'.

As we discussed earlier, in *The Call Centre* documentary Nev parades what he describes as 'a desperate female' around the call centre trying to find her a date. This behaviour is shocking to see, yet as the programme unfolds it becomes clearer how these practices have developed. How does management determine if someone can make sales during an interview? The ephemeral qualities needed to be a good seller are difficult to quantify. So managers and supervisors turn to increasingly bizarre justifications for their approach. In Nev's case it seems to boil down to an assessment of a worker's 'confidence'. In practice, this involved walking a woman around the call centre and asking the other workers if they would employ her. Nev explains it is also 'to see if any of the boys fancy you', explicitly objectifying the woman. Thus anyone who immediately opposes this kind of behaviour is selected out, as they will not get the job. Afterward, this criticism is undermined in the way already discussed; anyone offended must be failing to 'get the joke'.

DISCIPLINE

The sexist environment in the call centre put additional pressures on workers' behaviour. The management of the labour process also extended to disciplinary control of the body. In certain types of work this is more straightforward, while in others less so. Foucault's understanding of this is attentive to the subtleties at work. He explains how disciplinary control

> does not consist simply in teaching or imposing a series of particular gestures; it imposes the best relation between a gesture and the overall position of the body . . . good handwriting, for example, presupposes a gymnastics – a whole routine whose rigorous code invests the body in its entirety, from the points of the feet to the tip of the index finger.[22]

The physicality of the call-centre labour process does not seem that important at first. However, throughout training the physical aspects of a 'good' phone call are regularly reiterated. Workers are not allowed to sit slouching at the desk making calls. The supervisors explain that an upright posture must be maintained at all times, keeping the head lifted to project the voice. It is not simply a case of reading the words out loud. The voice itself requires modulation throughout the script. Trainees get printed scripts and annotate them with the required pace, tone, pauses, emphasis and indications of where to freely elaborate. It is regularly stated that standing and gesticulating can add the ephemeral 'good' quality to calls. Trainees have to observe the top sellers and emulate their delivery. I struggled to understand how mimicking posture and hand movement would lead to sales. Even so, my own best results all involved a physical aspect. I developed a routine: standing up at the start of the call, ensuring that my body was moving, gesturing as if addressing someone in person, with specific movements and exaggerated facial expressions. While this bizarre performance worked for me, each worker had to develop their own style.

The affective component of the labour process proves problematic for management. This aspect is not like the finished commodity leaving the Fordist production line. No two interactions on the phone are ever exactly the same. So no one strategy can ensure a sale in each and every encounter. The use of emotion and humour are by definition subjective and receive different responses. Thus, achieving discipline over the labour process is particularly difficult. The attempt begins with the scripting. This takes place away from the call-centre floor, a process shrouded in mystery and not to be questioned. The script provides the skeleton of the conversation which is the fleshed out with different affects. The disciplinary role of the supervisor is to apply the 'principle of a theoretically ever-growing use of time'. This means 'exhaustion rather than use'. So rather than forcing workers to stay longer in the call centre, 'it is a question of extracting, from time, ever more available moments and, from each moment, ever more useful forces'.[23] In the context of sales this is an attempt to combine both quantitative and qualitative objectives. Workers must make more calls during their shift, and then seek to close sales in each and every one.

The buzz session is one example of how supervisors attempt to motivate workers in call centres. The two trainers who led these sessions always stressed how important it was to be in the right mood to sell. The problem for management is how you go about doing this. None of the workers want to be at work, as is common in these kinds of part-time jobs. Most have other interests, passions or things they would rather be doing. The buzz session is an attempt, as Carl Cederström and Peter Fleming argue, 'to inject life into the dead-zone of work'.[24] This means management actively encouraging workers to 'just be yourself!'. The characteristics discouraged in the Fordist workplaces of the past are now demanded: personality, quirks, different tastes and so on. Despite the regulation of the labour process, 'there is no better call center worker than the one who can improvise around the script'. This requires the worker to 'breathe life into a dead role and pretend their living death is in fact the apogee of life'.

Each shift began by gathering all workers together for a motivational session. We would pack into the small side room attached to the break area. Most of the workers squeezed along rows of worn sofas, the last to arrive stood awkwardly by the exit. These buzz sessions involved a range of staged 'fun' activities. The most common were alphabetical rule games. For example the 'going on a picnic game'. This involves a hypothetical picnic that the supervisors devise a rule for what you can bring. Each of the workers then asks if they can come with an item, receiving a yes or no in response. One by one the workers have to continue asking until everybody is accepted onto the picnic. The rules ranged from the simple (the same colour) to more complex alphabetical ordering. For example, the first letter of the item must start with the same first letter as the name of the person to the left. It is not clear what this has to do with sales, but the supervisors enjoyed watching workers squirm as they failed to guess.

The other activities involved more word games, general knowledge quizzes or the scintillating company rule competition. The motivation for participating was the possibility of leaving slightly early at the end of the shift if you won. This still did not alleviate the excruciatingly uncomfortable moments. At one point we had to sing 'Happy Birthday' to the elderly and quite confused grandmother of a supervisor. Another supervisor developed a penchant for interrogating workers about their personal lives. But the worst came with the discovery of a new iPhone app. It was a form of charades: one person (always a supervisor) holds the phone up to their forehead and points it to a group of people. It then displays an example to act out, sing or impersonate. But it differed from charades in that the iPhone camera records these performances. Unlike the other demeaning games, the trainer could then replay the most embarrassing moments. The glee with which supervisors started this game was an uninviting start to the buzz session.

While these encounters seem bizarre and 'remote from the large-scale shifts reshaping a waning late-capitalism' there is an interesting insight captured here. These attempts at enthusing workers are 'novel forms of regulation' focused 'on those moments of life that once flourished beyond the remit of the corporation'.[25] The challenges of management in the call centre thus feed into the buzz sessions. There is a twofold realisation. First, it is only when 'workers had checked-out (either literally or mentally) that they begin to feel human again and buzz with life'. Second, 'that call center work requires high levels of social intelligence, innovation and emotional initiative'. So various attempts emerge that try to 'find a way of capturing and replicating that buzz of life . . . on the job'.[26] This explains examples like this in the call centre:

The workers looked at the floor anxiously, feigning smiles but knowing that something pretty awful was about to happen. They were told to form a circle as Carla – the 'team development leader' – prepared to deliver a pep-talk, which would have been funny if not for the sadistic glint in her eye. 'As you all know, life at Sunray is more than just a job, it's all about fun and enjoying yourself, here you can really shine and be yourself!' The workers shifted nervously as she bleated on, 'And it's all about color and fun . . . OK guys, let's do it!'. 'Oh Jesus,' muttered one worker with blue hair and an anarchist tattoo on his wrist. Carla hit PLAY on her outdated CD player and we all began to sing Kermit the Frog's only Top-10 single: 'Why are there, so many, songs about rainbows, what makes the world go round . . . someday we'll find it, the rainbow connection, the lovers, the dreamers and me . . .'[27]

Management is concerned with more than just the participation of workers in these activities. It is not enough to take part: the worker must take part in a particular way. Ostensibly it is about 'fun', but it also involves a 'coercive nature'. Failing to take part in a genuine way risks one's labelling as 'a party-pooper', which is 'the most serious crime you could commit, even worse than taking these exercises to the extreme'.[28] Thus these attempts to intensify the labour process involve new affective demands for workers. It is not enough to sell your labour-power – nor even to work hard during that time – you must also enjoy the process. To return to Marx, the regime of real subsumption colonises life beyond work. Capital, vampire-like,[29] sinks its teeth into the emotions as well as the bodies of workers. The demand for authenticity is a significant pressure for workers, not only in their performance on the phone, but also to the evaluative gaze of management. The labour process is therefore disciplined with a range of different 'tactics'. These involve, as Foucault argues, 'the art of constructing, with located bodies, coded activities and trained aptitudes, mechanisms in which the product of various forces is increased by their calculated combination'.[30]

Another of these tactics is the '1-2-1' meeting. Besides the supervisor's presence on the call-centre floor, this is an important aspect of management control. Once a week each worker has to come to a '1-2-1' meeting in a separate room. Although the name implies four people, there were only two in the '1-2-1' coaching meeting. After being beckoned into the room, the worker was presented with a performance sheet. It formed the basis of the discussion with the supervisor. The worker's performance is then dissected with various suggestions about how they can improve. It always involved stipulating new targets. Throughout my time at the call centre I kept a record of the '1-2-1' meetings. I always asked for a photocopy, saying that I wanted to study it further. While this was true, it also gave an inflated impression of my commitment. The advice I received was often contradictory, highlighting again the difficulty in teaching workers to sell.

The '1-2-1' meetings were structured around a one-page form divided into five sections. The first details the 'Performance on targets/objectives' set in the last meeting with tick-boxes. The second section lays out the 'New targets/objectives'. Along with plenty of space there is a reminder that failure to reach these can result in disciplinary action. It also includes a 'SMART action plan'. Rather than an opportunity for intelligent planning, SMART is a mnemonic for setting *specific, measurable, attainable, relevant* and *time-bound* goals. Yet instead of a 'SMART action plan' I only ever received a list of positive and negative comments. Arguably, none of these ever met the requirements of the mnemonic. The third section records 'attendance/timekeeping', the fourth 'training/ development needs', and the fifth 'behaviours/attitude', each with space for notes and any actions required. The form finishes with space for signatures of the worker and supervisor, agreeing to the analysis and outcomes.

The first '1-2-1' meeting detailed my performance in vague terms. My SMART action plan stated:

Does well to elaborate/expand on F+B. F+B uses first name well. Pace good, pauses decent. Natural and conversational. Add okays and greats after F+B. Add more energy in tone. Add emphasis on key words. Use assertive okays. Need a more assertive tone. Does well to take on feedback and apply. C&R stay assumptive, close and move on with script.

There was not much else on the feedback form other than ticks in boxes, targets and one line explaining the need to 'stay/sound confident, project voice!'. Throughout the forms there is a heavy use of acronyms. For example, F+B (features and benefits), C&R (clarify and reassure), and DD (DirectDebit). Then at the end all I needed to do was sign my name in agreement. The advice given in all my '1-2-1' meetings tended to be similar. Most of the meeting is an attempt to make the worker auto-critique their performance. For example, the common question 'how do you think you can improve? What more could you be doing? How else could you have approached that call?'. A selection of my 'SMART action plans' shows how this developed over my time at the call centre. Jamie (they often began with my name)

... has improved his script delivery. More natural and flowing, conversational. More assertive around DD page. Confidently C&R and close, advance C&R training will help.
Stay assumptive when C&R'ing. Don't lose confidence (Hear this in his voice), Natural and conversational through DD. F+B use pauses in the right places = let cust digest info. Keep pace steady and constant. Use a more reassuring/firm tone (take control). E.g. Use Okays! Greats and customer name.
... has got off to a great start this week (well done and keep this up). Needs to focus on improving his performance and keeping it constant. Aim for 4 more sales this week. Use training materials such as advance C&R and put this into practice. Stay confident when C&R'ing/close and stay positive. Sound more assertive, firm tone.

After these examples the '1-2-1' meetings started becoming less frequent. They only picked up again once my performance stopped improving. As the feedback explains:

Pauses are good, as is pace. Don't pause for too long, not allowing customer to interrupt, just let the script flow. Good use of positive words, don't over use positive words as it loses its purpose. Don't offer quote straight away, follow C&R procedure. Great use of okays. Do well to sell on F+B. Apply training, adv C&R. Change mentality, approach to selling on competition leads. Don't get defeated, objections will always come up, stay positive. Confidence.

... can sometimes get defeated when doing C&R, closing, needs to have more belief and be more assertive, rather than saying it for the sake of it. Needs to start improving performance, gets close to his target, then gets defeated, keep up confidence.

These excerpts from the '1-2-1' feedback sheets again highlight the difficulty for supervisors. How can they provide constructive feedback that can actually improve sales for workers? The encouragement to be 'confident' or 'assertive' is hard to disagree with, but there is little elaboration about what this actually means during a phone call.

Sales Feedback Sheet

1. Call intro (alert, focused, not talking outside the call)
2. Script delivery (natural and conversational, using first name, pace, energy, pausing)
3. Confidence (assertive okays, assumptive tone)
4. Assertiveness (taking control, closing)
5. Rapport (use of rapport building)
6. Selling on Benefits (features to benefits, key word emphasis, sounding enthusiastic, pausing after benefits, positive words, okays)
7. TCF and compliance (not selling on cooling off period, offering quote on a second objection)
8. Timeliness (spending appropriate time on Free Offer (no longer than 6 mins), and pitch)
9. C&R (acknowledgement, dealt with specific objections, probed, closed after C&R)
10. Behaviours (positive use of language, positive body language, sitting up straight, and adapting to client)

The 'Sales Feedback Sheet' is also used by supervisors while they listen into calls. The sheet has ten areas required for 'effective selling', each with a number of options that are either ticked if they are achieved during the call or underlined if not. There is also a space for additional comments, divided into positive and corrective. The feedback sheet, like the '1-2-1' meetings, seem almost deliberately vague. The aim is apparently not to encourage a particular method of selling or train a homogeneous group of workers. The emotional and affective part of the labour process is complex, for example, valuing of unique characteristics and prizing qualities such as 'personality'. These instruments encourage a kind of quasi-Maoist auto-critique. Workers have to constantly repeat where they have gone wrong and how they will improve. The mantra is repeated at the start of shifts, in training sessions, and the '1-2-1' meetings. This process shifts the emphasis onto the worker as active agent in every potential sale on the phone. It rests on a notion of the customer without agency: they do not really know what they want, so the worker must convince them. Thus every call has the potential to be a sale, so long as the worker internalises and repeats this combination of self-help phrases and management buzzwords.

THE PANOPTICON

The analogy of the Panopticon is used frequently in the academic literature on call centres. Often these involve arguments about control, either its totalisation or the effect of minimising resistance. Jeremy Bentham first discussed the Panopticon as an architectural structure that would allow 'a new mode of obtaining power of mind over mind, in a quantity hitherto without example'.[31] The now familiar construction of the central observation post with individual cells around it, allowed 'the apparent omnipresence of the inspector . . . combined with the extreme facility of his real presence'.[32]

It is worth looking at Bentham's writing before moving on to discuss Foucault's developments. Bentham argues that when dealing with workers: 'whatever be the manufacture, the utility of the principle is obvious and incontestable, in all cases where the workmen are paid according to their time'.[33] He foresaw an application for the Panopticon to remedy the indeterminacy of labour power. Bentham compares this to pay 'by the piece' which he regards as the superior method of payment for work. In this case, the workers' interest 'in the value of' their 'work supersedes the use of coercion, and of every expedient calculated to give force to it'. This is a move away from direct control, instead providing workers with rewards to motivate themselves. It is also an attempt to get workers to internalise the demands of work. In the call centre the employer purchases labour-power for a set time and pays an hourly rate for shifts. However, the sales bonus introduces an element of piece-work.

The call centre Panopticon is not recreated exactly along the lines described by Bentham. There is no central tower from which the supervisors can simultaneously observe all workers, while remaining unobserved themselves. The computer surveillance is clearly analogous, offering the potential to interrogate each worker without their knowledge. Yet the arrangement of the call-centre floor is also reminiscent of the Panopticon. Each row of desks has a supervisor seated at the end. From here they can observe individual workers, both their physical performance and their computer screens. Bentham expresses concern for finding a method to allow the inspector to view out of the tower while also examining their own ledger of accounts, something that is difficult without providing illumination that would reveal the inside. A complex 'lantern' is considered 'pierced at both elevations with small holes . . . no larger than the aperture of a common spying-glass, and, like that, closed by a piece of glass, which if necessary might be coloured, or smoked, or darkened by a blind'.[34] The computer screens of the supervisors operate in a much more simple way. While the worker's computer screen is clear, the supervisors have privacy screen filters installed. This filter creates a narrow viewing angle, so the screen can only be viewed from directly in front; therefore the supervisor can view other screens – and various monitoring programmes even allow this remotely – while their own remains hidden. They are free to browse Facebook and look at 'funny' pictures of cats. Unfortunately for them this sometimes became apparent as the filter cannot prevent conversations between supervisors being overheard.

Bentham's discussion of punishment is also worthy of consideration. A critic claimed prisoners would disprove the omnipresence of the inspector through experimentation. In response Bentham spells out a frightening response:

> Will he? I will soon put an end to his experiments: or rather, to be beforehand with him, I will take care he shall not think of making any. I will single out one of the most untoward of the prisoners. I will keep an unintermitted watch upon him. I will watch until I observe a transgression. I will minute it down. I will wait for another: I will note that down too. I will lie by for a whole day: he shall do as he pleases that day, so long as he does not venture at something too serious to be endured. The next day I produce the list to him. – You thought yourself undiscovered: you abused by indulgence: see how you were mistaken. Another time, you may have rope for two days, ten days: the longer it is, the heavier it will fall upon you. Learn from this, all of you, that in this house transgression never can be safe. Will the policy be cruel? – No; it will be kind: it will prevent transgressing; it will save punishing.[35]

What is notable about this example is the role of punishment. It is not just a case of catching someone breaking the rules. Rather, 'in Bentham's eyes, punishment is first and foremost a spectacle: it is insofar as punishment is not intended for the punished individual, but for all others, that the execution of the punishment is a spectacle.'[36]

There is an example from the call centre that illustrates the use of this kind of spectacle. A worker was caught pretending to make phone calls. He was going through the motions, yet whenever someone picked up the phone he immediately ended the call. The worker thought he was getting away with this, so continued for most of the shift. The supervisors identified the problem from the call records. He was immediately fired mid-shift. Precarious employment contracts allow this kind of summary punishment.

There is no protection and the contract can be terminated at a moment's notice. The supervisors did not stop with the sacking. They called everyone into a special meeting in the conference room to explain what had happened. For thirty minutes the supervisors created a spectacle of shouting. This reiterated how workers who broke the rules would be made an example of. After all, the aim of the Panopticon is, as Miran Božovič argues, to 'deter the innocent from committing offences by producing an appearance through reality'.[37] The analogue conception of the Panopticon must therefore create the fiction of omnipresence. The advent of computer surveillance means the fiction of the ever-watching supervisor could become reality. Even if they were to miss something at the time, the records can be scoured for transgressions after the fact.

This disciplinary logic combines with the demand for workers to auto-critique. If discipline were perfected architecturally, there would be no further need for these. Indeed, auto-critique takes on an almost gratuitous aspect considering the number of ways in which workers can be subjected to the management gaze. It is at this point worth turning to the notion of the 'electronic panopticon' that Sue Fernie and David Metcalf use,[38] beginning with Foucault's notion specifically:

> the perfect disciplinary apparatus would make it possible for a single gaze to see everything constantly. A central point would be both the source of light illuminating everything, and a locus of convergence for everything that must be known: a perfect eye that nothing would escape and a centre towards which all gazes would be turned.[39]

This is the ideal type of surveillance found in architectural form in Bentham's account. Yet this total notion of surveillance is not what management is attempting to achieve. As Foucault argues, 'the disciplinary gaze did, in fact, need relays'. So, surveillance became conceptualised as a 'pyramid was able to fulfil, more efficiently than the circle . . . it had to be broken down into smaller elements, but in order to increase its productive function: specify the surveillance and make it functional'.[40] It is therefore necessary to focus on the function of surveillance in the call centre, rather than the general potential.

The role of surveillance at work developed alongside the changes in production. Foucault identifies how in 'the régimes of the manufactories' it 'had been carried out from the outside by inspectors, entrusted with the task of applying the regulations'. This method – one that once produced the reports Marx studied for the chapter on the working day – gave way to something else. The development of factories required 'an intense, continuous supervision; it ran right through the labour process'. With the development of new machines and techniques, it 'became a special function, which had nevertheless to form an integral part of the production process, to run parallel to it throughout its entire length'. This embedding of supervisors throughout the productive process is similar to capital being written into machines. The result is that the 'specialized personnel became indispensable, constantly present and distinct from workers'.[41] Foucault articulates clearly how the supervisory function becomes embedded in the production process. The development in call centres thus builds on a long history of integrating supervision into the productive process.

The notion of the Panopticon continues this integration of supervision and production to a new level. Foucault argued that the major effect of the Panopticon was 'to induce in the inmate a state of conscious and permanent visibility that assures the automatic functioning of power'. The 'perfection' of that power 'should tend to render its actual exercise unnecessary'. Finally, those subject to it 'should be caught up in a power situation of which they are themselves the bearers'.[42] But is it possible to apply this architectural prison model to a workplace? In the call centre workers are subjected to an audible, visual and even electronic 'field of visibility'. It is made abundantly clear to workers that this is the case. But do they then 'assume responsibility for the constraints of power'; do they 'make them play spontaneously play upon' themselves; do they 'inscribe' upon themselves 'the power relation in which' they 'simultaneously play both roles'; and ultimately 'become the principle of' their 'own subjection'?[43]

This paints a picture of an unchecked management, whose power leaves workers helpless. The only alternative seems to be fleeing from the call centre, the advantage being what Marx ironically describes as a doubly free worker – free to choose who to sell their labour to, and additionally freed from the ownership of capital or means of production.[44] It is worth returning to the quote from Alan McKinlay and Phil Taylor, that 'the factory and the office are neither prison nor asylum, their social architectures never those of the total institution.[45] The potential of the Panopticon for surveillance, controlling and intensifying the labour process is clear. To be able to 'diffuse the locus of supervision from the individual who can not be everywhere at once to a roaming gaze that can capture subjects and analyze their movements in multiple places at once.[46] That would be the dream of factory foreman of the past.

NEW MANAGEMENT TECHNIQUES

The metaphor of the Panopticon can extend beyond the workplace to take on broader implications. Massimo De Angelis argues that 'a socially pervasive market order' – like that found in contemporary capitalism – 'presents organisational and disciplinary characteristics that are similar to those of a prison, not just any prison', but 'the panopticon'. He remarks that some might 'find this comparison odd, if not paradoxical.[47] On a deeper comparison, the contribution becomes clear. It focuses on the way in which both are disciplinary mechanisms in which individual 'freedom is limited to a choice from a given menu and they are prevented from defining the context of their interaction.[48] This is particularly useful because it connects the management techniques in the call centre with the broader experiences of neoliberal capitalism.

The Panopticon itself was conceived of as a physical building. Yet it 'can be interfaced with the outside world through an administrative device, bookkeeping and the publication of accounts'. This provides a way for signals to be read from outside. On this basis it can encourage competition between different organisations. One potential signal is that 'bad management is demonstrated by loss of profit'. An example of this, even beyond the sphere of production, can be found with the proliferation of metrics and measurements in universities. These operate internally, on the level of individuals and departments with the REF (Research Excellency Framework), NSS (National Student Survey) and local feedback mechanisms. Then these are aggregated and used to construct league tables, pitting departments and universities against each other. Both the supervised and the supervisor become caught in the mechanism of surveillance. The Panopticon and neoliberal capitalism both involve 'impersonal mechanisms of coordination of individual subjectivities that give form to social labour'. While Bentham found that the impersonal quality imbued the Panopticon with the ability to inspect, Hayek's conception of the market emphasised 'abstract rules of conduct, which bind together private individuals so that there is no need for them to develop common aims'.[49] For the Panopticon the observation tower mediated between individuals, distributing punishments and rewards. Now it is money and prices that play the mediating role.[50]

These processes of commodification and competition have intensified greatly since the 1970s. The changes that have taken place since then are often broadly labelled as neoliberalism. The problem with this categorisation is that it can imply a break from the normal operation of capitalism. Neoliberalism, rather than capitalism, becomes the target of critique. Keeping this in mind it is still important to consider the changes of the past few decades. David Harvey argues that neoliberalism is 'in the first instance a theory of political economic practices that propose that human well-being can best be advanced by liberating individual entrepreneurial freedoms and skills within an institutional framework characterized by strong private property rights, free markets, and free trade'.[51] These 'political economic practices' have risen to a position of hegemony since the 1970s. The result has been programmes of 'deregulation, privatization, and withdrawal of the state from many areas of social provision'. The result of these forced 'neoliberal freedoms have, after all, not only restored power to a narrowly defined capitalist class. They have also produced immense concentrations of corporate power'.[52] This is a key point in Harvey's definition. Neoliberalism is not an aberration. The capitalists have been winning, on the whole, in the class struggle since the 1970s. The working-class movements of the past have suffered significant defeats. Not only that, but the possibilities for new movements have been hamstrung.

This restoration of class power involved sustained attacks on freedom. As Harvey argues, 'financial power could be used to discipline working-class movements',[53] and a devastating assault on the working class was waged, continuing today. It also involved the aggressive 'privatization' that forms 'the cutting edge of accumulation by dispossession'. This process can be identified in the response to the 2008 financial crisis: widespread austerity programs that involve attacks on workers' wages and conditions, slashing of public spending and the privatisation of public services such as health and education. It is in this context that De Angelis argues neoliberal capitalism can be understood as

> a system of interrelated virtual 'inspection house', which we may call the 'fractal panopticon' . . . each panopticon, that is each set of interrelationships of control and resistance defined by a scale of social action, is in turn a singularity within a series of singularities, which stands in relation to each other in such a way that their action constitutes a 'watchtower' that is external to them, thus forming a greater panopticon – and so on in, in a potentially infinite series.[54]

This regime of surveillance utilises new technologies. The past few decades have seen many new innovations, along with drastic reductions in costs. As Harvey argues, neoliberalism 'requires technologies of information creation and capacities to accumulate, store, transfer, analyze, and use massive databases to guide decisions in the global marketplace'.[55] Beyond directly benefiting capital accumulation, these methods are increasingly taken up elsewhere. For example, a UK police force has been experimenting with 'predictive policing'. This involves 'a mingling of criminology, anthropology and mathematics designed to stop crimes before they take place'.[56] It evokes images of the *Minority Report*-style 'pre-crime'. Instead of humans with pre-cognitive powers to see the future, there are databases and algorithms.[57]

It is this general context in which call centres should be understood. A deregulated financial environment combining with technologies of surveillance and control, The lack of an organised working-class movement means the mutations of management are left relatively unchecked. The point here is not to overemphasise the strength of management in the workplace. After all, the mutations of management are not necessarily a sign of strength. For example, as Luc Boltanski and Eve Chiapello have argued in their study of management thought:

> Capitalism cannot find any resources within itself with which to justify grounds for commitment . . . to maintain its powers of attraction, capitalism therefore has to draw upon resources external to it, beliefs which, at a given moment in time, possess considerable powers of persuasion, striking ideologies, even when they are hostile to it.[58]

There is a capacity for management to absorb criticism and subvert it. Instead of this signalling victory on the part of management, it indicates that the problem of gaining consent in capital accumulation remains very real.

To witness managers discussing the alienation of work is at first a confusing phenomenon, yet it makes the thoroughgoing critique of contemporary work even more crucial. The new management techniques, including those detailed above, aim to further motivate workers. This involved insights 'gleaned' from the 'growing industry of self-help and new-age spirituality'. What can now be called 'liberation management' starts from the position that 'no one can exploit workers better than workers themselves'.[59] There is no longer the same fear of absenteeism there was in the Fordist workplace. The binary of present and absent is no longer so clear. In this way it is a return to the Taylorist obsession with the inevitability of soldiering. However, the new demands of this work mean that 'every fiber of your organism to always be switched on, the enemy of production is what human resource managers like to call presenteeism: being present only in body with every other part of you being far, far away'.[60]

The risk of 'presenteeism' is clear for managing affective forms of service work. The experience is understood by 'even a child' that 'knows that the smile and "have a great day" from a customer-service-worker is fundamentally creepy.'[61] This is similar to the 'Uncanny Valley' that occurs with the simulation of emotion by robots or computers. The 'phenomenon implies that virtual characters approaching full human-likeness will evoke a negative reaction from the viewer, due to aspects of the character's appearance and behavior differing from the human norm.'[62] The ability to fool people into believing that an emotion is real is a difficult challenge. The same can be true for people expressing fake emotions: not only is the emotion itself called into question, but it can create a negative experience for the recipient. Call-centre work imposes demands on the delivery and maintenance of packages of affects. The supervision is therefore no longer limited to where, how and what we do on a task, or how long it takes. It reaches into an emotional level: is the worker deploying the correct emotions? Are they genuinely feeling those emotions? This introspection shifts the balance of power in the workplace: fault lies not with the boring tasks and poor conditions, but instead with the worker for failing to expose or express genuine emotions.

This mode of management is exemplified in the film *Office Space* (tagline: 'Work Sucks').[63] The protagonist works in a bland office, consigned to an individual cubicle. His job involves updating bank software to ensure compliance with the new date format after 1999 (to help deal with the so-called 'millennium bug' feared for the new century). Suffice to say he is not satisfied with his work. The worker is harassed by eight different managers for forgetting to put a new coversheet on one of his reports. To each one of the managers he admits his mistake and they remind him of the memo and the necessity of coversheets. The main plot involves the worker being hypnotised. At the sudden death of the hypno-therapist, he is left permanently unworried about work and free to express himself. Leaving aside the need for this plot device, it does raise an important critique. The worker launches into a tirade against the pointless non-work of memos. His straight-talking is taken, quite unintentionally, as a sign of his business strength. The worker explains: 'Yeah, I just stare at my desk; but it looks like I'm working. I do that for probably another hour after lunch, too. I'd say in a given week I probably only do about fifteen minutes of real, actual, work.'[64] The critique of work continues as the office workers leave for a coffee break. At the chain restaurant they meet a new character who is also harassed by her boss. The company regulations state that workers must wear fifteen pieces of 'flair', additional items on their uniform that show their personality. The waitress is taken aside by the manager and asked why she is only wearing fifteen pieces of 'flair'. When she asks if this is a problem, the manager replies:

> Now, you know it's up to you whether or not you want to just do the bare minimum. Or . . . well, like Brian, for example, has thirty seven pieces of flair, okay. And a terrific smile . . . People can get a cheeseburger anywhere, okay? They come to Chotchkie's for the atmosphere and the attitude. Okay? That's what the flair's about. It's about fun.[65]

In this encounter the demand for 'flair' does not seem to be fun. As Mark Fisher argues, this demand is 'a handy illustration of the way in which "creativity" and "self-expression" have become intrinsic to labor' and moreover how there are now 'affective, as well as productive demands on workers'.[66] For management it is difficult to observe and measure how creative a worker's self-expression is, resulting in the 'attempt to crudely quantify these affective contributions'.

The intensification of the labour process is linked to a method of reward and punishment in the call centre. The quality control (QC) team listen into every successful sales call and a selection of other calls. After a sale, QC summons a worker by placing a small laminated card on their desk. This is meant to avoid interrupting the phone call but it comes across as quite ominous. The worker then has to sit on small fold-out stool by the QC desks. This is an infantilising experience (and, for me, also was quite an awkward one given my height – I'm 6ft 3ins). The worker is then expected to listen back to the recording of their call and guess what rating the call has been given, before the positive and negative aspects are detailed by QC. If the call is green the worker receives a raffle ticket and is entered into a prize draw. The draw took place every couple of months and prizes included £100 of Selfridges vouchers or a mini-Wii games console.

The company made various attempts to encourage worker participation on and off the call-centre floor. There were prizes awarded for making sales, usually vouchers for High Street shops. Another example was the introduction of 'theme months'. The first was 'spring break' which involved some cosmetic changes to the call centre, much to the excitement of the supervisors. Colourful banners and posters were plastered over the walls, with the addition of inflatable palm trees, animals and beach balls scattered around. The supervisors insisted the workers wear garish fake flower garlands while at work. On one day a supervisor mixed up an industrial quantity of non-alcoholic punch which was served up in novelty plastic cups with cocktail umbrellas. At one point I asked why this was happening, which was met with the simple response: 'Why not?'.

The non-financial incentives in the call centre extended beyond redecoration. Every Friday the company bought a large amount of junk food, delivered to the office for everyone to eat during their final break of the day. There were paid trips to restaurants or even to bars. During my initial training period, the sales team were taken out to a Nando's chicken restaurant after a shift. The supervisors emailed out the invitations a few days before. As I was fairly new at the call centre – or, more specifically, because I had not yet made enough sales – I did not get an invite. The supervisors handed out menus during the shift which made it obvious who was performing well enough to go. This was embarrassing and was clearly a method used by the supervisors to exert pressure on our performance. They even allowed those invited – about half of the trainees – to finish early and gather together to talk about the meal, leaving those not invited to continue making our calls. All of these incentives aimed to retain workers at the company, and to reduce the high levels of turnover.

In these ways, management attempted to reconcile the contradiction between quality and quantity, through both incentives and the application of processes of control. I also observed instances of reducing explicit control in the call centre in order to encourage higher quality. There was an insistence on elaborating on the script at certain points to make it sound more natural, but this always happened within defined limits. The same is true of the process for dealing with objections called 'clarify and reassure' (C&R), a particular form of emotional labour. Though this is not scripted on the computer, two paper sheets were provided – 'basic' and 'advanced' – which explained how to deal with objections. This was only to be done in accordance with strict rules: a maximum of three attempts, the first attempting to handle the objection (a negative response to an attempted pitch), the second offering a quote but then trying to C&R again, the third (if unsuccessful) ending by sending a quote.

THE MANAGEMENT OFFENSIVE

The challenges of management in the call centre stem from the phenomenon of 'soldiering' – the attempts by workers to avoid reaching their productive potential by setting a slower pace, for example. In response, management experiments with different strategies and tactics to overcome it. To understand this it is worth returning to Marx. He noted how the exchange of the commodity of labour power between the buyer (the capitalist) and the seller (the worker) appears as straightforward. Yet, once this transaction is followed 'into the hidden abode of production', it is here that 'the secret of profit-making must at last be laid bare'.[67] The transaction that has taken place is different to that of other commodities. The buyer is purchasing a potential, something only to be realised once it is put to work in production. This indeterminacy of the labour process is crucial for understanding the workplace. Once the capitalist has 'purchased a given quantity of labour power' they 'must now "stride ahead" and strive to extract actual labour from the labour power' they 'now legally own'.[68]

The apparently simple exchange of labour power on the market becomes complicated in the 'hidden abode' of production. As Richard Edwards argued, in the workplace, conflict exists because the interests of worker and those of employers collide . . . control is rendered problematic because unlike the other commodities involved in production, labour power is always embodied in people, who have their own interests and needs and who retain their power to resist being treated like a commodity.[69]

The workplace is therefore a 'contested terrain', to quote the title of Edwards's book. There are three component parts that form a 'system of control' or 'the social relations of production within the firm'. The first is 'direction', the way in which workers are instructed to complete tasks. The script and the automatic call dialler structure this for the call-centre worker. The second is 'evaluation', how the employer supervises and assesses worker performance. For example, the electronic surveillance systems, metrics and call listening. The third is 'discipline', the methods management use 'to elicit cooperation and enforce compliance with the capitalist's direction of the labour process'.[70] In the call centre this is a combination of bonuses and punishments. The buzz sessions, the '1-2-1' meetings and the threat of summary dismissal. These three aspects provide a starting point for understanding management in the call centre.

The indeterminacy of the labour process dictates that management attempt control. It becomes important the moment the capitalist attempts to realise the potential purchased. The combination of these two factors is not straightforward. For example, Paul Thompson argues that 'complications arise when attempts are made to specify how control is acquired and maintained'.[71] He draws on Marx's notions of 'factory despotism' mentioned earlier and the 'real subordination of labour'. This involves organising the workplace with a 'hierarchical chain of command'. It is 'given a material framework when capital can use science and machinery to control labour through the production process itself'.[72] This claim seems particularly applicable in a call centre, with the pace and volume of calls dictated by technology. This entails the shift from formal subsumption (the exchange of commodified labour power from seller to buyer) to real subsumption of labour under capital.[73] This real subsumption involves capital reorganising the labour process, the workplace and social relations. Or, in other words, workers become really subordinated to capital.

The process of subordination entails the new management techniques we have discussed so far. This involves control, but the concept can be understood in two different ways. Both in 'an absolute sense, to identify those "in control", and in a relative sense, to signify the degree of power people have to direct work'.[74] This nuance is an important theoretical consideration. In the workplace the manager is formally in control, yet still has to achieve this in practice. Goodrich uses the notion of a 'frontier of control' in the workplace to capture this dynamic.[75] Imagine the workplace as a battlefield. On one side is management, and on the opposing side workers. The 'frontier of control' is like the invisible border between the two. Skirmishes can push this border further onto one side or the other. Attempts to do this provoke a response, while gains in one area can be lost in others. The location of the frontier is not a given, rather it is in flux and constituted through struggle.

This fluctuating struggle for control in the call centre has led to the implementation and integration of increasingly sophisticated technology. The question of this technology poses a problem for what a non- or post-capitalist call centre would be. Given that the technical organisation of the labour process is deeply intertwined with capital and managerial imperatives, how could this be conceived of in another way? As Burawoy argues, 'in reality, machinery embraces a host of possibilities, many of which are systematically thwarted, rather than developed, by capital'.[76] These possibilities are difficult to comprehend in the call centre due to the fact its current operation appears to leave little option for workers to take back control. In different kinds of workplaces, the question of workers' control has frequently emerged, as detailed in numerous examples found in an edited volume by Immanuel Ness and Dario Azzellini. In particular, they note how critical Marxists have understood 'workers' control and councils as the base of a self-determined socialist society'.[77] Yet the call centre – and especially high-volume sales call centres – do not appear as an obvious target for self-management. Consider, for example, Burawoy's explanation of how

> an automatic system of machinery opens up the possibility of the true control over a highly productive factory by a relatively small corps of workers, providing these workers attain the level of mastery over the machinery offered by engineering knowledge, and providing they then share out among themselves the routines of the operation, from the most technically advanced to the most routine.[78]

What would the achievement of workers' control look like in a call centre? The answer is probably that most workers would like to stop making unsolicited phone calls, turn off the system and leave to do something else. The problem is that the vast majority of call centres – and especially sales call centres – produce little in the way of social value. It is possible that call centres could be put to an instrumental use during periods of struggle or any moment that mass participation may be needed: trying to mobilise large numbers of people at short notice or finding out information about what is happening in a particular area. Yet beyond that the social utility of call centres is not clear, particularly given that most of the technology is developed specifically to introduce new means to control workers.

The development and introduction of technology in the call centre has provided ample opportunities for management to engage in detailed surveillance and control. The labour process results in a clear and discrete output that is easily measured and recorded: the phone call. The widespread use and low cost of digital technologies has made the storage and instant playback of phone calls a reality for management, alongside statistics on call duration, break length, time between calls and so on. Sue Fernie and David Metcalf argue that call centres have become organised like an 'electronic panopticon'.[79] They argue that the 'possibilities for monitoring behaviour and measuring output are amazing to behold – the "tyranny of the assembly line" is but a Sunday school picnic compared with the control that management can exercise in computer telephony'. To do so, the analysis must take into account 'both the voluntary dimension of labour and the managerial need to elicit commitment from workers'.[80] Otherwise it can 'disavow the possibilities for collective organisation and resistance'.

The vast array of data that can be collected still requires human input to interpret and act upon it. If this were not the case, there would not be so many supervisors required on the call-centre floor. Management continues to require this human component, since 'no electronic system can summon an agent to a coaching session, nor highlight the deficiencies of their dialogue with the customer'. The scripting is a logical extension of Taylorism, as it represents 'a qualitative transformation in the degree to which management attempts to exert control over the white-collar labour process'. It is this which Taylor and Bain argue 'represents an unprecedented level of *attempted* control which must be considered a novel departure'.[81]

4

MOMENTS OF RESISTANCE

This chapter takes up the challenge of studying resistance in the call centre, shifting the analytical focus onto something deliberately hidden. Aspects of the labour process and the way it is managed – the most obvious being the specifics of exploitation – are obscured or mystified, and resistance takes place in a particular context. As the previous chapter on management detailed, there are multiple ways in which workers are monitored and controlled in the workplace, including the timing of the labour process to the second, and the call centre: the workplace is overdetermined by surveillance and control, while infractions and failure to cooperate with management is often punishable by sacking.

The aim of this chapter is twofold: to understand how a researcher can begin the search for covert resistance, and to present more of my own experience on the call centre floor. This first-hand ethnographic research will be used to highlight the different forms of resistance from the point of view of the workplace itself. For the first part a visual analogy can provide a useful starting point: how can we *see* resistance in the workplace? Tim Strangleman has discussed the ways in which researchers have 'seen' work,[1] highlighting how Nick Hedges and Huw Beynon's *Born to Work* sought to do so by combining photographs and text to try and reveal the secrets of the workplace, or as they put it, to 'seek out the scene of the crime'.[2] In a similar vein, Bolton et al. handed out disposable cameras to child workers who then documented their own experiences of work, providing a window into a world that is usually hidden from sight.[3] While visual methods were not possible in this case, the chapter draws on a visual analogy to begin the analysis that is sensitive to the subtleties of resistance. This is a challenge that the Italian Workerists – the innovators of the workers' inquiry discussed earlier – sought to take up. As Gigi Roggero explains: 'the problem of co-research as a style of militancy is exactly to produce new glasses, through which to see what is not immediately visible and perceivable, as well as what it can be or what it could become.'[4]

In order to craft and focus these new analytical glasses, the first part of this chapter discusses what is meant by resistance, examining the different forms it can take. In particular, this means broadening out the understanding of resistance to cover more than just trade union membership and strike action. This is the first step in sharpening the analysis, with the second examining the relationships between the labour process and resistance. The chapter then moves on to discuss the ethnography, considering the different moments of resistance found on the call-centre floor. These are understood in relation to Kate Mulholland's framework of *'Slammin' Scammin' Smokin' an' Leavin'* – or 'cheating, work avoidance, absence and resignation'.[5] These different moments are then discussed and explored as examples of the refusal of work. This refusal is considered as a potential way to transform the high turnover of workers from a weakness to a potential strength.

WHAT IS RESISTANCE?

In order to see resistance in the workplace it is necessary to consider what could constitute resistance, while simultaneously remaining attentive to any new or emergent forms. Before putting on these new analytical glasses it is worth pointing out that there has often been a blinkered approach to signs of resistance that views certain indicators, like official trade union membership statistics, as representative of the whole. This is a view limited by blinkers because it obscures much of the overall picture, and like the role for blinkers in domesticating animals, it also has a pacifying effect. As George Rawick has argued, figures of 'formal organization' – like those of membership levels, newspaper subscriptions, participation in electoral politics and so on – are often taken as indicators. However, what is really needed is to uncover the details of how many man-hours were lost to production because of strikes, the amount of equipment and material destroyed by industrial sabotage and deliberate negligence, the amount of time lost by absenteeism, the hours gained by workers through the slowdown, the limiting of the speed-up of the productive apparatus through the working class's own initiative.[6]

This highlights the plurality of other activities and practices in the workplace that are not captured by union membership. It also draws attention to another important reminder: resistance at work is not only limited to the strike. In many ways the strike – the temporary suspension of the labour process achieved by workers withdrawing their own labour – is the archetypal form of resistance at work. It is a collective, visible and antagonistic rupture of the relationship between labour and capital, bringing contradictions to the fore with a clear dividing line. It conjures up images of physical picket lines (with or without braziers), protests and solidarity. However, between the placid workplace and the all-out strike there are a range of practices – some collective, others individual – that are worthy of sustained attention.

The difficulty in spotting other acts of resistance is no accident. At the point of the strike it is obvious to managers what is happening: the labour process is halted. In response pay is withheld and the dispute takes shape: demands, counter-demands and negotiations. However, acts of sabotage or slowdown, for example, are not necessarily things that workers would want to advertise to the boss. While that might be satisfying, it would bring the conflict to a head and in casualised workplaces could lead to an immediate sacking. In this difficult context it is worth considering the struggles of people in even worse conditions. For example, Edward B. Harper's study of lifelong indentured servants found that

most characteristically expressed discontent about their relationship with their master by performing their work carelessly and inefficiently. They could intentionally or unconsciously feign illness, ignorance, or incompetence, driving their masters to distraction. Even though the master could retaliate by refusing to give his servant the extra fringe benefits, he was still obliged to maintain him at a subsistence level if he did not want to lose his investment completely. This method of passive resistance, provided it was not expressed as open defiance, was nearly unbeatable.[7]

The existence of this low-intensity conflict in a context in which the indentured worker seems to be relatively powerless is important. Even if there were no outward signs of conflict, below the surface there can still be practices of resistance, expressed in a necessarily covert manner. Similarly, James C. Scott's study of peasant resistance found that 'open insubordination in almost any context will provoke a more rapid and ferocious response than an insubordination that may be as pervasive but never ventures to contest the formal definitions of hierarchy or power'. Therefore, peasants engaged in 'everyday' forms of resistance, because, like most subordinated people, this form of resistance 'is the only option'.[8]

The context of everyday resistance in the contemporary workplace is different. Unlike the indentured servants or the peasants described above, the worker, and in this case the call-centre worker, struggles in different conditions. Karl Marx, as discussed in the previous chapter, ironically defined workers as doubly-free under capitalism.[9] They do not *have* to be in a particular workplace, but economic compulsion – rather than physical coercion – forces workers to choose one. The impact of this is discussed by Braverman, who describes how

> the hostility of workers to the degenerated forms of work which are forced upon them continues as a subterranean stream that makes its way to the surface when employment conditions permit, or when the capitalist drive for a greater intensity of labor oversteps the bounds of physical and mental capacity. It renews itself in new generations, expresses itself in the unbounded cynicism and revulsion which large numbers of workers feel about their work, and comes to the fore repeatedly as a social issue demanding solution.[10]

In this passage Braverman discusses the way in which the labour process creates resistance even if it is not obviously apparent. The notion of resistance continuing as 'a subterranean stream' bubbling under the surface captures an important dynamic. The problem is that there is no divining rod that can guide the search for resistance below the surface, but by approaching the search from the perspective of the labour process itself, we can (at least) make a start.

Before moving on to discuss specific examples of resistance stemming from the labour process, it is worth briefly reviewing how resistance can be conceptualised in the workplace. For example, Randy Hodson provides a useful definition of worker resistance, that 'any individual or small-group act intended to mitigate claims by management on workers or to advance workers' claims against management'.[11] This struggle between workers and management can be conceptualised as battle over the 'frontier of control' in the workplace,[12] that Richard Hyman describes as 'a frontier which is defined and redefined in a *continuous* process of pressure and counter-pressure'.[13] This situates resistance as a result of the dialectic of struggle between labour and capital, taking place inside the labour process. It therefore includes sabotage[14] or the more general acts that can be categorised as 'the withdrawal of cooperation'.[15]

Yet forms of resistance exist beyond the dialectic between control and resistance. Even if workers were not acting as 'fully conscious agents engaged in class struggle, in seeking to control, management did'. This notion of class struggle in the workplace, that occurs whether workers are actively fighting it or not, is particularly useful. However, when considering what fighting might actually involve there are a range of practices that can be included. The theoretical model of control and resistance can miss other practices, for example 'misbehaviour'.[16] This can be broadly defined as 'anything you do at work you are not supposed to do',[17] which in a call centre encompasses quite a wide range of activities. To narrow it slightly, it can include behaviours such as 'incivility, sabotage, culture, humour, leadership or harassment' which should be 'analysed as acts of resistance in their own right'. Importantly, misbehaviour provides a way for workers to deal with the pressure of the labour process, for example to 'get back' at management or simply allow workers to 'get by' working under harsh conditions.[18] To this can also be added the importance of simply 'having a pop' at management – something that will be returned to later in this chapter and the next.

It is important to consider the connection between the specificities of the labour process in different jobs and the new forms of resistance that can emerge. An interesting example of this can be found with the Cathay Pacific airline flight attendants' smile strike. The workers drew on the fact that the company advertised its 'service with a smile' to engage in a specific form of work to rule – only completing what is stipulated in a contract, something that can be very disruptive as many jobs actually require more than this. The workers engaged in a smile strike, refusing to deploy the emotional labour described by Arlie Hochschild.[19] In addition to this the workers also threatened to 'stop providing meals, snacks and beverages like alcohol'. As Tsang Kwok-fung, the general secretary for the Cathay Pacific Airways Flight Attendants Union, remarked, 'we cannot smile because of the situation, because of how the company treats us'.[20] In many workplaces – call centres or offices immediately come to mind – the withdrawal of the smile would have little effect, but when it is a demand of the labour process it can become an effective point of contention.

Yet this creative approach to resistance could also be developed for call centres. Refusing to participate in certain aspects of the call, the greeting for example, or refusing to 'smile down the phone' could have a similar effect.[21] For example, call-centre workers are increasingly becoming the main point of contact between a company and its customers. This means that workers can potentially damage the image and relationships of a company fairly quickly. Furthermore, regardless of whether this is conceived as a strategy, 'in subordinated work conditions, workers engage in a recipe of informal collective practices that are organically borne out of their daily work experiences'.[22] This creates a difficulty in identifying what forms these could take, but is an important reminder of the need to remain attentive to their emergence. The ability to build sustained resistance or the possibility of organisation hinges on whether or not strategies can be connected to embryonic and emergent struggles.

The nature of the labour process and the use of emotions in the call centre creates further complexities. Emotional labour draws on workers' personalities and emotions to extract additional profit. The process by which workers perform this is far from straightforward, yet it remains an undervalued skill. Call-centre workers, unlike other service workers, are limited to the extent that they can only express their emotions over the telephone. This makes the content of the phone call crucial to the profitability of the call centre, presenting workers with new opportunities to resist. The scripting for a sales call gives the impression of a standardised and regular call encounter, but in order to make sales there is a demand to go beyond this. The esoteric qualities of successful salespersons are hard to calculate or inculcate, therefore many managers engage in a strategy of hiring 'stars' that they 'assume have a flair for selling'.[23] This highlights the difficulty for management in the call centre, as there is no agreement about the best way to make a sale, nor is there any recipe to follow to do so.

The use of phone technology in the call centre also opens up other avenues. For example, Şafak Tartanoğlu found that workers' organisation in Turkish call centres was being built by subverting the labour process in new and creative ways.[24] Activists collectively rang into inbound call centres in what they called a 'call attack' and spoke to workers about organising, reaching a large number at the same time. This would then be followed up with meetings, leafleting and other traditional methods. The new use of the technology, originally designed to centralise and then maximise phone calls, also proved vulnerable to attempts at organising. Although this kind of tactic would not be possible in a predominantly outbound call centre, it highlights the importance of thinking creatively about the weaknesses or vulnerabilities of capital that might not be obvious at first.

MOMENTS OF RESISTANCE

My first experiences on the call-centre floor did not, as was expected, provide great insights into the practices of resistance.

Neither did the first few weeks of working there. Call-centre work is highly individualised. Calls are ultimately made by the worker, and the aim is to speak to one person and convince them to part with some money. However, working alongside others has a collective dimension, albeit with a number of factors that challenge this: the shift patterns can mean that you might only see other workers sporadically, the high turnover leads to some workers only lasting a very short time in the job, and it takes a while to become comfortable enough with the labour process to start talking to other workers between calls and engaging during the shift. As the first few weeks passed two things happened which began to clarify the analysis: the first was getting over the immediate fear of being fired for incompetence – avoiding an outcome in which the project repeats Robert Linhart's failed attempts on the assembly line – and the second was beginning to see the same people working day after day and getting to know them.[25]

The forms of resistance that I began to encounter can be conceptualised as different 'moments'. Drawing on Kate Mulholland's perceptive research on an Irish call centre it is possible to discuss four categories that can capture this informal resistance – three of which applied to the call centre in which I was working.[26] She describes the 'repertoire of resistance strategies' used by the call-centre workers as '*Slammin' Scammin' Smokin' an' Leavin'*' – or 'cheating, work avoidance, absence and resignation'. These forms emerge from the antagonism on the call-centre floor, in particular the 'fragmented work and new management initiatives' yet they 'reflect traditional patterns of work opposition'.[27] The following section will discuss the moments of resistance in the call centre using this framework from Mulholland, before considering the implications of these later in the chapter.

SLAMMIN', SCAMMIN', SMOKIN' AN' LEAVIN'

The first term used by Mulholland is '*Slammin'*', which she describes as the process of faking a sales encounter.[28] The workers 're-deploy "talk time" and the technology to fake sales thus highlighting how target driven productivity encourages them to search for short cuts'. She explains how the workers describe this 'with great amusement', yet 'their terse references to "flogging myself for nothing" are illustrative of the deep resentment they share over effort'. This form of resistance was simply not possible in my call centre. Due to the financial regulations that apply to selling insurance each successful sales call was digitally recorded and then scrutinised by the quality assurance team so fake calls would be easily detected. However, there was frequent discussion about the possible ways in which sales volumes could be boosted. The more outlandish involved considering getting friends to sign up to the insurance, selling to them to receive the sales bonus, then cancelling before the direct debit was due to be paid. The supervisors frequently reminded workers that this method of 'selling on cancellation' – although the instance they were referring to was trying to dupe customers into buying the product over the phone on the basis that they could always change their mind later – would result in disciplinary action. It is unquestionable that if there were a relatively reliable method to achieve fake sales this would have become popular as the pressure to make sales was constant.

The second and most common form of resistance is '*Scammin*'. It refers to the various attempts by workers to avoid work, whether by simply not turning up, pretending to be sick or leaving early without permission.[29] The shift structure was officially defined in strict terms: two slots of three-and-a-half hours, each with a fifteen-minute break, sandwiched around an hour-long unpaid break. But the exact amount of time that would be spent on the phone selling insurance was subject to a struggle between workers and supervisors. The supervisors tried to demand that workers should arrive fifteen minutes before their shift starts so that they would be ready for work despite the fact this was unpaid. There were then a number of other points of contention during the shift in which the length of time on the phone could be extended or reduced.

At the start of each three-and-a-half hour shift there was a buzz session with the supervisors. These played a motivational role as well as providing an opportunity for management to inculcate workers with the various rules of the workplace. The length of the buzz session was never officially defined and therefore it was at the discretion of the supervisors. This meant that as long as the games or discussion continued it could be stretched out. This involved a level of informal organisation as one individual worker could extend the session by asking more questions as the supervisors would catch on that they were trying to distract them and therefore cut the buzz session short. A successful extension involved a careful balancing act of feigning interest, posing questions and stimulating discussion. Over the time I spent in the call centre a collective approach emerged around this. Subtle cues would be exchanged under the gaze of the supervisors, a nod or raise of the eyebrows encouraging others to participate in the process. Although even the best attempts – which were then gleefully relayed to others in the breaks – could delay the start of work by at the most forty-five minutes, it was viewed as a significant victory. This flexibility existed because supervisors also did not have to work on the call-centre floor during this time, but ultimately they would be held responsible by their managers if the 'buzz sessions' became too long.

The supervisors allowed workers to leave early from a shift if they reached their sales targets. This was viewed by most workers as the best incentive to make sales, rather than any of the small prizes or games that could be played. It was common to see workers haggling with supervisors, trying to trade in vouchers or prizes to go home early instead. The most bizarre example of this was a worker's attempts to quantify the exchange rate of high-street vouchers with the value of labour, haggling over how much time off could be bought. This highlights how little workers enjoyed working at the call centre as any opportunity to leave would be seized upon, even motivating workers to make more sales. At one point during my time at the call centre the number of workers leaving early reached a peak. The call-centre manager organised a meeting with the supervisors to introduce new rules as the statistics showed that workers were only logged into the computers for 79 per cent of their paid time, the equivalent of one in five workers being completely absent. As one of the supervisors relayed to the workers this was 'unacceptable' as 'the company was paying loads of money per month for people to just sit at home'. While workers considered this a perfectly acceptable situation, unsurprisingly management did not. The new rules stipulated that no worker could leave before the last thirty minutes of the shift. However, this incentive had proved so useful for motivating workers to sell that supervisors began to circumvent the new rule by taking people off the call-centre floor for training in a separate room. The training involved playing games and was a reward; although workers would have to stay on site they did not have to use the phones and could then leave thirty minutes early.

There was constant tension over the length of the fifteen-minute mid-shift breaks. At first glance it appeared there would be no ability to contest this as the breaks were timed on each computer with a large counter displaying the time elapsed in minutes and seconds. Therefore, it should have been possible for a supervisor to bring up an individual worker's statistics and see if they have taken more than thirty minutes per day. However, the break-time setting on the computer was also used for '1-2-1' meetings with supervisors, training exercises, quality meetings after every sale and so on. The task of supervising breaks was furthered complicated by the fact that not all workers could take the break at the same time. Unfortunately, it was not possible to hang up mid-call when the break slot arrived, despite the temptation to do so. This meant that workers began to file off the call-centre floor gradually as the calls ended. The supervisors had to physically check the times on the individual computer screens, walking up and down the rows, to see if any worker was taking a longer break.

The reliance on visual checking created the possibility of extending the break-times. In order to leave the call centre to smoke or join the smokers' conversations, workers had to exit at the far side of the room. Upon returning, workers checked their computer screen to see how much time was remaining, and, if away from the gaze of the supervisor, they could quickly log in and out, resetting the timer. Then workers moved to the other side of the call centre where the break room was located. The supervisors would come into the break room to announce that timers were almost up, which would be disputed by individuals saying that they had come onto the break late. Most of the supervisors handled this badly; rather than formally disciplining workers they would continue to informally corral workers into returning, a process that could be strung out to extend the break. The main aim was to ensure not being caught with the break timer over fifteen minutes, which could result in formal disciplinary action. The final opportunity to maximise break time was to sit at the desk with the headset on and not log into the system until the supervisor cast their gaze along the worker's row. This could extend the break further, especially if the supervisor were busy corralling other workers into leaving the break room.

There was another type of moment that occasionally occurred during shifts. The computer system that distributed leads – the lists of numbers for the autodialling system to call – would run dry. It then required a supervisor to manually update the leads for each of the campaigns currently running. If the supervisor was not paying attention they would miss the error message popping up on workers' screens. The screen displayed a counter stating that it would check automatically after two minutes or on demand. The message would not appear for every worker, just for a section of those who were on the same campaign. This unexpected break could be extended for as long as each worker delayed telling the supervisor; however, they had to eventually inform them, as supervisors would notice either way. This collective misbehaviour involved similar cues to those used in the buzz session, glances and mouthing words across the call-centre floor. Most workers would take the impromptu break and then tell the supervisor after this rest, especially because reporting the problem straight away was generally frowned upon as it would take that choice away from others.

I did encounter more deliberate attempts at sabotage, although these remained covert and were rarely mentioned. The call centre had just enough headsets for workers on a typical day, so if any were to become damaged some workers might be moved off the call-centre floor. The wires connecting the headsets to the phone were fairly brittle and with a little effort could be sabotaged, but this could have unforeseen effects. During one shift I started with a '1-2-1' meeting and came late onto the call-centre floor. There were no spare headsets except a few with frayed cables that did not work properly – and had recently been under the care of other workers. I incorrectly assumed that this would mean I would not have to make calls during the shift, but the supervisor forced me to make calls balancing a regular handset on my shoulder. Under the threat of losing a day's pay I continued to call, now feeling like a bad parody of a 1990s stock trader raising my voice over the crackling line to be heard.

While there have been attempts to use sabotage as a guiding theoretical principle for understanding workplace resistance, these have been of limited success (for example, the work of Geoff Brown[30] and Pierre Dubois[31]). However, by arguing that 'anything less than complete conformity sabotages the capitalist project of maximising profit', this elevates all kinds of minor actions to the level of a major challenge to management.[32] As can be seen from the example above, minor and hidden incidents of sabotage may well provide a release for workers' frustrations, but they do not significantly undermine the process of capital accumulation in the call centre. The proliferation of computers in production has undoubtedly offered new opportunities for sabotage. One example can be seen in this incident:

> an overworked purchasing agent who maliciously ordered 2500 circuit boards and 1,000,000 batteries through a computer terminal. The circuit board manufacturer queried back because the boards were obsolete and no longer in production. However, 'several lorry loads of batteries arrived at the site before the stores manager began making enquiries regarding the purpose and storage of this large supply of batteries'.[33]

The prospect of destroying of a few call-centre headsets looks very minor in comparison!

There was also one case of a worker who attempted a more extreme form of '*Scammin*'' during work. He sat at his desk and would stretch out the time between calls, pretending to be taking notes about the calls. When a customer did pick up the phone he immediately hung up, albeit in the virtual form of clicking a button. One of the supervisors caught on to what he was doing, because it was flagged in his records as an anomaly that he was not spending any time on calls. After reviewing his call statistics they were able to identify his actions and he was summarily fired mid-shift on the call-centre floor. The supervisors immediately called all of the workers into the conference room for an emergency meeting. Over the period of at least half an hour, the fired worker – despite having already left the workplace – was made an example of. This show of managerial force was used to illustrate how the rules must be abided by, how they would find out if workers tried anything similar and that punishment would not be lenient.

The third form is a specific method of avoiding work by '*Smokin*'. This provides workers with the 'opportunity for an extra break, regardless of whether people smoked or not', interrupting management's schedule of work. Mulholland additionally found that 'the habit of meeting is also important for it encourages work group identity and a shared sense of grievance when workers discuss training, staff shortage, disappointments over pay, prize giving, the excessive monitoring, arbitrary discipline and not least productivity pressures'.[34] Therefore while smoking breaks may not at first seem that important, they act as 'informal meetings' with the potential to build collectivism on the basis of shared grievances, 'and as such are an antidote to individualizing strategies'.[35] There were two fifteen-minute statutory breaks per shift at the call centre where I was working. Most workers left the building and stood around the corner, regardless of whether they smoked or not. These meetings provided an opportunity to vent about the pressures of work away from the management gaze. The importance of these as moments of resistance was clear from the fact conversations would be cut short the moment a supervisor joined for their break.

The final form of resistance that Mulholland uses is quitting the job or '*Leavin*'.[36] Like many call centres, the one studied by Mulholland had a high staff turnover, with around eight per cent of the workers leaving each month. While '*Leavin*' might seem like the archetypal individual act it forms 'part of a more widespread pattern of work rejection'. Similarly, Marcel van der Linden discusses how, 'in a sense, a strike means a collective exit

– not with the intention of leaving for good, but to exert pressure temporarily. The 'distinction between "running away" and "fighting for better working conditions" is in reality rather fluid'.[37] This consideration of quitting the job as a form of unorganised resistance – and one that is not that different to striking – is key to understanding that call centres are not workplaces devoid of any form of struggle, despite their low levels of unionisation and officially sanctioned industrial action.

These moments of resistance in the call centre present methodological challenges for an undercover researcher. Each of the moments was a departure from how supervisors wanted workers to behave in the call centre. All of the workers participated to some degree in these actions and even though I was also a researcher – and in that sense an outsider in the workplace – I still needed to work and perform the labour process like the other workers. I engaged in the moments of resistance described above and therefore my presence involved an intervention. As Michael Burawoy has discussed in relation to workplace ethnographies, 'interventions' do not need to be minimised.[38] They 'create perturbations that are not noise to be expurgated but music to be appreciated, transmitting the hidden secrets of the participant's world'. The involvement of all of the workers in a form of misbehaviour – whether on their own or collectively, formally or informally – meant that not taking part in these would be an intervention in itself. I would likely have been labelled as the opposite of a troublemaker, someone likely to make problems for the other workers by following all of the rules which might expose them. The negative reactions that people received when they reported to supervisors that leads had run out ensured that they were more likely to engage in collective misbehaviour at the next opportunity. If the action was repeated a second time – which was never the case in my experience – presumably further social sanctions would be applied. In this sense, there was a form of unstated collectivity that emerged in the workplace.

The failure to be accepted by the other workers would have created a serious access problem. It is unlikely that other workers would have shared their experiences or discussed topics of resistance if they thought they would be reported to management. However, that is not the only reason to engage in the various moments of resistance. As Taylor and Bain have argued, in call centres 'it is difficult to escape the conclusion that the labour process is intrinsically demanding, repetitive and, frequently, stressful.'[39] The moments of resistance provide temporary respite from these characteristics of the labour process. The researcher who is working, like the other workers, is therefore also pushed by this dynamic into finding ways to ameliorate the situation. Therefore, I engaged in a number of these moments, partly out of choice to experience the labour process in the way that my co-workers did, and partly due to the highly pressurised target-driven environment. Vincent J. Roscigno and Randy Hodson recognise this dynamic when they argue that 'rather than such resistance being solely an effort to regain dignity in the face of personal insult and conflict with managers, resistance in such settings may be as much a function of frustration, boredom, and personal stress resulting from organizational chaos.'[40]

The defensive strand of resistance does pose problems for worker organisation. While 'telling the boss exactly what you think, or quitting, or finding small ways to mitigate the relentless pace of work can all be rewarding in the short run, these activities do little to challenge management's structural power in the call centre.'[41] However, the move towards activities that could form a challenge can start from these relatively minor actions. The path towards mounting successful workplace resistance has to build upon grievances, however minor they may appear. For example, issues such as access to communal break space, repairing broken equipment or repealing a particular punitive management rule all have the potential to build momentum and confidence. As Mulholland argues:

> Examples of this sort are a missed opportunity for the trade unions to take the initiative over what are conventional workplace issues, when the union has yet to transform this wellspring of conflict into an offensive against management.[42]

THE REFUSAL OF WORK

These moments of resistance provide a framework to discuss the various observed examples from the call centre where I was working. However, they also present a challenge, of how they could relate to a potential organisational form. The insights from Italian Workerism can shed some conceptual light on this. As Mario Tronti put in clear terms, 'we have to invert the problem'; instead of starting with capital, 'change direction, and start from the beginning – and the beginning is working-class struggle'.[43] The difficulty with this approach is that there are not a wide variety of open struggles from which to draw conclusions. A potential remedy is directing attention onto the class composition of workers in the call centre. As Gigi Roggero argues, 'our challenge is to begin once again from the blockages experienced by the struggles of the precarious' understanding how 'the political composition of the class is crushed within the sociological mold of its technical composition'.[44] This notion of class composition is an important contribution from the Italian Workerists. It begins with a consideration of technical composition: the organisation of the labour process, the use of technology and the conditions of the reproduction of labour power (the focus of previous chapters). Political composition, on the other hand, relates to the specific forms and relations of struggles, a complex factor continually subjected to processes of re-composition. These 'blockages' are therefore the result of the technical composition of the working class at a particular point, preventing sustained struggles and giving the surface impression of calm in many workplaces. For example, the limitation of most trade union demands to the questions of wages can result in the abandonment of struggle over the labour process itself. By failing to contest control over the organisation of work by management, workers themselves are left in a difficult structural position. The drastic shift in the frontier of control in the workplace means that it no longer appears as something that can even be contested, leaving significant power in the hands of management. However, these blockages facing precarious workers are neither permanent nor immovable. In seeking to shift the blockages it is first necessary to understand the conditions of the workplace and the class composition at particular points.

A particularly important matter to consider with precarious work is the question of turnover. High levels of turnover are a characteristic of the service-industry sector and are particularly acute in call centres. This poses a significant obstacle to organisation as networks that are built rapidly fall away as people drop out. However, this can be re-conceptualised by considering Marcel van der Linden's argument that the difference between 'running away' and 'fighting for better working conditions' is actually less than it might appear.[45] Rather than considering workplaces with high turnover as un-organisable, the problem can be turned on its head. As Mario Tronti argues,

> Obviously non-collaboration must be one of our starting points, and mass passivity at the level of production is the material fact from which we must begin. But at a certain point all this must be reversed into its opposite. When it comes to the point of saying 'No', the refusal must become political; therefore active; therefore subjective; therefore organised. It must once again become antagonism – this time at a higher level.[46]

The 'strategy of refusal' could begin from the moments of resistance discussed earlier in the chapter, whether it is calling in sick to work, leaving mid-shift, or simply not turning up to the workplace again. Therefore, the first challenge is to find the moments of resistance that are already taking place, attempt to understand how they could be turned into a refusal, and seek out the organisational forms that could develop this further.

The strategy of refusal builds on the notion of the flight from work. As Michael Hardt and Antonio Negri argue, 'the refusal of work and authority, or really the refusal of voluntary servitude, is the beginning of liberatory politics'.[47] However, they also add to this that 'the refusal in itself is empty'. Therefore, the key to answering the puzzle of contemporary class struggle is not only identifying those moments of resistance, but also understanding the potential of these lines of flight from work; simply refusing is not enough. This can be clarified by returning again to the empirical example. In the call centre there was a distinct lack of identification with the work. As described earlier, every worker had some alternative activity that they would have preferred to be doing. There were aspiring actors, musicians, students of all kinds of varied fields, but none who described call-centre work as their passion. The package of affects they had to use in the labour process bore no relation to what they actually wanted to be doing. The problem is that for the majority of workers who desire to do something more creative, most would struggle to support themselves in this pursuit alone. While the creative activities may produce value of different kinds, it is likely not to be that which will receive the remuneration necessary to reproduce their own labour power.

Call-centre work is particularly susceptible to the refusal of work and kinds of sabotage. In the broadest sense work under contemporary capitalism can be categorised into three types based on the direction of struggle (which is not say that these broad types supersede other analytical categories). The first is work in which the demand for workers' control does not makes sense. The call centre is an obvious example as it would be difficult to imagine why it would be brought under workers' control: who would you want to bombard with high speed sales calls? This is because the development of the call centre has been tied closely to the use of methods of surveillance, speed-up and control. Rather than seizing the means of production, a more attractive option is to simply go and do something else. The second kind of work is that which could be fulfilling and useful if it could be radically reorganised. An example of this is privatised care work. In the UK a large proportion of this kind of work is done on a highly casualised basis with low pay, often organised on a highly regulated basis in which limits are put on how long workers may spend with each user. If this work could be socialised and organised in a different way, it could have a significant impact on both workers and users. The third form is work in which workers retain a higher level of autonomy and the main aim would be to take control of the workplace and run it democratically. An example of this might be lecturers, who could still research and teach, but away from the pressures of managers. In these three cases there are clearly differences in the resistance that emerges and that might be successful. If there is an element of the work that is socially important, fulfilling or indeed enjoyable, then it is worth staying and fighting. In these cases, the flight from work does not take on the same importance. However, when work is stripped of these features almost entirely, then the refusal of work not only becomes a useful strategy, but it is also something that emerges organically from the labour process itself.

The development of capitalism and the application of technology to the productive process led many to identify the potential to drastically reduce the amount of time that people had to work. David Graeber notes that Keynes predicted in 1930 that by the end of the century the working week would be reduced to 15 hours.[48] Not only did this fail to materialise, but the opposite now seems to be true. The potential of technology has instead been exploited to make people work even more. In the place of declining manufacturing jobs there has been an increase in what David Graeber calls 'bullshit jobs'. These jobs are far removed from any fulfilling activity, so much so that many people find it difficult to explain what they are actually employed to do. This has implications for workplace struggle: what demands could or would be raised in this context? Although assembly-line work is repetitive and undoubtedly unappealing, the application of technology can vastly reduce the amount of labour required and machinery can be put to work for a variety of different ends. There are a range of jobs, often low-paid, that, if they were to disappear, the impact would be immediately felt: transport workers, nurses or refuse collectors, for example. For those working in 'bullshit jobs' it is 'not entirely clear how humanity would suffer [were they to] vanish. (Many suspect it might markedly improve.)'.[49]

The moments of resistance considered above are relatively isolated examples, although they have emerged organically from the labour process. My own experience on the call-centre floor provided the opportunity to encounter this range of different practices, elaborating how workers actually engaged in resistance. It is clear from the number and breadth of acts of resistance that occur below the surface, that there exists the potential for organised resistance in the call centre. The 'subterranean stream' that Braverman[50] refers to is bubbling away, although at present it does not seem obvious how it will reach the surface. In order to understand this further, the theme of the refusal of work which emerged during the research can be developed. The high levels of turnover in the workplace were a clear indication of this refusal, alongside the various attempts by workers to reduce the amount of time spent actually working – both directly by the workers themselves, and as rewards from management. This line of thinking draws on the contributions of the Italian Workerists to the notion of refusal of work as a strategy. The problem of turnover can then be seen in terms of the majority of workers' desire to do something other than call-centre work, conceptualising it as a 'bullshit job'.[51]

While this is an important starting point, the discussion of refusal still requires some sort of translation into practice. The act of leaving – whether through storming off the call-centre floor or just refusing to continue working – is therefore evidence of hostility to work and the lack of a collective channel for the changing of conditions. The struggle in the workplace is happening whether or not workers want to be involved, which means that it is often a struggle that they are losing. We will now move on to discuss the interventions and collective attempts that workers experimented with in the call centre, addressing the question of organisational forms and considering the potential means by which the tide of struggle could be turned.

5

PRECARIOUS ORGANISATION

We have so far discussed what it is like to work in the call centre, how management tries to control the labour process and different instances of resistance. The challenge now is to think through the problem of organisation. There was no formal worker organisation – trade union or otherwise – in the call centre (but as we have seen this does not mean it was not a site of collective struggle). There are two key issues here. The first is the state of trade unionism in the UK. Trade unions have a basic aim under capitalism: to secure, usually by collective bargaining, better conditions for workers. But in practice contemporary trade unionism seems to have lost it's 'unionateness': the 'commitment of an organization to the general principles and ideology of trade unionism',[1] failing to even secure these better conditions in many cases. As we will discuss in this chapter, it is therefore difficult to connect workplace resistance to official trade unionism.

The second issue is that even if a successful union branch was built, as Huw Beynon pointed out, 'trade unionism is about work and sometimes the lads just don't want to work. All talk of procedures and negotiations tend to break down here'.[2] This relates to a general lack of opportunities for political struggle over issues beyond the workplace. The failure of trade unions to intervene in the organisation of the labour process in call centres has left the frontier of control to be defined overwhelmingly by management. As Taylor and Bain argue, 'the future success of trade unions in call centres will depend in no small measure on their ability to contest and redefine the frontiers of control on terms desired by their members'.[3] This requires a break from the conception of unions as service providers for a shrinking base of members, and a move towards the building of combative organisations that are focused on workplace struggle.

The high turnover of workers in call centres presents a real and difficult obstacle for worker organisation. In addition to this, the tendency for management to victimise individual activists has a damaging effect on the longevity of campaigns. It is therefore necessary to try and conceive of forms of resistance and organisation than can be generalised on a larger scale. It is not possible to develop a strategy for unionising the currently non-union sectors based on only a small number of individuals. As Thompson and Ackroyd argue, 'It is not a case of "waiting for the fightback", romanticising the informal, or disregarding the capacity of unions to renew their own organisation and strategy'. Instead, 'we have to put labour back in, by doing theory and research in such a way that it is possible to "see" resistance and misbehaviour, and recognise that innovatory employee practices and informal organisation will continue to subvert managerial regimes'.[4] We have already discussed how the focus on resistance and misbehaviour can help to identify the ways in which challenges to management can be constructed. This has to be complemented by a strategic critique of contemporary trade unionism, not only to understand its failings, but as part of a demand to utilise trade union resources in an organising project that has workers' self-activity at its heart.

THE ATTEMPT TO ORGANISE IN THE CALL CENTRE

The possibility that the 'bullshit jobs' that Graeber discusses could be rejected on an organised basis today appears quite distant.[5] The level of struggle in the call centre where I was working was restricted to the moments of resistance discussed in the last chapter. However, what these moments do show is an unorganised resistance expressing a refusal and the tendency towards anti-work. This resistance can therefore be used to understand what kinds of strategies and tactics can develop from the experience of work itself.

The challenge of moving beyond sporadic everyday practices of resistance presents a series of problems. Michael Burawoy explains how 'institutions reveal much about themselves when under stress or in crisis, when they face the unexpected as well as the routine'.[6] This kind of active intervention into a call centre was undertaken by the Kolinko call-centre inquiry in Germany.[7] One of the explicit aims of Kolinko was to find and intervene in workers' struggle. This draws on the best elements of the workers' inquiry tradition in seeking to combine knowledge production with a form of organisation. The challenge for Kolinko was that they had trouble finding what they were looking for: 'the absence of open workers' struggles limited our own room for "movement"'.[8] They continue to argue: 'what is the point in leaflets and other kind of interventions at all if there is no workers' self-activity to refer to?'. These difficulties do not result in a failed research project however. As Burawoy points out, 'the activist who seeks to transform the world can learn much from its obduracy'.[9]

I had a number of isolated conversations with different workers in the call centre about organising collectively. The question of whether to move forward with a project of organisation was not one taken lightly. The act of discussing organising, let alone actually trying to organise, in a non-unionised workplace puts workers at risk of losing their jobs. As a researcher, the call-centre job was not my livelihood, nor was it somewhere I intended to be employed long-term, and so for me the impact of losing my job was not so serious. But an intervention on my part could potentially have had serious ramifications for other workers. It is important to remember that the workplace is not a laboratory. Therefore, sensitivity was required in my approach, alongside a recognition and prioritisation of the importance of workers' own self-activity in any organising process.

Throughout my time at the call centre I only ever encountered one other worker who had ever been a member of a trade union. I had the opportunity to speak with him regularly about the possibilities of organising in the call centre, as we both travelled home every day on the Tube to the same part of London. Our discussions focused on the likelihood of getting sacked by the company, what kind of demands we would make and the difficulties of getting other people on board. After a while these conversations began to move onto practical suggestions about organising in the call centre, which will be detailed below.

It was difficult to talk about trade unionism with other call-centre workers. That did not mean that politics was absent from the workplace. For example, in the wake of the killing of Drummer Lee Rigby, a British Army soldier, on the streets of Woolwich, South London in 2013,[10] anti-racism and anti-fascism became common talking points during our breaks. There was discussion of how people could oppose the English Defence League, a right-wing protest group, and although no one had been on a demonstration before, there was a good conversation about going together to one in the future. These political interventions began to open up a space to discuss the possibilities for resistance, but also to identify which people to speak to further.

The majority of the workers were students or graduates and had a limited connection to the student movement of 2010. The political situation that most had grown up in was the wake of the Labour government's invasion of Iraq, the financial crisis of 2008–9, the MPs' parliamentary expenses scandals of 2009 and the inner-city London riots of 2011. Neither trade unions nor the traditional avenues of social democracy were discussed as vehicles for change. This did not mean that there were not a wide variety of grievances. The topics discussed included low wages, bullying supervisors, the cost of housing in London, extortionate landlords, overpriced transport and student debt among others.

During a shift one of the trainees who started at the same time as I passed me a hand-drawn cartoon of the undercover boss consultant with a speech bubble saying 'you'll lose your job son!'. This was the beginning of more serious discussions about how we could organise in the workplace. He stated that he did not care whether he lost his job and suggested that we could meet with some other people for a drink after work. The first discussion away from the workplace – other than the smoking breaks – took place in a nearby pub. A group of us who worked the same shifts would often go for a drink at the end of work, but from then on these became more political with discussions about what building a union would involve and why it was worth doing. One person in the group argued that the job wasn't really that bad, and after all 'if it ain't broke don't fix it!' and 'I'm worried about ruining the atmosphere in the office'. The cartoonist argued that he had 'always been in the union, you don't want to wait until it is too late'. He elaborated that 'the worst thing about work is when people are rude. When I was at [company] and in [the union] they wouldn't do it because of the union. To me, joining a union is about respect'. We discussed who else we could get together for another chat after work.

The next time we met was after a Saturday shift, opting for lunch nearby. The discussion began by explaining what being in a trade union would involve, and the necessarily clandestine activity was quite off-putting to some people. The closest approximation that one person could arrive at was that the union would be 'like Dumbledore's army'.[11] (It speaks volumes that the closest comparison to trade unionism for this individual was taken from a fantasy story.) Another person had been involved in the staff forum – a kind of management-run scheme to discuss problems at work – and had been arguing for the London Living Wage.[12] He agreed that organising collectively might be a good idea, but at least wanted to try the staff forum first.

The clandestine nature of organising was clearly an obstacle, but for some it was also a source of enthusiasm while working a boring job. Over a week of secretive conversations and invitations, we organised the largest and most successful meeting in a pub near the call centre. In the best tradition of exciting meetings there were too few seats and not enough space around the table. A spot at the back of the pub seemed suitable, if only slightly too noisy for an easy discussion. After the meeting got underway one of the other workers nudged me and pointed to something on the wall. Alongside the hipster decorations and bookshelves was a tattered red Soviet-era communist flag mounted in a frame. One of the workers then pointed it out, saying: 'I guess that's appropriate isn't it!'. Appropriate perhaps, but it was also somewhat surreal to have our first official meeting under a commodified version of a communist symbol. The discussion that ensued was wide-ranging, but often came up against a stumbling block: there was little sense of how a group of workers could begin to effect change in the workplace, or even what specifically might be contested.

The attempt to begin building some kind of organisation involved trying to join a trade union.[13] After finding out about how to join the trade union from the union's website, I called the membership telephone number. I explained over the phone that I was a call-centre worker and interested in joining, and was told that this could only be done by email or post, in an ironic moment of one call-centre worker speaking to another. I submitted my application by email and did not receive a reply for a few weeks, after which I got an email confirming my membership and the telephone number for a branch organiser. After missing each other a few times due to the nature of shift work I made contact with the organiser. She informed me that I had been added to a combined, geographically defined branch that covered a wide area and different employment types. Unfortunately, I had missed the last branch meeting a few days before which had been cancelled anyway for low attendance. I was shocked to find out that the next meeting would not take place for three months. After a brief discussion the organiser offered to help organise a room in a pub near the workplace to host a meeting – something we had already been doing. She also offered to post membership forms, of which three arrived in a hand-addressed envelope a few days later.

There was a real difficulty in making a connection between the trade union and our workplace. The leap from our independent collective meetings to joining an external organisation was a difficult one. This problem was greatly exacerbated by the high turnover in the call centre. The length of time it took to start having meetings with the union meant that a number of the people initially involved had left the call centre during this phase.

LEARNING FROM OTHER STRUGGLES

The example discussed here highlights many of the difficulties of organising in call centres. The official response of trade unions to the new conditions and structures of the work has been varied, with Bob Russell suggesting that trade unionism in call centres is 'embryonic'.[14] Enda Brophy detailed the experience of 'Collettivo

PrecariAtesia',[15] a workers' collective in Rome, formed in 2004 in one of the largest call centres in Europe. The workers were classified as 'freelancers' as 'they technically rented their workstations and were paid by the call, but management set their shifts at six hours a day, six days a week'. The workers were therefore not entitled to a range of contractual rights, including the right to unionise, to strike, holiday or sick pay, or even maternity leave. One worker described 'seeing women forced to work during their eighth month of pregnancy lest they lose their position'. The Collettivo began to organise in the call centre and used a kind of 'digital sabotage'. The workers organised a number of strikes subverting their status as freelancers to leave work without the permission of management. The result of the campaign, which spread across a range of Italian call centres, was a reclassification of the workers as employees, and compensation. However, as a result of the campaign every member of the Collettivo lost their job.[16]

One of the lessons from the Kolinko inquiry is that despite the best intentions of researchers it is not always possible to find open struggle in a workplace to engage with.[17] We have discussed so far some initial attempts to organise, but it would be quite a stretch to label them as successful examples. At the start of my research I was introduced to someone who had led a strike in a call centre: Michael, the same person interviewed earlier in the book. The interview sheds some further needed light on the possibilities for organising and some of the details of how different actions were organised.

Michael had worked at various call centres, both in the UK and abroad, but the interview focused on one example in particular. This was a charity-fundraising call centre and 'could have anything up to about five hundred people on their books'. The conditions for the workers in the call centre were typical for the sector as '100 per cent of it was running on zero-hour contracts'. Michael explained how the experience of working at a charity-fundraising call centre compared to a previous job:

It was the first time that I had worked in an environment where the work was non-stop and regimented. And so before that I worked for fifteen years in the civil service and, you know, even though there was of course a level of factory standards it was never as controlled.

It is worth noting that the civil service has a recent history of trade union militancy, with the PCS (Public and Commercial Services) union being involved in a number of national strikes and campaigns. Michael had been active in the union in his previous workplace and had developed a practical experience and knowledge of trade unionism. He summarised the experience of the labour process in the call centre:

It's almost the pressure to hit targets, do you know what I mean? There never seemed to be a couple of hours without worrying about whether you were up on them. The targets for those would be just so high and also the targets in terms of the amount of calls that you need to make are so high, those were really, really draining.

This experience is similar to that of the call centre I worked in and is typical of the high-volume outbound type, creating the 'assembly-line in the head' and 'always feeling under pressure and constantly aware that the completion of one task is immediately followed by another'.[18] The reality for workers is that of a regimented labour process driven by quantitative targets, despite the fact that in this example the aim of the labour process is to solicit charity donations.

The behaviour of management in our call centre followed a similar pattern to what we have discussed so far. Although there was not an analogous 'Nev' figure, the approach tended towards the despotic. In addition to the surveillance methods common in call centres, management exerted their power in various ways:

There were all sorts of rules. I mean for instance hanging coats on the back of your chair was banned, little things like that. Constantly listing things that people couldn't do. I've seen people being chased into toilets because they have their phones on them and stuff like that! All these things you can do with or without the computers.

This bullying style was indicative of a workplace in which the 'frontier of control' lay mostly in the hands of management.[19] This behaviour had the potential to limit workplace resistance, but the aggressive tactics also became a grievance for workers. The first instance of resistance that Michael referred to came as a response to management:

> There was one guy, an Irish guy, he had been there for years and they said he had been skipping calls. Now the operations manager kind of got involved in it and it was obvious that they were trying to catch him out and it was obvious that they wanted to get rid of him. And it was also quite clear that here was someone who was seen as someone who would stand up to managers. That is a big fear for them that someone would stand up. It was before we had really had a go at organising the union. He was in the Labour party and a trade unionist anyway.

This example highlights the hostility of management to the first stages of organisation in the workplace. If an individual worker is singled out to be a problem, or likely to 'stand up' to managers, steps can be taken to increase the supervision with a view to terminating employment. This fear of victimisation can be used to prevent workers taking the first steps to organise collectively. However, victimisation of workers is not necessarily a straightforward process for management:

> I think there had been attempts beforehand, before I had got there, and I think people had joined from there and it had kind of fell away. It made it quite difficult to go to the union about it when they kind of sacked him at the start and basically, yeah, they sacked him on the spot for fraud. They called it fraud! He was skipping calls, that was fraud. And what he said was: the system had kind of, the reason it sounded like he had skipped the calls, was because [his] screen had frozen. And at the initial

hearing the HR guy, who obviously didn't know what he was talking about, said: if your screen was frozen then everyone else's would have on all the campaigns, they would all freeze, all have done the same. And so what we did, one of the first things we did as a union was we had a kind of a letter or a petition saying, well, it was a survey. When the system goes down, does your screen freeze? We did this survey, we turned up about forty of these surveys in the appeal hearing [laughter], and so they had to kind of accept that, so he got reinstated. And that was kind of a big win for us.

The reliance on the electronic surveillance of the labour process proved problematic for management. As they were not experienced with the labour process, management, compared to the workers, lacked knowledge of the systems. The workers organised their own survey, arming them with the evidence to fight the victimisation. This first step was important in two regards: firstly, it highlighted a weakness on the part of management, and secondly it developed the confidence of the workers to oppose a decision by management. This opening challenge questioned the authority of management and provided a defence against the threat of victimisation.

The confrontation provided the impetus for the workers to launch an organising project in the call centre. Michael was able to draw on his previous experience as a trade unionist in the civil service, explaining how 'when I first started there and I had this sort of thing, I'm in a workplace, the first time I had gone in I saw there was an opportunity here to have a go at building a union from scratch'. It was therefore a deliberate choice to start organising in the call centre, but Michael's knowledge and practical experience had to be reapplied in this new context. The workers in the call centre initially received very limited support from the trade union, unlike Michael's previous experiences in the civil service. The trade union had a combined branch that the workers joined and at its monthly branch meetings it 'would be lucky to get ten or fifteen people, out of four thousand'. Michael explained that when he joined the branch 'It wasn't outward looking at all, it was really pretty much, you know, service providers. And, you know, they would provide people to go and represent people at a disciplinary and so on, which is fair enough'. The lack of support from the established trade union meant that the initial attempts at organising had to be undertaken independently by the workers at the call centre.

The workers began to organise in the call centre informally. While they did recruit other workers to the trade union, they also relied on informal meetings to develop networks in the workplace:

> When I first got there was an attempt to get a few people together in a pub and have a bit of a chat. The thing was, the union, I didn't know a few people and it wasn't until I had been there a few months. The issue that came up really was the one of pay. It was while I was having a smoking break, which, you know, smoking, you should really take [it] up if you want to organise! [laughter] Well, that's kind of a clue, really, isn't it? If you go outside for a break with the smokers, that the kind of place to be really.

The smoking area and the pub became important sites for these first discussions about organising. The pub – despite not being an accessible location for all workers – provided a useful opportunity as it was removed from the workplace and workers might be meeting there anyhow after a shift. The smoking area provided a regular opportunity to meet with different workers throughout the shift, temporarily away from supervision. Similarly, Mulholland references 'Smokin'' specifically as a form of resistance in her study. Identifying and exploiting the moments where workers meet collectively away from management supervision is an important and replicable starting point.[20]

The dispute at Michael's workplace developed after the workers came into contact with someone who worked in one of the company's other call centres. They discovered that each of the sites were on different pay scales. There was outrage at the fact they were receiving less pay than workers doing the same job at a different site. This formed the basis for the campaign:

... even though this is the last thing you should do, you know, when you're starting to organise, to go for an issue that is seen as being unwinnable [laughter]. But it was just too deeply felt, you couldn't really avoid it. So we just got people together in a pub, we thought maybe five or six people would turn up. In fact over twenty people turned up. So we decided that we would agitate around pay but there were a whole load of other issues, one of them was around bullying, and so taking that one which didn't go down very well.

Michael explained that the issue of pay was 'seen as being unwinnable'. This was partly due to the charity fundraising that the call centre was engaged in. As mentioned earlier, the managers would apply a kind of 'moralism' to workers: soldiering at work would only hurt the charity, a pay rise would mean less money for the charities, and so on. The 'moralism' that surrounds charities can be deployed by management in an attempt to encourage workers or deflect their grievances. This is despite the fact that charity call centres, in general, are not charities themselves. Instead they are a sector of outsourced call-centre operations which compete for contracts to raise money on behalf of charities. The call centre is therefore itself a profit-making venture. Michael and the other workers started an investigation, looking through the company's accounts to prove that a pay rise could come from the profits rather than the funds raised for the charities.

The identification of a demand for the campaign was an important development. However, there remained obstacles:

It was difficult that people were part time. But again as long as you have got a core of people that are kind of trying to speak to the new people coming in, that are constantly involved in trying to build, being at the forefront of fighting on these issues, then you can still get people in. See, the thing is, in terms of the kinds of numbers on the books and so on, it was going to be really, really difficult to get the numbers that we would need to get a kind of recognition, but we actually did win stuff. We actually won the first pay rises in there for six years and that was over the threat of walkouts and of the threat of cancelling our shifts at the same time. But as we were doing it there were moments when you were like, what is the point of doing this? We'll never break through, etc. But I think that people feel that it was very, very important that it was done, that we had that, and also that when it came to a disciplinary [hearing] there was someone, there were people who were trained up through the union to represent people, you know, the bread and butter stuff. I think when we won the pay thing, then lots of people joined the union afterwards.

These obstacles are typical of the experience of organising in casualised private-sector workplaces. What is interesting about this quote is that Michael does not gloss over the problems and highlights the importance of attention to detail on 'the bread and butter stuff' and the experience of a success. The combination of these two factors was important for the campaign. The success proved that it was worth getting organised and raised confidence. The attention to detail meant that every opportunity to organise was exploited to its fullest potential, focusing on that potential rather than the limitations.

Michael detailed the practicalities of finding opportunities to organise on the call centre floor. One of the most important examples was

to make an announcement about the union in what they called the break-out area. Someone would stand up, usually me or the couple of others that would do it, and we would make an announcement about it. And it would usually go down really, really well! But of course as well we would publish leaflets, newsletters and that kind of stuff.

The workers held their own organisational buzz sessions. Instead of the management-led buzz sessions that Cederström and Fleming argue are an attempt 'to *inject life into the dead-zone of work*',[21] the workers seized the opportunity to inject organising into the break-time. These interventions required significant confidence on the part of individual workers at first, especially considering how the threat of victimisation still hung over the call-centre floor. These acts were shifted into collective interventions when the workers started planning them together and writing leaflets to hand out. Michael explains that the leaflets were

> mainly about whatever was happening in the call centres, we would do articles about, you know, the wrap time, or how the pay campaign was going, but also we would put in stuff about the anti-fascism or some other political campaign.

The interventions at the breaks provided a wider audience for the workers who were organising. It allowed the move from a smaller group to wider networks at the call centre. The workers began to meet regularly outside of the call centre:

> We would have meetings in a pub afterwards, basically right after the shifts ended, so at least once a month we would meet in the Wetherspoons and we would all gather round trying to listen, you know, all repeating stuff to each other. But we managed to get a separate room upstairs booked as we got some money from the union and they would do stuff like pay for that. There were times as well where when the system went down it was an opportunity to go around the call centre and talk to people. Alongside talking to people in all the breaks and that. Actually some of the best times were when on a Saturday after a shift, loads of people would go to the pub afterwards and you could chat to everyone away from work.

Once the regular meetings had started, the relationship with the trade union improved. The union began to provide resources and logistical support to the workers. Despite this, the overwhelming majority of the activity was led at a rank and file level. These interventions at the call centre were not without risks, however. Although the break-time speeches and leaflets were identified as an important part of the project they could also easily become a point of confrontation.

One of these confrontations took place at the height of the campaign. There was now a network of collective organisation spread across the call centre with regular meetings. As Michael describes it,

Basically we would take up issues and there was a guy who had got suspended for his apparent behaviour in a briefing. There were a number of people who were upset about it. It was someone who wasn't the easiest, he was a kind of a 'Marmite' guy, not everyone kind of liked him and that, but he was in the union. But that didn't matter because as the union we tried to establish a principle that actually an attack on this person was an attack on the union. So we had a big meeting to discuss our position etc. And I wrote up a piece and I put it in [a socialist newspaper] and stupidly put my name next to it. And next thing I know I get this phone call. I'd just come back from [union] conference. And they said, 'Right, you have written an article and it has your name on it, it's in [a socialist newspaper], and it is bringing the name of [the company] into disrepute, you are therefore suspended and later you will have a hearing' and so on.

The threat of victimisation that had hung over the call centre had returned with a vengeance. Michael had been targeted for something that had happened outside of the call centre and became the focus of an attempt to break the workers' nascent organisation. The establishment of the trade union principle of 'an attack on this person was an attack on the union' meant that the workers were prepared for a defence campaign:

And so word got out and within a day of my suspension we had organised a meeting in a pub of about fifty people and people were very, very angry and saw it as an attack on our right to organise, which is great, it is fantastic. And as I said, someone who had been there for years, it was a coach basically, and she said 'Do you know what, I'm not going to do my shift until you get [Michael] back'. So for my hearing, we had taken a few people to the [union] branch meeting and argued for a strike ballot, we got a protest outside the hearing. And people came from different charities and stuff, and I was involved in going round getting solidarity, getting speeches we had people in our meeting speaking from [a charity] who were out on strike at the time and a group of them came down, a group from the RMT [the transport workers' union] came down, about fifty people all in all. A number of people came before their shifts, came down from work and it was good. I remember people also, the next meeting we had was quite big, and I think we agreed that we would kind of go for a day of people not working their shifts and so on, and that's when we called a strike.

The campaign was able to build links both inside and outside of the call centre. The prospect of being able to call a strike in the call centre shows how the level of organisation had grown significantly from the early conversations in the smoking area or the pub after work.

The existence of workers' self-organisation in the call centre provided the means for a collective response to victimisation. Despite this, as Michael explains,

It was very difficult because that's when a lot of people started, a lot of people who had been key to building the union were concerned, and actually the chief executive came and sat on the shop floor he was calling in, even though, union recognition was going to be over his dead body, he was calling in people who were reps in the union, mainly the young union reps, all the union reps, and kind of saying, 'Look, [Michael's] only got himself to blame' and all this kind of stuff, this is what he wanted, he created this situation, all this kind of shit, so it all became really tense! Lots of tense phone calls, really difficult because I had to do stuff on the outside as well. But also there is that point as well where you worry about the momentum. If we don't do something quite sharpish, you know we will lose that momentum. But other things have happened, there was an article in the third sector, in the magazine for charities. I was going round doing meetings in various union meetings to speak about my victimisation. I was in Oxford and invited to speak at [the union] branch there, I was on the way back from there,

I heard that there was an MP who had raised it as an early day motion [laughter]. 'This is disgraceful, this kind of victimisation' and so on. It was an attack on trade unionism. It was very shortly after that they rang, I got a phone call that said from the chief operations officer that, although he was spitting feathers, he gave me my job back. It is interesting, I think it was the pressure about how they would be seen, especially to the charities and so on, the bad press, that moralism flipped over the other way. And it was great returning, but they went for me a few more times after that again [laughter]. But then again I had done my five years at that point, which is about as much as I could take!

The example of how the campaign won the reinstatement raises a number of issues. The campaign was not limited to industrial action within the workplace itself. The workers sought to build links across other trade union branches but also more broadly within the labour movement. While these kinds of action are commonplace, they can play an important role in generalising forms of struggle and confidence. The use of leverage in campaigns – that is, applying pressure outside of the workplace – had an important effect. The ability to exert pressure via customers, through the media or in public relations, can be used to strengthen a campaign. Particularly in the example of charities, there is a susceptibility to this kind of action due to the moral aspects.

The interview finished with a set of comments reflecting on the experience of trying to build organisation in a call centre. Michael concluded:

I hope that some of the work we did remains. You just hope that people who went on to other workplaces saw something in it and carry it on elsewhere. It was interesting though, it was always the threat of doing stuff and people were always up for doing it. And as it turned out, each time we got the desired result before it got to that, so we never got to test it out. I'm not sure what would have happened, I'm not exactly sure! [laughter] It is a lot of hard work. Looking back, I think that if there was one thing that I could have done, it would have been to harden up more people, you know, so there were more than a few key individuals, because what happens if they are not there anymore? Well, that is a difficult process, isn't it?

The experience of the campaign that Michael led shows that successful organisation is possible in a high-volume sales call centre. Particularly notable is the combination of traditional modes of trade union organisation and creative innovations relating to the labour process in the call centre. A number of challenges to organising are detailed specifically, but the high turnover emerges as the most important. As noted earlier, Marcel van der Linden's notion that 'the transition between "running away" and "fighting for better working conditions" is in reality rather fluid' is very relevant in this case.[22] This can be seen in Michael's comment that he had 'done' his 'five years at that point, which is about as much as I could take!', and which is significantly longer than most workers were prepared to remain at the call centre I worked in. However, the idea that the experience of organising is not limited to a specific time or place is incredibly important. Michael applied his previous experiences from the civil service to the call centre, and hoped that workers in the call centre 'who went on to other workplaces and that saw something in it [would] carry it on elsewhere'. Even projects that fail can form part of the process of organising in the future, lessons being learnt from failures as well as successes. The challenge at this stage is to understand how continuity can be achieved: both within the same workplace and between different workplaces.

UNDERSTANDING PRECARIOUS LABOUR

In order to understand how struggle could develop in a call centre it is crucial that we address the precariousness of labour. By any measure the employment relations in the call centre were insecure. During my time at the call centre I could have been fired at any point as my employment contract offered no security. The majority of the workers were either in a similar position or employed through a temp agency. This lack of job security posed a significant challenge for organising. The term precarity has been used to describe the conditions of insecure employment, but the application of the term "precariousness" is both more unwieldy and indeterminate than most'. If anything can be said 'for certain about precariousness, it is that it teeters', which points towards 'some of the tensions that shadow much of the discussion about precarious labour'.[23] Pierre Bourdieu explains that 'casualisation of employment is part of a mode of domination of a new kind, based on the creation of a generalized and permanent state of insecurity aimed at forcing workers into submission, into the acceptance of exploitation'.[24]

This definition provides an important starting point for the discussion of precarity, yet the arguments about the existence of a 'precariat' put forward by Guy Standing has done much to muddy the waters.[25] Richard Seymour argues that Standing's formulation of the precariat 'remains at best *a purely negative, critical concept*', but this is not to say that the term should be completely rejected.[26] The problem with the concept is that 'its advocates want it to do far more than it is capable of doing – that is, naming, describing, and explaining a developing social class'. Precarious employment is not new, as is evident from the description by a dock worker in 1882, 'dock labouring is at all times a precarious and uncertain mode of living'.[27] Furthermore, the imbalance of power between capital and labour has meant that the period of secure employment for men in Western Europe under the Fordism of the 1960–1970s is an exception to the rule historically. If it is not a new phenomenon then it is necessary to consider how conditions of precarity have arisen or could be overcome. The defeat of trade unions under Thatcher signalled the beginning of neoliberalism, involving attacks on workers' terms and conditions, the dismantling of the welfare state through the reduction of government spending and the opening up of public services to market forces.[28] So while the precariousness of labour in general is built into capitalism, this has been greatly exacerbated by the weakening of trade unions and the fact that 'precarity is built into neoliberal capitalism, in which growth is predicated on financial risk and indebtedness'.[29]

The experience of contemporary precarity has to be understood as part of the shift away from the patterns of production and consumption of Fordism. In terms of employment, Angela Mitropoulos argues that the 'flight from "standard hours" was not precipitated by employers but rather by workers seeking less time at work' and connects it to what 'the Italian Workerists dubbed the "refusal of work" in the late 1970s'.[30] This escape from the discipline of the Fordist labour market potentially alters the content of the struggle. Anthony Iles warns of the risks of considering the struggles only 'in terms of battles for better legislation'. This attempt to win only employment reform 'misses the opportunity to investigate the tendency for self-organised (or "disorganised") labour to develop a more generalised struggle'.[31] It is in this way that the concept of precarity therefore takes on a political role in the autonomist tradition: it becomes a 'project to dismantle the mass worker as the central object for labour struggles and place it on the shoulders of the more encompassing but diffuse idea of the precarious worker'.[32]

In practice precarious employment has not led to a greater amount of leisure time for workers to enjoy. It may reduce – although 'not necessarily' – the 'actual amount of time spent doing paid work', but 'the post-Fordist worker' has to 'be continually available for such work'.[33] The time spent not working becomes devoted to searching and preparing for work. This leads Mitropoulos to argue that while Fordism sought to 'sever the brains of workers from their bodies', post-Fordist capitalism is 'characterised – in Foucault's terms – as the imprisonment of the body by the soul'. This notion is different to the orthodox Marxist conception of alienation. The perspective put forward by Berardi does not 'anticipate any restoration of humanity, does not proclaim any human universality, and bases its understanding of humanity on class conflict'.[34] This understanding of alienation as estrangement is not based on the loss of some kind of human essence. Instead it is a 'condition of estrangement from the mode of production and its rules, as refusal of work'. It is therefore, as Berardi puts it, to be 'seen as the condition of those who rebel assuming their partial humanity as a point of strength, a premise of a higher social form, of a higher form of humanity, and not as the condition of those who are forced to renounce their essential humanity'.[35]

Not all precarious workers are employed to do the same kinds of work, however. Kidd McKarthy suggests a distinction between 'BrainWorkers', those 'who are hired not for their general labour but for specialised skills or their creativity', and 'ChainWorkers', employed to work at large chain stores such as McDonalds. They are 'automatons and the only thing they have to sell is their labour'. The extension of rationalisation into the 'ChainWorkers' workplaces means that 'there is all the discipline of the factory with none of the interdependency and vulnerabilities which formerly allowed workers to fight back'.[36] The 'ChainWorkers' therefore face the largest structural barriers for organising. As Pollert and Charlwood have argued, the question of vulnerability is best understood with an emphasis on the conditions of 'low pay and non-unionism'.[37] The changes that have taken place in the labour market over the last thirty years have involved an increasing polarisation of the types of jobs available, with a growth in the number of low-paid jobs with bad conditions at the bottom.

The position of different precarious workers is uneven. Migrant workers, and in particular those without legal immigration status and therefore employment rights, are particularly at risk. There are also additional pressures on workers who attempt to balance paid work and unpaid work, for example workers carrying out home and family responsibilities as well as employment. This remains primarily a demand on women in the workforce and increases the likelihood of employment in non-standard jobs that are temporary or casualised. It is therefore possible to say that the most precarious and vulnerable are those in low-paid, 'non-standard' jobs, without trade union organisation as they are not covered by either of the 'three regulatory regimes – collective bargaining, employment protection rights and the national insurance system'.[38] Much academic literature is concerned with 'the unionized workforce', yet 'the non-unionized themselves, who comprise the majority of employees, have been marginalized', something that Pollert and Charlwood argue demands renewed attention.[39]

THE LIMITATIONS OF TRADE UNIONS

The problems of casualisation are compounded by the falling levels of trade union membership in the UK. The headline statistics for 2014 show that there were 6.4 million employees who were members of a trade union, with a density of 25 per cent. This is down from a peak of 13 million members in 1979, and a lower density than 1995 when it stood at 32.4 per cent. The membership is divided between 3.76 million in the public sector and 2.7 million in the private sector. Membership density in the public sector stands at 54.3 per cent whereas in the private sector it is only 14 per cent. Within these figures trade union members are likely to be older, with 38 per cent of members over the age of 50 compared with 28 per cent of employees.[40] It is therefore reasonable to argue that the general picture of trade unionism in the UK is bleak. Trade unions operate in a context of defeats. Thompson and Ackroyd argue that 'political action by a succession of Conservative admin-istrations has also clearly shaped the broader landscape'. They continue to argue that due to this, 'three significant dimensions of policy can be identified: a strategy of de-regulation of labour markets and promotion of a low wage, low skill economy as a means of attracting inward investment; competitive tendering and internal markets in the public sector; and the sustained legislative assault on union organisation, employment rights and collective bargaining'.[41]

The level of strike action can be used as an indicator of the confidence and combativity of the working class. The institutional figures for trade union membership are worrying and the figures for official strike days paint a similar picture. In the 1980s there was an average of 400 strike days lost per 1,000 workers annually.[42] Between 2003 and 2007 the average number of strike days per 1,000 workers had fallen to only 25.1.[43] The past few years have seen the trade union movement responding to government austerity programmes, which involved three dimensions: the Trade Union Congress organised a significant demonstration on 26 March 2011 in London which was followed by two large strikes in June and November later that year. These strikes involved 262,000 and

963,000 days lost respectively. Over 90 per cent of the lost working days in 2011 were in the public sector, and these two strike days overwhelmingly contributed to this. This represented an increase of four times the number of days lost through strikes compared to 2010. The TUC claimed that the November strike was the biggest for thirty years.[44] Although there have been public sector strikes in 2012 the number of strike days fell sharply from the high of 1.4 million to 250,000.[45]

The growth of employment in the service sector has not been matched by a growth in levels of trade unionism in this sector. Trade unions 'face considerable obstacles to extending their presence in private services, not least from hostile employers.'[46] However, Walters' study of part-time workers in retail organisations found less secure employment for workers was not necessarily a barrier to unionisation. The response from non-unionised workers in workplaces where there was a union was either that there had been no attempt to recruit them or they did not think that joining a union would achieve anything.[47] It is therefore possible to put forward an argument that does not consider the novelties of the service sector as insurmountable obstacles to unionisation. The failure to unionise service work is an outcome of class struggle, rather than an inevitable process. The victory of management lies in part in their ability to use 'the more hostile political and economic climate for trade unionism to undermine their power and legitimacy.'[48] This has often taken place without concerted attempts by trade unions to mount a serious counter-offensive. However, it is not the case that there are not examples of organised workers in the service sector. For example, flight attendants – the focus of Hochschild's research on emotional labour[49] – have effective trade union representation[50] and engaged in extensive industrial action in 2010 in the UK,[51] as well as the Cathay Pacific smile strike discussed in Chapter 4.

The context of call centres, with the high turnover of staff and extensive surveillance and control, is particularly hostile to trade unionism. Despite this there are 'generally sufficient opportunities available for workers to express their grievances, articulate their discontent, and thus resist efforts to shackle them.'[52] Bain and

Taylor – over ten years ago now – documented the development of trade union organisation in a number of different call centres. The question of developing strategies for organising the service sector remains on the whole unanswered in the UK.[53]

This will require an analytical focus on resistance at the workplace level. This cannot be put off until some point in the future, as Neil Davidson argues, 'for without the entry of the currently unorganised private sector workers into the trade union movement any revival of struggle will be unnecessarily weakened and limited, and their recruitment will not happen automatically.'[54] While there is a potential in re-thinking the relationship between worker and union there also has to be an awareness of alternative strategies that are currently being pursued inside of trade unions. The search for different ways to strengthen organisation, whether in the community or otherwise, still maintains a focus on organising. This stands in contrast to the growth of service unionism, in which the approach taken to building the union is quite different.

The possibilities for unionisation in the call centre have to be understood in the context of neoliberalism and the very low levels of unionisation in the private sector in the UK. Neil Davidson has argued that this has meant 'many working class people do not have the opportunity to develop "trade union consciousness", with all that means in relation to the likelihood of their holding left wing political positions and accepting the need for collective action to improve their condition.'[55] There are serious limitations in understanding the question of unionisation in these terms. Instead of pathologising the non-unionised worker it is worth considering the character of trade unions themselves. By drawing on Robert Blackburn's definition of 'unionateness' this can be explored further. It requires 'collective bargaining and the protection of the interests of members, as employees, as its main function, rather than, say, professional activities or welfare schemes . . . is independent of employers for purposes of negotiation . . . is prepared to be militant, using all forms of industrial action which may be effective.'[56] The basic features of trade union organisation are exactly the things that are being undermined by the shift towards service-based unionism. However, this operates in a contradictory context: the impetus to transform unions from above is not necessarily matched by support from below.

Service provision (offering options such as insurance, debt advice, helplines and discounts) is one attempt, driven from the top of the unions, to overcome falling membership rates. The required responses to the challenges facing unions have also been posed in terms of revival or renewal. The divorce of the national leadership from the conditions of the workplace is supposed to endow the leadership with the resources – and indeed the responsibility – for developing the strategies that could lead to a renewal. It appears that some of the strategies being developed by national union officers tend towards service provision. This can be seen on a larger scale, but also in smaller ways too. For example, the UCU (University and College Union) advertised a new online recruitment drive with the incentive that 'if a member joins using your link, your name will be automatically entered into a prize draw where you will have the chance to win a John Lewis hamper worth £200'.[57] It is worth noting that the John Lewis partnership[58] was started as an 'experiment in industrial democracy'.[59] But it has also been described as 'suffocatingly paternalistic in its apparent benevolence'.[60] This aspect of worker participation can therefore be understood as a 'response to the challenge of labour' which entails a 'blatant dislike of trade unionism'.[61] So, ironically, recruitment to the union is encouraged with a hamper from a famously anti-trade union company.

The concept of organising – perhaps opposed to selling services, though not necessarily so – is used to outline how union renewal could be achieved. This can refer to the introduction of specialist functions to represent different groups of workers, for example to cater specifically to the needs of casual workers. There is, however, an ambiguity in what is meant by the term organising. Melanie Simms and Jane Holgate illustrate this by arguing that the new approaches have 'tended to see organising as a "toolbox" of practices rather than as having an underpinning political philosophy or objective'. This has created a situation in which organising is being adopted without asking 'the fundamental question of what are we organising "for"?' The move towards focusing on organising is nevertheless positive.[62] The response by 'key policy makers at the TUC and in affiliate unions' was to look towards 'US programmes such as the Organising Institute and Union Summer which were explicitly intended to attract underrepresented groups into the union movement.'[63] Part of the problem is that 'existing labor unions' – in the UK, as well as globally – 'have proved incapable of mobilizing mass rank-and-file militancy to resist the ongoing deterioration in workplace conditions and the systematic erosion of workers' power'. Immanuel Ness continues to point out that despite this, 'workers are developing new forms of antibureau-cratic and anticapitalist forms of syndicalist, council communist, and autonomist worker representation'. These experiments in new forms of organisation are important because they are 'rooted in the self-activity and democratic impulses of members and committed to developing egalitarian organizations in place of traditional union bureaucracies'.[64]

These first steps towards new forms of organisation could offer the potential to break the deadlock of austerity currently facing workers. However, the status of these as experiments limits them to potential effects rather than indicating something more substantial at this stage. It is important to remember, as Ralph Miliband argued, that 'left activists, generally speaking, have been a crucially important element in the labour movement and in the working class';[65] yet, at the same time, they are not the labour movement, nor are they working class. So while these emergent struggles are bursting forth at particular points, they are not generalising across large numbers of workplaces at this stage. The attempts by experienced, creative and already politicised workers to lead campaigns provide important inspiration, but can be particularly vulnerable to management strategies of victimi-sation. It is at this point that the conditions of precarity become particularly sharp. The attraction of the label of troublemaker, something which can happen quickly when a worker chooses to stick their head above the parapet, greatly intensifies the risk of being sacked. The longevity of these initial projects can be greatly reduced either by those at the core being forced out of the workplace or choosing to move on for other reasons.

The critique of the current state of trade unionism in the UK is not intended as a generalised criticism of trade unionism, partly because trade unionism operates within certain constraints and so would not develop an anti-work critique. Trade unions have been the subject of a sustained attack since the 1970s and perhaps what is notable is that, despite how low the levels of union membership are generally, the public sector is still relatively organised. However, it is necessary to highlight how trade unions have effectively failed to challenge the agenda of austerity and how most of their members are suffering from continuing attacks on their terms and conditions. The only signs of organised resistance have been the collection of one-day strikes, symbolic moments of action. However, as John Zerzan notes, 'as far back as 1952 a sociologist was advising management that "yearly strikes should be arranged, inasmuch as they work so effectively to dissipate discontent"'.[66] In this light the national strike days appear more of a cynical move by the trade union leadership. By giving up on the question of control of the labour process and instead limiting themselves to defensive campaigns, trade unions have failed to relate to the anger and resistance at a workplace level. They do, however, remain organisations in which arguments can be posed and organisational initiatives tried out – at least to some degree.

ANTI-WORK

In the context of 'bullshit jobs', it becomes important to understand the tendency toward the rejection of work. The theoretical basis of the anti-work perspective can be traced back to the Cuban Marxist Paul Lafargue. In a pamphlet, *The Right to Be Lazy* published in 1880, he argues that

> the proletariat, the great class embracing all the producers of civilized nations, the class which in freeing itself will free humanity from servile toil and will make of the human animal a free being, – the proletariat, betraying its instincts, despising its historic mission, has let itself be perverted by the dogma

of work. Rude and terrible has been its punishment. All its individual and social woes are born of its passion for work.[67]

Lafargue asserts that the expansion of the possibilities of non-work is central to the radical transformation of society by the working class. These involve not only the possibility of pursuing new creative endeavours; they even include just being lazy. Christopher Taylor argues that Lafargue's 'radicalization of laziness had a precedent in Karl Marx's own writing', yet despite Lafargue being Marx's son-in-law, the perspective has had a limited impact on the development of Marxist thought.[68] There has been a renewal of interest in autonomist Marxism and perspectives of anti-work, found for example in the writings of Kathi Weeks.[69] The flight from work described in Hardt and Negri's *Empire* is explicitly characterised by the authors as the product of French philosophy and Italian politics.[70] This understanding, as Christopher Taylor argues, 'elide[s] the connections between the development of radical Italian Marxism and the mid-twentieth-century work of C. L. R. James'.[71] We have already traced some of the connections between the Johnson-Forest Tendency (of which James was a leading member), *Socialisme ou Barbarie* and later the *Operaismo* which were important for the development of workers' inquiries. However, Taylor goes further, arguing that 'this appearance of similitude, however, intimates a deeper history of material connections, one in which an expansive circuit of transnational interaction and epistemic exchange linked the Caribbean to the Mediterranean'.

The analysis undertaken by the Johnson-Forest Tendency in the USA owed much to James. His 'approach to capitalism in Detroit derived from transnational sources and histories; he explored capitalism in the global North with creole eyes, placing the Fordist factory and the Caribbean plantation into a coincident time and space'.[72] The challenge posed by James in the Johnson-Forest Tendency, *Socialisme ou Barbarie* and the *Operaismo* entailed a critique of orthodox Marxism. For all three it also involved writing 'within and against an intellectual and institutional context in which Marxism was effectively redefined as a theory of distribution', a distortion of Stalinism stemming from the experience of state socialism. Work therefore became central and 'Soviet-style Marxism foreclosed any critique of work'.[73] The instance of workers' inquiry developed by James and the Johnson-Forest Tendency was an attempt to develop a thoroughgoing critique of contemporary work.

The theoretical development of workers' inquiry from James's study of the Haitian revolution[74] and application to workers in Fordist factories in Detroit is important, yet it leaves the question of what relevance this has to contemporary call-centre workers. The connection between slavery and Taylorism has been asserted by David Roediger and Elizabeth Esch.[75] As Christopher Taylor argues, the 'plantation slavery and Fordist capitalism appeared comparable to James because the latter reinscribed, reasserted, and internationalized the composition of work that had obtained in plantation societies'. He expands this by applying it to 'the transition to post-Fordist empire', arguing that it 'marks a renewed intensification and generalization of plantation-era processes by which capital attempted to impose work – a generalization and intensification that is negated through its refusal'.[76] Taylor also argues – and it is important to reiterate this here – 'while labor in a plantation society and labor in Fordist society are qualitatively different, the plantation and the factory are both constituted through an antagonistic dialectic, pitting a workforce striving for "universality" against the regime of labor in capitalism'.[77]

The opposition of the anti-work perspective to orthodox Marxism is a historical peculiarity. Marx himself studied the 'antagonistic social dynamics of postemancipation Jamaica' and 'would develop a robust antiwork perspective in the *Grundrisse*'.[78] While Negri's perspective was developed through a close reading of the *Grundrisse*, the figure of the slave remains absent in his anti-work politics. For Marx, the free slaves became the active subjects of two refusals: refusing slavery and then refusing wage labour.[79] Freed from the direct, forced exploitation of slavery they are unwilling to submit to indirect modes of exploitation. This experience in the Caribbean is the starting point for Marx's notion of anti-work, although he did not develop this in the same way as did either Lafargue or James. The anti-work perspective provides a critique that is not limited to the question of control of the labour process. In the context of 'bullshit jobs' it is possible, as Taylor argues, to go further than 'moralistic invocations of labor's value' that 'appear grotesquely comical'.[80] An 'Antiwork Marxism' holds potential in that it

> encourages us to laugh at this moralism, to take it for the farcical tragedy that it is, and to imagine new forms of life. If we listen carefully, we can detect in this laughter – resounding through Marx, James, and Negri – the resonant echo of free blacks in Jamaica, laughing with 'malicious glee' as the plantations around them crumbled.[81]

This perspective returns the focus to the activity of workers themselves. Instead of posing the question of resistance in the call centre as only a fight for small improvements to a job that is almost universally disliked, it also holds the potential to reassert a critique of work. This shifts the interpretation of workers in the call centre from being marginalised, only able to run away from the job, to active subjects refusing the current organisation of work.

6

CONCLUSION

The final stages of my workers' inquiry on the call-centre floor were particularly difficult. I had begun to average a reasonable number of sales per shift, and was on the cusp of 'graduating'. However, on a Friday night, all my shifts for the following week were changed: instead of three day shifts I received five nights and a Saturday shift. The next Friday, all of my shifts were again changed to the same pattern. Working every evening at the call centre, while reading and writing about call centres during the day, began to take its toll. I went through a number of shifts with no sales whatsoever. I had a tense '1-2-1' meeting with my supervisor about my performance. The SMART action plan only stated: 'Giving Jamie 2 weeks to improve his performance.' After a week my performance had not improved. The next '1-2-1' was self-explanatory:

> Jamie will have completed one of the two weeks given. By end of next week 2 weeks will be over, Jamie needs to have hit 0.25sph over this two-week period. Not achieving this may result in an HR meeting to review performance.

The shifts became increasingly stressful. The pressure to make sales increased with the constant exhortations from supervisors to 'smile while you dial!' which really was not helping. By then I had stopped wearing smart shoes to work and begun wearing trainers. The requirement to wear formal footwear was bizarre, given it is a call centre and no one on the end of the phone would ever see you – and seemed to be introduced as a punishment so that wearing your own clothes could then become a reward for top sellers. It felt like a minor victory over management.

The general atmosphere in the call centre had also begun to deteriorate. The number of 'red' calls increased to the point that the supervisors lost their monthly bonuses. One of the other workers mentioned after a shift that she was genuinely considering asking someone to punch her in the face halfway through the shift so she could leave early. A number of workers – including the one remaining person who had trained with me – were placed on probation for failing to meet sales targets. The number of challenging phone calls that I experienced seemed to be increasing. In part, this was a reflection of austerity. More and more potential customers told stories of how they were now working reduced shifts, suffering pay cuts and worried about being made redundant. While this provided a glimpse into the conditions for many people across the UK, they were also real people on the other end of the line who you then have to try and push to buy insurance.

During the buzz session for the shift we had been shouted at by the supervisors for the general level of performance in the team. I interjected, making a sarcastic comment and telling the supervisors not to shout at me. My final '1-2-1' meeting was, unsurprisingly, quite hostile. I was made to sign the feedback form including the statement that 'Jamie should have a more positive attitude towards his role. Made negative comments on C&R during buzz session, doesn't give other agents a good impression'. I was repeatedly questioned by the supervisor about why I could not reach my targets. I said the problem was that I did not like pressuring people into buying insurance that they did not want or need. The supervisor replied, 'Fine, this job isn't for everyone!' and became defensive. In a somewhat bizarre turn of events, the supervisor then attempted the C&R process to convince me otherwise, applying the same sales techniques that I had used myself.

At the end of the probation period I had fallen far short of the targets I had been given. After an HR meeting – which was surprisingly brief – I was no longer employed by the company. My own refusal had come to the fore, and although my exit was slightly earlier than originally planned, it still meant that I was one of the longest-lasting workers in my training cohort.

REFLECTIONS ON WORKERS' INQUIRY

At the start of the book we examined a number of different moments of workers' inquiry from Marx, the Johnson-Forest Tendency, *Socialisme ou Barbarie*, the *Operaismo*. What we have discussed so far is an attempt to adapt this method for studying a contemporary workplace. Although Marx's call for an inquiry would not have been appropriate for the research here, the theoretical justification he articulated remains important. Marx's argument for the project is twofold: Marxists need to develop an analysis of the conditions of the working class, but this is best achieved by workers themselves who are themselves capable of transforming said conditions.

I had no previous contact with workers in the call centre before becoming employed there. This had important implications for the method. While the contributions of the Johnson-Forest Tendency and *Socialisme ou Barbarie* represented a development of the approach, it was not possible to use the form of working-class documentary that Dunayevskaya described as the 'full fountain pen' method.[1] To illustrate the difficulties of this, I met up again with a group of workers after we had all left the call centre. As a group we had tried to organise in the call centre and had met regularly after work (see Chapter 5). During my time at the call centre the question of research had come up a number of times: supervisors could not care less what I did with my time outside of work and the other workers were not particularly interested in the subject of my research. Researchers often attribute a level of importance to their own research that is not shared by others, assuming that because they spend so much time on it others will want to know all about it too. I explained to the other workers that I was writing about call centres and explained some of the research questions. This was met with puzzled responses: why would anyone want to write about call centres? A few in the group thought that it might be worthwhile to consider our experiences of trying to organise, but none of them wanted to read anything that I had written. In a sense, the refusal of work continued even after leaving the call centre. We continued to have discussions that informed the writing of this book, yet the experience echoed the challenge found by *Socialisme ou Barbarie*: 'workers simply did not write'.[2]

The lack of contact with workers at the beginning of the project posed an immediate access challenge. Not only did I not have access to workers with whom to collaborate on an inquiry, but nor did I have a sense of which workplace would be suitable to study. The method therefore had to begin as an inquiry 'from above'.[3] Applying to work at a range of call centres through online applications meant the choice of workplace was relatively random, yet it followed the same route that other workers took to find casualised call-centre work. The main focus of the research has been the call centre that I was working in, which, like other empirical examples, has features both specific and general. In particular, it is worth noting that it was a high-sales operation (and therefore involved greater pressures than other variations) and was based in London. However, there are a number of dynamics that emerged in the research that can be generalised, and we will be discuss these further below. To broaden the scope of my findings, I also worked in another call centre before this one, interviewed a number of people who had worked in different locations and types of call centres (one of which was discussed in detail in Chapter 5).

The debates in the journals of the *Operaismo* informed the development of this inquiry. It is clear that an inquiry 'from below' was not possible at the start of the research, as, Vittorio Rieser argues, 'it requires being in a condition where you are pursuing enquiry with workers that you are organizing or workers that are already organized'. The intention was to begin with the inquiry 'from above' and seek to move towards one 'from below' and 'develop a co-research project in the call centre'.[4] The decision to find employment in the call centre was taken with two objectives: to undertake a detailed ethnography of the labour process and to meet other workers. By these measures the project achieved its aims. It was able to produce a detailed and rich ethnographic account of the experience of the labour process, management and the moments of resistance in the call centre. While I met and organised with different workers during my time at the call centre, it was not possible to develop it into a co-research project. I discussed ideas and strategies with a number of workers but this remained informal. The difficulties outlined earlier in trying to involve workers in a more formal manner are not surprising. The refusal of work was not limited to a rejection of working at the call centre itself. It also extended outside the workplace: not wanting to talk, read or write about call centres after work ended.

This experience is similar to that of the Kolinko call-centre inquiry discussed previously.[5] The intention of their project was to find struggles to engage and intervene in. Yet they conclude by saying that 'the absence of open workers' struggles limited our own room for "movement"'. While there were the moments of resistance to relate to in the call centre the experience was far removed from that described by Michael in Chapter 5. The decision to begin organisation at the call centre was taken collectively by a small group of workers. However, it was catalysed by an intervention that I made. As Michael Burawoy argues, 'interventions create perturbation that are not noise to be expurgated but music to be appreciated, transmitting the hidden secrets of the participant's world'.[6] The attempts to build organisation would have been pointless if the other workers were not interested or prepared to be involved. The discussions that we had at the initial stages were particularly useful for the research, as was seeing how organisation developed and the challenges it faced. What is clear is that the nature of work has changed and so have the forms of resistance.

The central argument of this book has been that call-centre workers do resist. This has been discussed by examining the labour process, management, resistance, the refusal of work and the possibilities for organisation. The book began with a discussion of the BBC documentary *The Call Centre*[7] and the film *The Wolf of Wall Street*.[8] The brief glimpses into *The Call Centre* leave much missing from the picture, which is no surprise given its intention to entertain or amuse. It is interesting – in a depressing way –

that this kind of work is presented as an object of humour, in a similar way to the example of *Undercover Boss*,[9] also discussed earlier. The proliferation of such programmes is closely tied up with questions of power, in part because the only time we tend to hear these workers' voices is during the scripted encounters that attract so much frustration, and partly as it is swept up in the drive to commoditise new sphere of social life through the lens of reality television. The narrator introduces *The Call Centre* by explaining that 'with a sales floor simmering with stress, sex, and success . . . there's never a dull day when you work at this Swansea call centre'. However, rather than this being an incisive analysis of work, it is indicative of the reality-TV format in general as 'it was clear that working class participants were being recruited for entertainment purposes'.[10] Therefore it is no surprise that a format which created a series like *Benefits Street*[11] is unlikely to offer an insight into working-class self-activity and the possibility of social or political change. The narrative of *Benefits Street* reinforces the class-based notion of an undeserving poor; in *The Call Centre* resistance to Nev seems futile.

The cold call has become part of the experience of living under late capitalism. The regularity with which I receive unsolicited calls from anonymous workers trying to peddle some pointless product is astonishing: PPI repayments, accident compensation claims, mobile or broadband packages, even some which are more straightforward scams. I seem to invariably get sales calls while writing. This adds a dimension to call-centre work that it is almost universally reviled, both by those who have experienced working at it or those on the other end of the phone. When presenting aspects of the book at academic conferences, I am always surprised at the number of anecdotal stories that people want to share afterwards. But the aim of this book has been different to any of these shows: it is neither an exploitation of the conditions for entertainment, nor is it limited to finding novel ways that customers have dealt with the annoyance of cold calls. Instead the book has sought to combine a detailed ethnography of a particular call centre with a discussion of how resistance and organisation can and does develop.

THE LABOUR PROCESS

The theorisation of the labour process started from the ethnographic research on the call-centre floor. It provides an account of what it is actually like to be employed in a workplace that subjects workers to intense surveillance and aggressive sales targets. This meant a non-stop process of making calls with strictly observed breaks precisely measured in time down to the second. It involved making terrible jokes over and over again, while faking laughter each time in the hope of securing more insurance sales. It demanded sitting through demeaning buzz sessions and excruciating '1-2-1' sessions that force the worker to perform an auto-critique, internalising management nonsense. It meant speaking to a person waiting for dialysis or another who had just lost their baby to leukaemia with a supervisor standing over you filled with glee at the prospect of an easy sale. The intention was to present, like Romano did for the manufacturing plant in *The American Worker*, an analysis that 'never for a single moment permits the reader to forget that the contradictions in the process of production make life an agony of toil for the worker'.[12]

The labour process in the call centre was organised along Taylorist management principles. For Frederick Taylor this meant that the 'task specifies not only what is to be done, but how it is to be done and the exact time allowed for doing it'.[13] The scripting of the call encounters represents a clear example of the separation of conception from execution in the labour process. There was a contradiction between the qualitative demands for high customer service and the quantitative demand to increasing the number of sales, a feature identified by Taylor and Bain in their conclusion that 'even in the most quality driven call centre it is difficult to escape the conclusion that the labour process is intrinsically demanding, repetitive and, frequently, stressful'. The findings of the book confirm their conclusion that the labour process creates the experience for workers of 'an assembly-line in the head'.[14]

The implication of this process for workers was articulated through the concepts of emotional and affective labour. When Nev explained that 'happy people sell, miserable bastards don't', he hinted at the complexity of this.[15] The transformations that have taken place in the contemporary economy have involved a shift from the exploitation of the bodies of workers during the Fordist mode of production to exploiting the minds and emotions of workers in increasingly larger numbers. While Hochschild's concept of emotional labour is an important starting point for this process, capturing the additional components of the labour process in service work,[16] it is problematic in terms of the conclusions for authenticity and self. This is clarified further by the distinction between '*brain workers*' and '*chain workers*'.

While highly skilled '*brain workers*' use 'communication, invention and creation', the '*chain workers*' like those in call centres are 'people who sit at their terminals in front of a screen, repeating every day the same operation a thousand times', and 'relate to their labor in a way similar to industrial workers'.[17] The call-centre worker is therefore an appendage to a new kind of machine. No longer faced with the same physical demands of the assembly line, the new demand is for a repetition of the same performance trying to convince people to part with their money for insurance over the phone. The reaction to this is not the loss or alienation of some part of the self; rather it is a 'condition of estrangement from the mode of production and its rules, as refusal of work'.[18] In the call centre, like many of the 'bullshit jobs' David Graeber describes,[19] it is not a question of seizing back the means of production in order to fulfil the workers' potential, but resistance is more likely to take the form of refusal.

MANAGEMENT

The role of management in the call centre has been detailed in this book. We began with the figure of Nev, declaring that 'Napoleon . . . a dictator' was his inspiration.[20] However, this ridiculous statement was not just a performance for the TV programme; it also indicates how much power managers and supervisors have on the call-centre floor. Goodrich's notion of the 'frontier of control' as a contestable line between workers and management in a workplace was difficult to trace.[21] The use of technological methods of control and supervision in the call centre has increased the power of management: logging time on calls, recording all conversations for immediate playback, timing breaks to the second and generating statistical reports. The lack of trade union organisation created the conditions at the call centre in which management power developed relatively unchecked. In this context it is easy to over-generalise and it is worth bearing in mind Taylor and Bain's point that this 'represents an unprecedented level of *attempted* control which must be considered a novel departure'.[22]

The metaphor of the Panopticon – which has been frequently referred to in the literature – was used to illustrate the process of surveillance and control in the call centre. Returning to Bentham's Panopticon writings[23] before looking at Foucault,[24] the Panopticon was here used as a theoretical metaphor to explore the empirical research in detail. The Panopticon – both physically and in terms of processes – maps easily onto the organisation of the call centre; however it is important to note that the 'factory and the office are neither prison nor asylum, their social architectures never those of the total institution'.[25] The features of the call centre as a site in which the 'dynamic process of capital accumulation' takes place means that it can understate 'both the voluntary dimension of labour and the managerial need to elicit commitment from workers'. This leads to a problematic analysis, one which can 'disavow the possibilities for collective organisation and resistance'.[26] However, as we have discussed, if these limitations are taken into account, the metaphor of the Panopticon can be used effectively to illustrate what management attempts to achieve on the call-centre floor.

The example of the undercover consultant illustrates how supervision in the call centre remains a challenge despite all of the different methods at management's disposal. The computer surveillance methods create vast quantities of data; however, a lack of knowledge about the labour process itself limits that data's usefulness. Therefore, an undercover consultant was employed by the call centre to go through the training process and work on the floor to find novel ways to intensify the labour process. The process seemed remarkably similar to the reality TV show *Undercover Boss*,[27] yet without the cameras the consultant was prepared to offer insights into the thought processes of management.

Management's undercover research follows in the footsteps of Taylor's Midvale Steel Company experiments, in which he argued that 'managers assume . . . the burden of gathering together all of the traditional knowledge which in the past has been possessed by the workmen and then of classifying, tabulating, and reducing this knowledge to rules, laws, and formulae'.[28]

These challenges are clear from the ethnography on the call-centre floor. The power of supervisors in the call centre tends towards creating bullying and often sexist behaviour. Yet when the ability of supervisors to motivate workers to increase their sales is considered another picture emerges. The record of the '1-2-1' meetings I had with supervisors indicates a lack of knowledge about how sales are made or what kind of encouragement can be used. The task of management to motivate workers who do not want to be at work is captured by Cederström and Fleming's analysis of the buzz session as an attempt 'to *inject life into the dead-zone of work*'.[29] The reliance on empty rhetoric and a form of quasi-Maoist auto-critique indicates a management that is far from all-powerful. The refusal of work – most often expressed in high staff turnover – is recognised as a 'moderate concern' by 55 per cent of call centres surveyed by Income Data Services, with managers offering thirty-four different responses to address it.[30] At my call centre this was clear from the widespread practice of granting workers permission to leave work early as a motivational incentive. When this factor is focused upon, the power of management in the call centre seems greatly reduced: in the end, without workers on the phones it is certain that no sales will be made.

RESISTANCE

The main aim of this book was to discover whether workers resisted in call centres. This required the development of an analysis that was sensitive to the wide variety of forms that this resistance could take. There was a wide variety of covert forms of resistance used by workers at the call centre, captured in Kate Mulholland's categories of '*Slammin' Scammin' Smokin' an' Leavin'*' – or 'cheating, work avoidance, absence and resignation'.[31] The first moment of resistance discussed by Mulholland was '*Slammin*'; the process of faking a sales encounter. This moment is the only one that does not map directly onto a form found at our call centre, other than one rare example. This is due in part to the financial regulation applied to selling insurance. However, frequently the topic was raised in conversations of how a sale could be faked, and the supervisors regularly pointed out that 'selling on cancellation' was a disciplinary offence.

The second form of resistance was '*Scammin*'. This involved the various attempts by workers to avoid work. This was found to be incredibly common at the call centre. During the shift there were a number of opportunities to extend time off the phones: from the lunch break, buzz session, training, to the shorter breaks. This should have not been possible due to the electronic surveillance; however, the supervisors misused the system, for example, by logging training or buzz sessions as breaks. This meant that the actual time on the break was harder to gauge and could therefore be extended. Informal organisation emerged with strategies to stretch out the buzz sessions, not inform supervisors of leads running dry, or re-setting the break timers.

The third form is a specific kind of work avoidance known as '*Smokin*'. Almost all of the workers at the call centre would leave the workplace during the fifteen-minute in-shift breaks, whether they smoked or not. The importance of this is indicated by Mulholland, who argues that 'the habit of meeting is also important for it encourages work group identity and a shared sense of grievance' that can develop 'when workers discuss training, staff shortage, disappointments over pay, prize giving, the excessive monitoring, arbitrary discipline and not least productivity pressures'.[32] This was the case at the call centre. The initial conversations about organising began during the smoking breaks, along with general venting about a range of grievances, away from the supervisory gaze.

The final form of resistance is '*Leavin*', or quitting the job. This was very common at the call centre, with every worker I started with leaving the job before the end of my research project. Although '*Leavin*' might seem like the archetypal individual act it forms 'part of a more widespread pattern of work rejection'[33] and, as identified by Marcel van der Linden, the exit from work is not vastly dissimilar to a strike: the 'transition between "running away" and "fighting for better working conditions" is in reality rather fluid'.[34] This final form is crucial for the present analysis of resistance in the call centre. While it is often seen as an expression of the structural weakness of call-centre workers, it is possible to reverse the understanding in a way that returns agency to the workers. It is also an indicator of a generalised refusal of work.

These moments of resistance complicated the empirical research. My relationship to acts of resistance required an intervention, whether by choosing to take part or not. Michael Burawoy, as discussed earlier, argues that 'interventions' do not need to be minimised. They 'create perturbations that are not noise to be expurgated but music to be appreciated, transmitting the hidden secrets of the participant's world'.[35] If I had not been working on the call-centre floor it would not have been possible to uncover the covert acts of resistance, although '*Leavin*' is such a widespread phenomenon it is difficult to miss. The forms of resistance are reminiscent of Braverman's description of 'the hostility of workers to the degenerated forms of work which are forced upon them' and continue 'as a subterranean stream that makes its way to the surface' at certain points.[36] The '*Leavin*' that Mulholland refers to is the moment the water rushes upward – the event that consolidates all of the small acts of resistance that build up over time.

The question of high staff turnover, and '*Leavin*'[37] as a form of resistance in the call centre, was developed into the theme of the refusal of work. This is understood theoretically as an important phenomenon that represents workers exercising their limited choice, rather than an indication of their inability to organise. The phenomenon is characteristic of many service-sector jobs but it is particularly prevalent in call centres. While it poses a significant obstacle to building formal organisation in a workplace it can also be an untapped source of collectivity. As a shared experience, which also leads to common forms of action, it holds the potential to catalyse informal organisation.

The problem of high turnover can also be reversed from an inhibiting factor to a potential strength. Through an investigation of the connection between Paul Lafargue and C. L. R. James, and the link that Christopher Taylor identifies between *Operaismo* and the Caribbean, an argument can be posed about the possibilities of an anti-work politics. If there is a historical connection between modern management techniques and slave owners, an analysis of the development of struggle between these forms and their subjects is also important. The search to uncover the subjects of revolt is therefore the search for those engaging in a refusal: from the slave, to the Fordist worker, to the precarious worker seeking to regain some autonomy. The anti-work perspective provides a critique that is not limited to the question of control of the labour process – indeed, the possibility of control is absent at this point anyway. In the context of 'bullshit jobs'[38] it is possible, as Christopher Taylor argues, to go further than 'moralistic invocations of labor's value' that 'appear grotesquely comical'.[39]

The analysis of the technology in the call centre has important implications for translating the traditions of trade unionism into new contexts. To pose the question of workers' control in the call centre is quite different to its application to the factory, the hospital or the university. It is difficult to imagine how the call centre could become part of a revolutionary process with 'workers' control and councils as the base of a self-determined socialist society'.[40] The refusal of work in the call centre is connected to the centre's specifically capitalist organisation. The call centre strips telephonic encounters of all the social dimensions of communication that cannot be instrumentalised. There could be a strategic role for call centres during a period of struggle or when mass participation is needed, but would they continue after that?

ORGANISATION

The theme of organisation emerged tentatively throughout the course of this project. No formal union organisation was established at the call centre. It is possible that a longer project at the workplace could have developed and tested forms of organisation in collaboration with other workers, but as we have discussed above, my own exit from the call centre prevented this. The refusal of work and high staff turnover in the call centre interacted with the precarious conditions under which workers were employed. However, this precarity should not be understood as an exceptional form of employment relations under capitalism. Apart from a relatively brief period of Fordist employment for men in Western Europe and the USA in the 1960s and 1970s, the working class has historically relied on insecure employment. But the rise of neoliberalism and the collapse of the Fordist model led to a transformation of employment relations, particularly with the way in which precarity is 'built into neoliberal capitalism'.[41] The relationship between capital and labour has always been marked by a level of precarity. The extension of this beyond the traditional working class means that this phenomenon has now become more common.

The state of contemporary trade unionism is important to consider in two ways: the first is that given that trade unions have been facing a sustained ideological attack since the 1970s – alongside serious defeats for organised labour – the continued existence of trade unions can be considered a success. However, the relegation of trade unionism to a great degree to the public sector represents a failure to relate to workplace resistance in the private sector. This criticism is intended as part of a constructive debate about the future of trade unionism, rather than holding rank and file trade union members responsible for the class-based project of neoliberalism or regarding union leadership as having failed in some way. As Taylor and Bain argue, 'the future success of trade unions in call centres will depend in no small measure on their ability to contest and redefine the frontiers of control on terms desired by their members'.[42] This means a radical shift from the union as a service provider towards one led by workers engaged in workplace conflict.

The interview conducted with Michael (discussed in Chapter 3) provides a powerful example of workers' self-organisation. Despite the threat of victimisation of activists by management in the call centre, the workers developed strategies to build formal and informal organisation in the workplace. The combination of detailed, persistent work and tangible victories proved successful in this example. However, the approach relied on pre-politicised activists with the experience and drive to follow through their initial attempts. What is particularly notable was the combination of traditional modes of trade union organisation and creative innovations relating to the labour process in the call centre. A number of challenges to organising were detailed specifically, but high staff turnover emerges as the most important. As has been noted, there is not that much of a difference between leaving the workplace permanently and doing so temporarily as part of a strike.[43] As Michael concluded, by the end he had had enough of working in a call centre – despite his stint being much longer than that of most workers at the call centre. However, the recognition of how the experience of organising is not limited to a specific time or place is incredibly important. Michael applied his previous experiences from the civil service to the call centre, and hoped that workers in the call centre would apply the tactics and organisation elsewhere. Even projects that fail can form part of the process of organising in the future, lessons being learnt from failures as well as successes. The problem at this stage is developing an under-standing of how that continuity can be encouraged.

FINAL THOUGHTS

So where does this lead us? Throughout this book we have presented an in-depth ethnography and theoretical analysis of one call centre. The account found here is a different repre-sentation to that found in *The Call Centre*, in that it focuses the analytical lens on the resistance of workers. The class composition of the workers is understood through two dimensions; first, a highly regulated labour process to which advanced technologi-cal methods of surveillance and control have been applied, and second, a relationship between workers and supervisors that is defined by the relatively unchecked power of management. The political composition that is related to this, but not defined by it, is more complex. The workforce is young and predominantly female. There were no traditions among them of trade unionism or organised politics. Despite this the workforce was *political*. Although none of the workers in the call centre had had any prior experience of taking part in organised workplace struggles or social movements, the temporary but repetitive expressions of the refusal of work were almost universal. These workers were unburdened by the experiences of working-class defeats, and did not feel the 'tradition of all dead generations' weighing 'like a nightmare' upon them.[44] A process of political recomposition takes place with the experiences of struggle – whether successful or not – in the workplace. The creativity of these workers is what holds the potential to form organisation in new and disruptive ways.

The workers did resist in the workplace. The labour process created the opportunity for different forms of resistance and these came to be connected to forms of organisation. The significance of this argument is that the majority of workers in the UK are employed in jobs with no recognised trade union representation. So far the transformation of contemporary work has not been widely met with new and innovative forms of workers' organisation. It does not matter if workers see themselves as 'fully conscious agents engaged in class struggle; in seeking to control, management did'.[45] In the context of continuing austerity, the questions of where resistance will come from and who can be subjects of social change are both of great importance.

The analysis of the methods of surveillance and control confirms much earlier research in the relevant fields: management has been able to create a highly controlling environment in call centres, often without an organised response from formal trade unions. The precarious employment conditions have been conceptualised as part of the long history of struggle between capital and labour, a relationship which is always precarious to some degree for workers, yet can become more or less intensely so. In a situation in which workers are not organised into formal trade unions the experience of precarity is particularly sharp. It is for this reason that finding small acts of resistance in a call centre, like those identified by Mulholland, are so important. This book has gone beyond just identifying these moments of resistance, instead analysing each as expressions of refusal. The implications extend beyond this one call centre: even when workers are faced with numerous challenges and obstacles, the possibility for resistance remains.

The next task is to undertake further projects using a similar method. Call centres are certainly not the only type of workplace that employs workers on precarious contracts with low pay and poor conditions. Also, not all call centres are subjected to the same regimes of control. The call-centre labour process relies on integration with other such processes, particularly those that produce and distribute the commodities being sold. The call centre is therefore not central to capital accumulation, but provides new ways to realise profits. However, outgoing sales call centres do highlight important tendencies that are beginning to define many different industries that are central to capital accumulation. There is a pressing need for in-depth studies of workplace resistance in other contexts that can shed light on the contemporary challenges of organising. As we discussed earlier, there has been a renewed interest in workers' inquiries. While there are a number of debates about the use of the method and its potential role in the analysis of contemporary work, what is needed are further attempts at workers' inquiries. These can either be conducted where researchers take on work themselves, in areas where they have contact with workers already, or in workplaces where they want to make contact with workers. In so doing, researchers can aim to take up the challenge that Marx laid out in the concept of the workers' inquiry, but also in his call for a '*ruthless criticism of the existing order*, ruthless in that it will shrink neither from its own discoveries, nor from conflict with the powers that be'.[46]

NOTES

CHAPTER 1

1. *The Call Centre* [Documentary, Reality-TV] BBC, 2013, www.bbc. co.uk/programmes/b03mtjjh
2. *The Wolf of Wall Street* [Biography, Comedy, Crime] Paramount Pictures, 2014.
3. *The Call Centre*, BBC, 2013.
4. *The Wolf of Wall Street*, Paramount Pictures, 2014.
5. C. L. Goodrich, *The Frontier of Control* (London: Pluto Press, 1975).
6. *The Call Centre* (2013).
7. *The Wolf of Wall Street* (2014).
8. *Ibid.*
9. *Ibid.*
10. Hilary Osborne, 'Call Centres in BBC3 Programme Hit with £225,000 Fines', *The Guardian*, 18 June 2013, www.theguardian. com/money/2013/jun/18/call-centres-bbc3-programme-fines
11. Mark Fisher, *Capitalist Realism* (Winchester: Zero Books, 2009), p. 63.
12. *Ibid.*
13. Franz Kafka, *The Castle* (London: Penguin, 2000), p. 65.
14. Fisher, *Capitalist Realism* (2009), p. 65.
15. *Ibid.*, p. 64.
16. Enda Brophy, 'The Subterranean Stream: Communicative Capitalism and Call Centre Labour', *Ephemera*, Vol. 10, No. 3/4 (2010), p. 471.
17. *The Call Centre* (2013).
18. Phil Taylor and Peter Bain, '"An Assembly Line in the Head": Work and Employee Relations in the Call Centre', *Industrial Relations Journal*, Vol. 30, No. 2 (1999), p. 109.
19. I contacted one of the producers in an attempt to find out more about the show. It took a considerable search to even identify the producers, and the only way to contact one was through Twitter. After a brief discussion he agreed to talk, but then never responded to my subsequent questions.

20. Real Bergevin, Afshan Kinder, Winston Siegel and Bruce Simpson, *Call Centers for Dummies* (Mississauga, Ontario: John Wiley and Sons Canada, 2010), p. 1.

21. *Ibid.*, p. 1.

22. *Ibid.*, p. 11.

23. *Ibid.*, p. 23.

24. Karl Marx and Friedrich Engels, *Manifesto of the Communist Party* (1848), www.marxists.org/archive/marx/works/1848/communist-manifesto/index.htm

25. Claude S. Fischer, *America Calling: A Social History of the Telephone to 1940* (Berkeley: University of California Press, 1992), p. 268.

26. Bergevin et al., *Call Centers for Dummies* (2010), p. 12.

27. Taylor and Bain, '"An Assembly Line in the Head"' (1999), p. 102.

28. *Ibid.*, p. 5.

29. Julia O'Connell Davidson, *Privatisation and Employment Relations: The Case of the Water Industry* (London: Mansell, 1993).

30. Vaughan Ellis and Phil Taylor, '"You Don't Know What You've Got till It's Gone": Re-Contextualising the Origins, Development and Impact of the Call Centre', *New Technology, Work and Employment*, Vol. 21, No. 2 (2006), p. 3.

31. Neill Marshall and Ranald Richardson, 'The Impact of "Telemediated" Services on Corporate Structures: The Example of "Branchless" Retail Banking in Britain', *Environment and Planning A*, Vol. 28, No. 10 (1996), p. 1848.

32. Ellis and Taylor, '"You Don't Know What You've Got till It's Gone"' (2006), p. 6.

33. *Ibid.*

34. Peter Bain, Aileen Watson, Gareth Mulvey, Phil Taylor and Gregor Gall, 'Taylorism, Targets and the Pursuit of Quantity and Quality by Call Centre Management', *New Technology, Work and Employment*, Vol. 17, No. 3 (2002), p. 4.

35. *Ibid.*, p. 6.

36. Karl Marx, *Capital: A Critique of Political Economy Vol. 1.* (London: Penguin Books [1867] 1976): pp. 167–8.

37. Marx, *Capital* (1867), p. 201.

38. Ellis and Taylor, '"You Don't Know What You've Got till It's Gone"' (2006), p. 5.

39. Miriam Glucksmann, 'Call Configurations: Varieties of Call Centre and Divisions of Labour', *Work, Employment & Society*, Vol. 18, No. 4 (2004), p. 802.

40. *Ibid.*, p. 804.

41. *Ibid.*, p. 805.
42. *Ibid.*, p. 807.
43. Bergevin et al., *Call Centers for Dummies* (2010), p. 12.
44. *Ibid.*, p. 800.
45. Ursula Huws, Nick Jagger and Peter Bates, *Where the Butterfly Alights: The Global Location of eWork* (London: Institute for Employment Studies, Report 378, 2001).
46. Glucksmann, 'Call Configurations' (2004), p. 807.
47. *Ibid.*, p. 801.
48. Phil Taylor and Peter Bain, 'Call Centre Offshoring to India: The Revenge of History?', *Labour and Industry*, Vol. 14, No. 3 (2004), pp. 15–38.
49. Holman, D., Batt, R. and Holtgrewe, U., 'The Global Call Centre Report: International Perspectives on Management and Employment (executive Summary)' (2007), www.ilr.cornell.edu/globalcallcenter/upload/GCC-Intl-Rept-UK-Version.pdf, p. 1.
50. *Ibid.*, p. 5.
51. *Ibid.*, p. 1.
52. Kiran Mirchandani, *Phone Clones: Authenticity Work in the Transnational Service Economy* (London: ILR Press, 2012).
53. Holman et al., *The Global Call Centre Report* (2007), p. 40.
54. *Ibid.*, p. 41.
55. Office for National Statistics, *EMP04: All in Employment by Status, Occupation and Sex. Labour Force Survey* (London: Office of National Statistics, 2013a), www.ons.gov.uk/ons/rel/lms/labour-force-survey-employment-status-by-occupation/index.html
56. Glucksmann, 'Call Configurations' (2004), p. 797.
57. UNISON, 'Call Centres' (2014), www.unison.org.uk/at-work/energy/key-issues/call-centres/the-facts
58. Income Data Services, *Pay and Conditions in Call and Contact Centres 2012/13* (London: IDS, 2012), p. 9.
59. *Ibid.*, p. 116.
60. *Ibid.*, p. 63.
61. *Ibid.*, p. 56.
62. *Ibid.*, p. 59.
63. Bergevin et al., *Call Centers for Dummies* (2010), p. 12.
64. Kate Faulkner, Paul Bentley and Lucy Osborne, 'Shame of the Charity Cold Call Sharks', *Daily Mail*, 7 July 2015, www.dailymail.co.uk/news/article-3151533/Shamed-charity-cold-call-sharks-Britain-s-biggest-charities-ruthlessly-hound-vulnerable-cash-try-opt-receiving-calls.html

65. Phil Taylor, Chris Warhurst, Paul Thompson and Dora Scholarios, 'On the Front Line', *Work, Employment & Society*, Vol. 23, No. 1 (2009), p. 7.

66. See, for example, Huw Beynon, *Working for Ford* (Harmondsworth: Penguin, 1973); Michael Burawoy, *Manufacturing Consent* (Chicago: University of Chicago Press, 1979); Anna Pollert, *Girls, Wives, Factory Lives* (London: Macmillan, 1981); Ruth Cavendish, *Women on the Line* (London: Routledge & Kegan Paul, 1982).

67. For a longer and more in-depth discussion of this, see Jamie Woodcock, '"Smile Down the Phone": An Attempt at a Workers' Inquiry in a Call Centre', *Viewpoint Magazine*, Vol. 3 (2013) and Jamie Woodcock, 'The Workers' Inquiry from Trotskyism to Operaismo: A Political Methodology for Investigating the Workplace', *Ephemera*, Vol. 14, No. 3 (2014), and the other articles in these special issues.

68. Marx, *Capital: A Critique of Political Economy Vol. 1* ([1867] 1976), p. 344.

69. David Harvey, *A Companion to Marx's* Capital (London: Verso, 2010), p. 141.

70. Marx, *Capital* ([1867] 1976), p. 397.

71. Michael Lebowitz, *Following Marx: Method, Critique and Crisis* (Boston: Brill, 2009), p. 314.

72. Harry Cleaver, *Reading* Capital *Politically* (Brighton: Harvester Press, 1979), p. 58.

73. Karl Marx, *A Workers' Inquiry* (1880), www.marxists.org/archive/marx/works/1880/04/20.htm

74. *Ibid.*

75. E. P. Thompson, 'History from Below', *Times Literary Supplement*, 7 April 1966.

76. Gayatri Chakravorty Spivak, 'Subaltern Studies: Deconstructing Historiography', In *Selected Subaltern Studies*, edited by Ranajit Guha (New York: Oxford University Press, 1988).

77. Sheila Rowbotham, *Hidden from History: 300 Years of Women's Oppression and the Fight against It* (London: Pluto Press, 1977).

78. Asad Haider and Salar Mohandesi, 'Workers' Inquiry: A Genealogy', *Viewpoint Magazine*, Vol. 3 (2013), http://viewpointmag.com/2013/09/27/workers-inquiry-a-genealogy

79. Marcel van der Linden, 'Socialisme ou Barbarie: A French Revolutionary Group (1949–65)', *Left History*, Vol. 5, No. 1 (1997), pp. 7–37.

80. C. L. R. James, Raya Dunayevskaya and Grace Lee, *State Capitalism and World Revolution* (Detroit: Facing Reality Publishing Committee, 1950).
81. Cleaver, *Reading* Capital *Politically* (1979), p. 62.
82. Paul Romano and Ria Stone, *The American Worker* (Detroit: Facing Reality Publishing Company, 1946).
83. Paul Romano, 'Part 1: Life in the Factory', in *The American Worker* (1947), www.prole.info/texts/americanworker1.html
84. Charles Denby, *Indignant Heart: A Black Worker's Journal* (Detroit: Wayne State University Press, 1989).
85. Marie Brant and Ellen Santori, *A Women's Place* (New Writers, 1953).
86. Martin Glaberman, *Punching Out* (Detroit: Correspondence Publishing Committee, 1952).
87. Martin Glaberman, *Union Committeemen and Wildcat Strikes* (Detroit: Correspondence Publishing Committee, 1955).
88. Haider and Mohandesi, 'Workers' Inquiry: A Genealogy' (2013).
89. Kent Worcester, *C. L. R. James: A Political Biography* (Albany: State University of New York Press, 1995), p. 125.
90. Cornelius Castoriadis, 'An Interview with Cornelius Castoriadis', *Telos*, Vol. 23, Spring (1975), p. 131.
91. Paul Romano, 'L'ouvrier Américain', *Socialisme ou Barbarie*, Vol. 1 (1949).
92. van der Linden, 'Socialisme ou Barbarie' (1997), p. 19.
93. Claude Lefort, 'Proletarian Experience', *Socialisme ou Barbarie*, no. 11. trans. *Viewpoint Magazine* (1952), http://viewpointmag.com/2013/09/26/proletarian-experience
94. George Vivier, 'La Vie en Usine', *Socialisme ou Barbarie* (1952).
95. Cleaver, *Reading* Capital *Politically* (1979), p. 64.
96. van der Linden, 'Socialisme Ou Barbarie' (1997), p. 32.
97. Stephen Hastings-King, 'Looking for the Proletariat: Socialisme ou Barbarie and the Problem of Worker Writing', *Historical Materialism*, Vol. 71 (2014), pp. 105–6.
98. van der Linden, 'Socialisme ou Barbarie (1997), p. 20.
99. *Ibid.*, p. 7.
100. Cleaver, *Reading* Capital *Politically* (1979), p. 64.
101. Maria Turchetto, 'From "Mass Worker" to "Empire": The Disconcerting Trajectory of Italian Operaismo', in *Critical Companion to Contemporary Marxism*, edited by J. Bidet and S. Kouvelakis (Boston: Brill, 2008), p. 287.

102. Dario Lanzardo, 'Intervento Socialista Nella Lotta Operaia: l'Inchiesta Operaia di Marx', *Quaderni Rossi*, vol. 5 (1965), pp. 1–30.
103. Paul Romano, 'L'operaio Americano', *Battaglia Comunista* (1955).
104. Cleaver, *Reading Capital Politically* (1979), p. 66.
105. Steve Wright, *Storming Heaven: Class Composition and Struggle in Italian Autonomist Marxism* (London: Pluto Press, 2002), p. 35.
106. *Ibid.*
107. Wright, *Storming Heaven* (2002), p. 23.
108. *Ibid.*, p. 54.
109. Frederick Taylor, *The Principles of Scientific Management* (New York: W.W. Norton, 1967), p. 36.
110. Harry Braverman, *Labor and Monopoly Capital: The Degradation of Work in the Twentieth Century* (London: Monthly Review Press, 1999), p. 60.
111. Quoted in Wright, *Storming Heaven* (2002), p. 38.
112. Quoted in Gigi Roggero, 'Romano Alquati — Militant Researcher, Operaist, Autonomist Marxist — Has Passed Away, Age 75', *Fuckyeahmilitantresearch* (2010), http://fuckyeahmilitantresearch. tumblr.com/post/502186794/romano-alquati-militant-researcher-operaist
113. Marx, *Capital* ([1867] 1976), p. 340.
114. Quoted in Haider and Mohandesi, 'Workers' Inquiry: A Genealogy' (2013).
115. Mario Tronti, *Operai e capitale*, 2nd ed. (Turin: Einaudi, 1971), p. 89, quoted in Antonio Negri and Michael Hardt, *Commonwealth* (Cambridge, MA: Harvard University Press, 2009), p. 291.
116. Cleaver, *Reading* Capital *Politically* (1979), p. 66.
117. Francois Matheron, 'Operaismo', *Generation Online* (1999), www.generation-online.org/t/toperaismo.htm
118. *Ibid.*
119. *Hotlines – Call Centre | Inquiry | Communism* (Duisburg: Kolinko, 2002).
120. David Harvey, *A Brief History of Neoliberalism* (Oxford: Oxford University Press, 2007), p. 38.
121. Enda Brophy, 'The Subterranean Stream: Communicative Capitalism and Call Centre Labour', *Ephemera*, Vol. 10, No. 3/4 (2010), p. 474. This refers to the utopian perspective of Daniel Bell, *The Coming of Post-Industrial Society: A Venture in Social Forecasting* (New York: Basic Books, 1973).
122. Brophy, 'The Subterranean Stream' (2010), p. 471.
123. Goodrich, *The Frontier of Control* (1975).

CHAPTER 2

1. See Richard Murphy, 'Vodafone's Tax Case Leaves a Sour Taste', *The Guardian*, 22 October 2010, www.theguardian.com/commentisfree/2010/oct/22/vodafone-tax-case-leaves-sour-taste
2. *Glengarry Glen Ross* [Drama] Zupnik Cinema Group, 1992.
3. Robert Linhart, *The Assembly Line* (Amherst: University of Massachusetts Press, 1981), p. 27.
4. The analysis of the class nature of Russia was an important point of distinction between the Communist Parties and Trotskyist groupings. The theory of State Capitalism was the source of the break from the Fourth International which later spurred attempts at workers' inquiries.
5. Braverman, *Labor and Monopoly Capital* (1999), p. 60.
6. *Ibid.*, p. 82.
7. Taylor, *The Principles of Scientific Management* (1967), p. 39.
8. Braverman, *Labor and Monopoly Capital* (1999), pp. 79, 81.
9. Taylor and Bain, '"An Assembly Line in the Head"' (1999), p. 102.
10. *Ibid.*, p. 115
11. *Ibid.*, p. 110.
12. *Ibid.*, p. 108.
13. *Ibid.*, p. 116.
14. *Ibid.*, p. 109.
15. *Ibid.*, p. 103.
16. Arlie Russell Hochschild, *The Managed Heart: Commercialization of Human Feeling* (Berkeley: University of California Press, 2012), p. 7.
17. Taylor and Bain, '"An Assembly Line in the Head"' (1999), p. 103.
18. *The Call Centre* (2013).
19. Franco Berardi, *The Soul at Work: From Alienation to Autonomy* (Los Angeles: Semiotext(e), 2009) p. 21.
20. *Ibid.*, p. 84.
21. *Ibid.*, p. 85.
22. Kerry A. Lewig and Maureen F. Dollard, 'Emotional Dissonance, Emotional Exhaustion and Job Satisfaction in Call Centre Workers', *European Journal of Work and Organizational Psychology*, Vol. 12, No. 4 (2003), pp. 366–92.
23. Karl Marx, *Economic and Philosophic Manuscripts of 1844* (1844), Marxists.org/archive/marx/works/1844/manuscripts/labour.htm
24. Marx, *Capital* ([1867] 1976), p. 614.

25. Bertell Ollman, *Alienation: Marx's Conception of Man in a Capitalist Society* (Cambridge: Cambridge University Press, 1977), p. 138.
26. Karl Marx, *Grundrisse* (London: Penguin [1857] 1973), p. 706.
27. Berardi, *The Soul at Work* (2009), p. 35.
28. Christian Marazzi, *Capital and Affects: The Politics of the Language Economy* (Los Angeles: Semiotext(e), 2011), p. 21.
29. *Ibid.*, p. 25.
30. Berardi, *The Soul at Work* (2009), p. 188.
31. *Ibid.*, p. 87.
32. Marx, *Economic and Philosophic Manuscripts of 1844* (1844).
33. Ollman, *Alienation* (1977), p. 131.
34. Marx, *Economic and Philosophic Manuscripts of 1844* (1844).
35. Berardi, *The Soul at Work* (2009), p. 39.
36. *Ibid.,* p. 44.
37. Tronti, 'The Struggle against Labour' (1972), p. 22.
38. Berardi, *The Soul at Work* (2009), p. 46.
39. *Ibid.*, p. 59.
40. Taylor and Bain, '"An Assembly Line in the Head"' (1999), p. 111.
41. Braverman, *Labor and Monopoly Capital* (1999), p. 62.
42. Marazzi, *Capital and Affects* (2011), p. 76.
43. Taylor and Bain, '"An Assembly Line in the Head"' (1999), p. 108.
44. *Ibid.*, p. 109.

CHAPTER 3

1. *The Call Centre* (2013).
2. Bergevin et al., *Call Centers for Dummies* (2010).
3. *Undercover Boss* [Documentary, Reality-TV], Channel 4, 2010, www.channel4.com/programmes/undercover-boss
4. *Back to the Floor* [Documentary, Reality-TV] BBC, 1997.
5. Hugh Dehn, 'UK: Back to the Floor', *Management Today*, 1998, www.managementtoday.co.uk/news/411264/UK-Back-floor
6. Quoted in *ibid.*
7. *Undercover Boss* (2010).
8. Toby Miller, 'Foucault, Marx, Neoliberalism: Unveiling Undercover Boss', in *Foucault Now*, edited by J. D. Faubion (Cambridge: Polity Press, 2014), p. 200.
9. Braverman, *Labor and Monopoly Capital* (1999), p. 63.
10. Taylor, *The Principles of Scientific Management* (1967), p. 36.
11. Quoted in Braverman, *Labor and Monopoly Capital* (1999), p. 70.

12. Michael is a pseudonym. His identity is kept anonymous as there is a risk of damaging his future employment prospects.
13. Michael Burawoy, *The Politics of Production* (London: Verso, 1985), p. 47.
14. Quoted in Braverman, *Labor and Monopoly Capital* (1999), p. 134.
15. Braverman, *Labor and Monopoly Capital* (1999), p. 137.
16. *Ibid.*, p. 134.
17. Michel Foucault, *Discipline and Punish: The Birth of the Prison* (London: Penguin, 1991), p. 144.
18. *Ibid.*, p. 145.
19. *Ibid.*, p. 150.
20. *Ibid.*, p. 151.
21. Goodrich, *The Frontier of Control* (1975).
22. Foucault, *Discipline and Punish* (1991), p. 152.
23. *Ibid.*, p. 154.
24. Carl Cederström and Peter Fleming, *Dead Man Working* (Winchester: Zero Books, 2012), p. 10.
25. *Ibid.*, p. 11.
26. *Ibid.*, p. 9.
27. *Ibid.*, p. 10.
28. *Ibid.*, p. 16.
29. Marx, *Capital* ([1867] 1976), p. 342.
30. Foucault, *Discipline and Punish* (1991), p. 167.
31. Jeremy Bentham, *The Panopticon Writings* (London: Verso, 1995), p. 31.
32. *Ibid.*, p. 45.
33. *Ibid.*, p. 80.
34. *Ibid.*, p. 106.
35. *Ibid.*, p. 105.
36. Miran Božovič, 'Introduction', in *The Panopticon Writings*, by Jeremy Bentham (London: Verso, 1995). p. 4.
37. *Ibid.*, p. 8.
38. Sue Fernie and David Metcalf, *(Not) Hanging on the Telephone: Payment Systems in the New Sweatshops* (Centre for Economic Performance: London School of Economics, 1997), p. 3.
39. Foucault, *Discipline and Punish* (1991), p. 173.
40. *Ibid.*, p. 174.
41. *Ibid.*
42. *Ibid.*, p. 201.
43. *Ibid.*, p. 203.
44. Marx, *Capital* ([1867] 1976), p. 272.

45. Alan McKinlay and Phil Taylor, 'Foucault and the Politics of Production', in *Management and Organization Theory*, edited by A. McKinlay and L. Starkey (London: Sage, 1998), p. 175.
46. R. Danielle Egan, 'Eyeing the Scene: The Uses and (Re)Uses of Surveillance Cameras in an Exotic Dance Club', in *Culture, Power, and History: Studies in Critical Sociology*, edited by S. Pfohl et al. (Leiden: Brill, 2006), p. 205.
47. Massimo De Angelis, *The Beginning of History: Value Struggles and Global Capital* (London: Pluto, 2007), p. 194.
48. *Ibid*, p. 195.
49. *Ibid.*, p. 206.
50. *Ibid.*, p. 212.
51. Harvey, *A Brief History of Neoliberalism* (2007), p. 2.
52. *Ibid.*, p. 38.
53. David Harvey, *The New Imperialism* (Oxford: Oxford University Press, 2003), p. 157.
54. De Angelis, *The Beginning of History* (2007), p. 216.
55. Harvey, *A Brief History of Neoliberalism* (2007), p. 3.
56. Paul Peachey, 'The Real Minority Report? Kent Constabulary Tests Computer Program to Predict Crime', *The Independent*, 4 October 2013, www.independent.co.uk/news/uk/crime/the-real-minority-report-kent-constabulary-tests-computer-program-to-predict-crime-8744940.html
57. *Minority Report* [Film] Twentieth Century Fox, 2002.
58. Luc Boltanski and Eve Chiapello, *The New Spirit of Capitalism* (London: Verso, 2007), p. 20.
59. Cederström and Fleming, *Dead Man Working* (2012), p. 4.
60. *Ibid*, p. 7.
61. *Ibid*.
62. Angela Tinwell, Mark Grimshaw, Debbie Abdel Nabi and Andrew Williams, 'Facial Expression of Emotion and Perception of the Uncanny Valley in Virtual Characters', *Computers in Human Behaviour*, Vol. 27, No. 2 (2010), p. 741.
63. *Office Space* [Film] Twentieth Century Fox, 1999.
64. *Ibid*.
65. *Ibid*.
66. Fisher, *Capitalist Realism* (2009), p. 40.
67. Marx, *Capital* ([1867] 1976), pp. 279–80.
68. Richard Edwards, *Contested Terrain: The Transformation of the Workplace in the Twentieth Century* (New York: Basic Books, 1979), p. 12.

69. *Ibid.*
70. *Ibid.*, p. 18.
71. Paul Thompson, *The Nature of Work: An Introduction to Debates on the Labour Process* (London: Macmillan, 1989), p. 123.
72. *Ibid.*, p. 124.
73. Marx, *Capital* ([1867] 1976), pp. 1019–38.
74. Andrew L. Friedman, *Industry and Labour: Class Struggle at Work and Monopoly Capitalism* (London: Macmillan, 1977), p. 45.
75. Goodrich, *The Frontier of Control* (1975).
76. Burawoy, *The Politics of Production* (1985), p. 53.
77. Immanuel Ness and Dario Azzellini (eds), *Ours to Master and to Own: Workers' Control from the Commune to the Present* (Chicago: Haymarket Books, 2011).
78. Burawoy, *The Politics of Production* (1985), p. 53.
79. Fernie and Metcalf, *(Not) Hanging on the Telephone* (1997), p. 3.
80. Taylor and Bain, '"An Assembly Line in the Head"' (1999), p. 103.
81. *Ibid.*, p. 109.

CHAPTER 4

1. Tim Strangleman 'Ways of (Not) Seeing Work: The Visual as a Blind Spot in WES?', *Work, Employment & Society*, Vol. 18, No. 1 (2004), p. 187.
2. Nick Hedges and Huw Beynon, *Born to Work: Images of Factory Life* (London: Pluto, 1982), p. 7.
3. A. Bolton, C. Pole and P. Mizen, 'Picture This: Researching Child Workers', *Sociology*, Vol. 35, No. 2 (2001), pp. 501–18.
4. Gigi Roggero, 'Notes on Framing and Re-inventing Co-research', *Ephemera*, Vol. 14, No. 3 (2014), p. 521.
5. Kate Mulholland, 'Workplace Resistance in an Irish Call Centre: Slammin', Scammin' Smokin' an' Leavin'', *Work, Employment & Society*, Vol. 18, No. 4 (2004), pp. 709–24.
6. George Rawick, 'Working Class Self-Activity', *Radical America*, Vol. 3, No. 2 (1969), p. 29.
7. Edward B. Harper, 'Social Consequences of an Unsuccessful Low Caste Movement', *Social Mobility in the Caste System in India: An Interdisciplinary Symposium*, ed. James Silverberg, Supplement no. 3, Comparative Studies in Society and History (The Hague: Mouton, 1968), pp. 48–9.

8. James C. Scott, *Weapons of the Weak: Everyday Forms of Peasant Resistance* (New Haven: Yale University Press, 1987), p. 33.
9. Marx, *Capital* ([1867] 1976), p. 272.
10. Braverman, *Labor and Monopoly Capital* (1999), p. 104.
11. Randy Hodson, 'Worker Resistance: An Underdeveloped Concept in the Sociology of Work', *Economic and Industrial Democracy*, Vol. 16, No. 1 (1995), p. 80.
12. Goodrich, *The Frontier of Control* (1975).
13. Richard Hyman, *Industrial Relations: A Marxist Introduction* (London: Macmillan, 1975), p. 26.
14. John M. Jermier, 'Sabotage at Work', *Research in the Sociology of Organizations*, ed. Nancy DiTomaso, vol. 6 (Greenwich, CT: JAI Press, 1988).
15. Paul K. Edwards and Hugh Scullion, *The Social Organization of Industrial Conflict* (London: Basil Blackwell, 1982), p. 154.
16. Paul Thompson and Stephen Ackroyd, 'All Quiet on the Workplace Front? A Critique of Recent Trends in British Industrial Sociology', *Sociology*, Vol. 29, No. 4 (1995), p. 617.
17. Stephen Ackroyd and Paul Thompson, *Organisational Misbehaviour* (London: Sage, 1992), p. 2.
18. Diane van den Broek and Tony Dundon, '(Still) Up to No Good: Reconfiguring the Boundaries of Worker Resistance and Misbehaviour in an Increasingly Unorganised World', *Relations Industrielles/Industrial Relations*, Vol. 67, No. 1 (2012), p. 99.
19. Hochschild, *The Managed Heart* (2012).
20. Huffington Post Canada, 'Cathay Pacific Smile Strike: Cabin Crews Threaten to Withhold Services Over Pay Dispute', *The Huffington Post*, 13 December 2012, www.huffingtonpost.ca/2012/12/13/cathay-pacific-smile-strike_n_2292796.html
21. Taylor and Bain, '"An Assembly Line in the Head"' (1999), p. 103.
22. Mulholland, 'Workplace Resistance in an Irish Call Centre' (2004), p. 709.
23. *Ibid.*, p. 716.
24. Şafak Tartanoğlu, 'The Conditions and Consequences of Informal Organisation in Turkish Call Centres', International Labour Process Conference, 13–15 April London (2014), www.ilpc.org.uk/Default.aspx?tabid=6135&absid=921
25. Linhart, *The Assembly Line* (1981).
26. Mulholland, 'Workplace Resistance in an Irish Call Centre (2004), pp. 709–24.

27. *Ibid.*, p. 713.
28. *Ibid.*, p. 714.
29. *Ibid.*, p. 718.
30. Geoff Brown, *Sabotage: A Study in Industrial Conflict* (Nottingham: Bertrand Russell Peace Foundation for Spokesman Books, 1977).
31. Pierre Dubois, *Sabotage in Industry* (London: Penguin Books, 1979).
32. Thompson and Ackroyd, 'All Quiet on the Workplace Front?' (1995), p. 616.
33. Quoted in Hodson, 'Worker Resistance' (1995), p. 92.
34. Mulholland, 'Workplace Resistance in an Irish Call Centre' (2004), p. 719.
35. *Ibid.*, p. 720.
36. *Ibid.*
37. Marcel van der Linden, *Workers of the World: Essays toward a Global Labor History* (Leiden: Brill, 2008), p. 179.
38. Michael Burawoy, 'The Extended Case Method', *Sociological Theory*, Vol. 16, No. 1 (1998), p. 14.
39. Taylor and Bain, '"An Assembly Line in the Head"' (1999), p. 110.
40. Vincent J. Roscigno and Randy Hodson, 'The Organizational and Social Foundations of Worker Resistance', *American Sociological Review*, Vol. 69, No. 1 (2004), p. 34.
41. Brophy, 'The Subterranean Stream' (2010), p. 477.
42. Mulholland, 'Workplace Resistance in an Irish Call Centre' (2004), p. 720.
43. Mario Tronti, *Operai e capitale*, 2nd ed. (Turin: Einaudi, 1971), p. 89 quoted in Antonio Negri and Michael Hardt, *Commonwealth* (Cambridge, MA: Harvard University Press 2009), p. 291.
44. Gigi Roggero, *The Production of Living Knowledge* (Philadelphia: Temple University Press, 2011), p. 23.
45. van der Linden, *Workers of the World* (2008), p. 179.
46. Mario Tronti, 'The Strategy of Refusal', *Operai e capitale* (Turin: Einaudi, 1966), available at: http://libcom.org/library/strategy-refusal-mario-tronti
47. Michael Hardt and Antonio Negri, *Empire* (London: Harvard University Press, 2001), p. 204.
48. David Graeber, 'On the Phenomenon of Bullshit Jobs', *Strike Magazine*, 17 August 2013, http://strikemag.org/bullshit-jobs
49. *Ibid.*
50. Braverman, *Labor and Monopoly Capital* (1999).
51. Graeber, 'On the Phenomenon of Bullshit Jobs' (2013).

CHAPTER 5

1. Robert Blackburn, *Union Character and Social Class* (London: Batsford, 1967), p. 18.
2. Beynon, *Working for Ford* (1973), p. 140.
3. Phil Taylor and Peter Bain, 'Trade Unions, Workers' Rights and the Frontier of Control in UK Call Centres', *Economic and Industrial Democracy*, Vol. 22, No. 1 (2001), p. 62.
4. Thompson and Ackroyd, 'All Quiet on the Workplace Front? (1995), p. 629.
5. Graeber, 'On the Phenomenon of Bullshit Jobs' (2013).
6. Burawoy, 'The Extended Case Method' (1998), p. 14.
7. Kolinko, *Hotlines - Call Centre | Inquiry | Communism* (2002).
8. *Ibid.*, p. 23.
9. Burawoy, 'The Extended Case Method' (1998), p. 17.
10. Sam Jones, Ben Quinn and Conal Urquhart, 'Woolwich Attack Prompts Fears of Backlash against British Muslims', *The Guardian*, 23 May 2013, www.guardian.co.uk/uk/woolwich-attack
11. From the *Harry Potter* stories. I was not aware of this reference at the time. For more information, see: http://joindumbledoresarmy.warnerbros.com
12. The London Living Wage is calculated as £8.55 per hour (and £7.46 for the rest of the UK) by the Living Wage Foundation, see: www.livingwage.org.uk
13. The name of the union, like that of the company, will remain anonymous.
14. Bob Russell, 'Call Centres: A Decade of Research', *International Journal of Management Reviews*, Vol. 10, No. 3 (2008), p. 206.
15. Brophy, 'The Subterranean Stream' (2010), p. 480.
16. *Ibid.*, p. 481.
17. Kolinko, *Hotlines – Call Centre | Inquiry | Communism* (2002).
18. Taylor and Bain, '"An Assembly Line in the Head"' (1999), p. 109.
19. Goodrich, *The Frontier of Control* (1975).
20. Mulholland, 'Workplace Resistance in an Irish Call Centre' (2004), p. 713.
21. Cederström and Fleming, *Dead Man Working* (2012), p. 10.
22. van der Linden, *Workers of the World* (2008), p. 179.
23. Angela Mitropoulos, 'Precari-Us', *Mute*, Vol. 2 (2005), p. 12.
24. Pierre Bourdieu, *Firing Back: Against the Tyranny of the Market 2*, trans. L. Wacquant, (London: Verso, 1998), p. 85 [Originally

published as *Contre Feux 2: Pour un movement social européen*, Paris: Éditions Raisons d'agir].

25. Guy Standing, *The Precariat: The New Dangerous Class* (London: Bloomsbury, 2011).

26. Richard Seymour, 'We Are All Precarious: On the Concept of the "Precariat" and Its Misuses', *New Left Project*, 2 October 2012, www.newleftproject.org/index.php/site/article_comments/we_are_all_precarious_on_the_concept_of_the_precariat_and_its_misuses

27. Quoted in *ibid.*

28. Harvey, *A Brief History of Neoliberalism* (2007), p. 12.

29. Seymour, 'We Are All Precarious' (2012).

30. Mitropoulos, 'Precari-Us' (2005), p. 13.

31. Anthony Iles, 'The Insecurity Lasts a Long Time', *Mute*, Vol. 2 (2005), p. 36.

32. Kidd McKarthy, 'Is Precarity Enough?', *Mute*, Vol. 2 (2005), p. 55

33. Mitropoulos, 'Precari-Us' (2005), p. 13.

34. Berardi, *The Soul at Work* (2009), p. 44.

35. *Ibid.*, p. 46.

36. McKarthy, 'Is Precarity Enough?' (2005), p. 57.

37. Anna Pollert and Andy Charlwood, 'The Vulnerable Worker in Britain and Problems at Work', *Work, Employment & Society*, Vol. 23, No. 2 (2009), p. 344.

38. Sandra Fredman, 'Women at Work: The Broken Promise of Flexicurity', *Industrial Law Journal*, Vol. 33, No. 4 (2003), p. 308.

39. Pollert and Charlwood, 'The Vulnerable Worker in Britain and Problems at Work' (2009), p. 357.

40. Department for Business Innovation & Skills, *Trade Union Membership 2014 Statistical Bulletin* (London: Department for Business Innovation & Skills, 2015), p. 5.

41. Thompson and Ackroyd, 'All Quiet on the Workplace Front?' (1995), p. 618.

42. Mark Carley, *Developments in Industrial Action 2003–2007* (European Foundation for the Improvement of Living and Working Conditions, 2008), p. 15.

43. *Ibid.*, p. 14.

44. Mark Carley, *UK: Annual Review — 2011* (European Foundation for the Improvement of Living and Working Conditions, 2012).

45. Office for National Statistics, *Labour Disputes – Annual Article 2012* (2013b).

46. Steve Williams and Derek Adam-Smith, 'Web Case: Trade Unions and the Prospects for Unionization in the Service Sector', in

Contemporary Employment Relations: A Critical Introduction, edited by S. Williams and D. Adam-Smith, 2nd ed. (Oxford: Oxford University Press, 2009).

47. Sally Walters, 'Female Part-Time Workers' Attitudes to Trade Unions in Britain', *British Journal of Industrial Relations*, Vol. 40, No. 1 (2002), pp. 49–68.
48. Williams and Adam-Smith, 'Web Case' (2009).
49. Arlie R. Hochschild, *The Managed Heart: Commercialization of Human Feeling* (Berkeley: University of California Press, 2012).
50. Marek Korczynski, *Human Resource Management in Service Work* (Basingstoke: Palgrave Macmillan, 2002).
51. Peter Walker, 'BA Flights Disrupted despite End of Three-Day Strike', *The Guardian*, 23 March 2010, www.theguardian.com/business/2010/mar/23/ba-flights-cancelled-strike
52. Williams and Adam-Smith, 'Web Case' (2009).
53. Peter Bain and Phil Taylor, 'Ringing the Changes? Union Recognition and Organisation in Call Centres in the UK Finance Sector', *Industrial Relations Journal*, Vol. 33, No. 2 (2002), pp. 246–61.
54. Neil Davidson, 'The Neoliberal Era in Britain: Historical Developments and Current Perspectives', *International Socialism Journal*, no. 139 (2013), p. 217.
55. *Ibid.*, p. 213.
56. Robert Blackburn, *Union Character and Social Class* (London: Batsford, 1967), pp. 19–20.
57. UCU, 'Help Make UCU a Stronger Union', UCU, University and College Union (2012), www.ucu.org.uk/index.cfm?articleid=6636
58. The John Lewis Partnership runs John Lewis department stores, Waitrose supermarkets and other businesses: employees are called 'partners' and benefit from a profit-sharing scheme: see www.johnlewispartnership.co.uk
59. John S, Lewis, *Partnership for All: A Thirty Four Year Old Experiment in Industrial Democracy* (London: Kerr-Cross Publishing, 1948).
60. Harvie Ramsay, 'Phantom Participation: Patterns of Power and Conflict', *Industrial Relations Journal*, Vol. 11, No. 3 (1980), p. 52.
61. Lesley Baddon, Laurie Hunter, Jeff D. Hyman, John Leopold and Harvie Ramsay, *People's Capitalism? A Critical Analysis of Profit-Sharing and Employee Share Ownership* (London: Routledge, 1989), p. 80.
62. Melanie Simms and Jane Holgate, 'Organising for What? Where Is the Debate on the Politics of Organising?', *Work, Employment & Society*, Vol. 24, No. 1 (2010), p. 157.

63. *Ibid.*, p. 159.
64. Immanuel Ness, 'Introduction', in *New Forms of Worker Organization: The Syndicalist and Autonomist Restoration of Class Struggle Unionism*, edited by I. Ness (Oakland, CA: PM Press, 2014), p. 1.
65. Ralph Miliband, *Capitalist Democracy in Britain* (Oxford: Oxford University Press, 1982), p. 13.
66. John Zerzan, 'Trade Unionism or Socialism: The Revolt against Work', *Solidarity*, no. 47 (1976), http://libcom.org/library/%EF%BB%BFtrade-unionism-or-socialism-revolt-against-work-john-zerzan
67. Paul Lafargue, *The Right to Be Lazy* (Chicago: Charles H. Kerr and Co. Co-operative, 1883), www.marxists.org/archive/lafargue/1883/lazy
68. Christopher Taylor, 'The Refusal of Work: From the Postemancipation Caribbean to Post-Fordist Empire', *Small Axe: A Caribbean Journal of Criticism*, Vol. 18, No. 2: 44 (2014), p. 1.
69. Kathi Weeks, *The Problem with Work: Feminism, Marxism, Antiwork Politics, and Postwork Imaginaries* (Durham: Duke University Press, 2011).
70. Hardt and Negri, *Empire* (2001).
71. Taylor, 'The Refusal of Work' (2014), p. 3.
72. *Ibid.*, p. 4.
73. *Ibid.*, p. 7.
74. C. L. R. James, *The Black Jacobins: Toussaint L'Ouverture and the San Domingo Revolution* (London: Penguin, 2001).
75. David R. Roediger and Elizabeth D. Esch, *The Production of Difference: Race and the Management of Labor in U.S. History* (New York: Oxford University Press, 2012), p. 141.
76. Taylor, 'The Refusal of Work' (2014), p. 11.
77. *Ibid.*, p. 7.
78. *Ibid.*, p. 14.
79. Marx, *Grundrisse* ([1857] 1973), pp. 325–6.
80. Taylor, 'The Refusal of Work' (2014), p. 17.
81. *Ibid.*, p. 17.

CHAPTER 6

1. Worcester, *C. L. R. James: A Political Biography* (1995), p. 125.
2. Stephen Hastings-King, 'Looking for the Proletariat: Socialisme ou Barbarie and the Problem of Worker Writing', *Historical Materialism*, Vol. 71 (2014), p. 106.

3. Vittorio Rieser, *The Political, Cultural Development and Main Reference Points* (2001), www.generation-online.org/t/vittorio.htm
4. *Ibid.*
5. Kolinko, *Hotlines - Call Centre | Inquiry | Communism* (2002).
6. Burawoy, 'The Extended Case Method' (1998), p. 14.
7. *The Call Centre* (2013).
8. *The Wolf of Wall Street* (2014).
9. *Undercover Boss* (2010).
10. Bev Skeggs and Helen Wood, *Reacting to Reality Television: Performance, Audience and Value* (New York: Routledge, 2012), p. 216.
11. *Benefits Street* [Documentary, Reality-TV] Channel 4, 2014.
12. Ria Stone, 'Part 2: The Reconstruction of Society', in *The American Worker* (1947), www.prole.info/texts/americanworker2.html
13. Taylor, *The Principles of Scientific Management* (1967), p. 39.
14. Taylor and Bain, '"An Assembly Line in the Head"' (1999), pp. 110, 109.
15. *The Call Centre* (2013).
16. Hochschild, *The Managed Heart* (2012).
17. Berardi, *The Soul at Work* (2009), p. 87.
18. *Ibid.*, p. 46.
19. Graeber, 'On the Phenomenon of Bullshit Jobs' (2013).
20. *The Call Centre* (2013).
21. Goodrich, *The Frontier of Control* (1975).
22. Taylor and Bain, '"An Assembly Line in the Head"' (1999), p. 109.
23. Bentham, *The Panopticon Writings* (1995).
24. Foucault, *Discipline and Punish* (1991).
25. Alan McKinlay and Phil Taylor, 'Foucault and the Politics of Production', in *Management and Organization Theory*, edited by A. McKinlay and L. Starkey (London: Sage, 1998), p. 175.
26. Taylor and Bain, '"An Assembly Line in the Head"' (1999), p. 103.
27. *Undercover Boss* (2010).
28. Taylor, *The Principles of Scientific Management* (1967), p. 36.
29. Cederström and Fleming, *Dead Man Working* (2012), p. 10.
30. Income Data Services, *Pay and Conditions in Call and Contact Centres 2012/13* (London: IDS, 2012), p. 59.
31. Mulholland 'Workplace Resistance in an Irish Call Centre (2004), p. 713.
32. *Ibid.*, p. 719.
33. *Ibid.*, p. 720.
34. van der Linden, *Workers of the World* (2008), p. 179.

35. Burawoy, 'The Extended Case Method', (1998), p. 14.
36. Braverman, *Labor and Monopoly Capital* (1999), p. 104.
37. Mulholland 'Workplace Resistance in an Irish Call Centre' (2004), p. 713.
38. Graeber, 'On the Phenomenon of Bullshit Jobs' (2013).
39. Taylor, 'The Refusal of Work' (2014), p. 17.
40. Ness, 'Introduction' (2011), p. 2.
41. Seymour, 'We Are All Precarious' (2012).
42. Taylor and Bain, 'Trade Unions, Workers' Rights and the Frontier of Control in UK Call Centres' (2001), p. 62.
43. van der Linden, *Workers of the World* (2008), p. 179.
44. Marx, *The Eighteenth Brumaire of Louis Bonaparte* (1852).
45. Thompson and Ackroyd, 'All Quiet on the Workplace Front?' (1995), p. 617.
46. Karl Marx, Letter from Marx to Arnold Ruge, September 1843 (*Deutsch-Französische Jahrbücher*, 1844).

REFERENCES

Ackroyd, S. and Thompson, P. (1992) *Organisational Misbehaviour*, London: Sage.

Back to the Floor (1997) BBC [Documentary, Reality-TV].

Baddon, L., Hunter, L., Hyman, J. D., Leopold, J. and Ramsay, H. (1989) *People's Capitalism? A Critical Analysis of Profit-Sharing and Employee Share Ownership*, London: Routledge.

Bain, P. and Taylor, P. (2002) 'Ringing the Changes? Union Recognition and Organisation in Call Centres in the UK Finance Sector', *Industrial Relations Journal*, Vol. 33 No. 2, pp. 246–61.

Bain, P., Watson, A., Mulvey, G., Taylor, P. and Gall, G. (2002) 'Taylorism, Targets and the Pursuit of Quantity and Quality by Call Centre Management', *New Technology, Work and Employment*, Vol. 17, No. 3, pp. 170–85.

Benefits Street (2014) Channel 4 [Documentary, Reality-TV].

Berardi, F. (2009) *The Soul at Work: From Alienation to Autonomy*, Los Angeles, CA: Semiotext(e).

Bergevin, R., Kinder, A., Siegel, W. and Simpson, B. (2010) *Call Centers for Dummies*, Mississauga, Ontario: John Wiley and Sons Canada.

Bentham, J. (1995) *The Panopticon Writings*, London: Verso.

Beynon, H. (1973) *Working for Ford*, Harmondsworth: Penguin.

Blackburn, R. (1967) *Union Character and Social Class*, London: Batsford.

Brant, M. and Santori, E. (1953) *A Women's Place*, New Writers.

Braverman, H. (1999) *Labor and Monopoly Capital: The Degradation of Work in the Twentieth Century*, London: Monthly Review Press.

Brown, G. (1977) *Sabotage: A Study in Industrial Conflict*, Nottingham: Bertrand Russell Peace Foundation for Spokesman Books.

Boltanski, L. and Chiapello, E. (2007) *The New Spirit of Capitalism*, London: Verso.

Bolton, A., Pole, C. and Mizen, P. (2001) 'Picture This: Researching Child Workers', *Sociology*, Vol. 35, No. 2, pp. 501–18.

Bourdieu, P. (1998) *Firing Back: Against the Tyranny of the Market 2* (trans L. Wacquant) London: Verso. [Originally published as *Contre Feux 2: Pour un movement social européen*, Paris: Éditions Raisons d'agir].

References

Božovič, M. (1995) 'Introduction', in *The Panopticon Writings*, by Jeremy Bentham, London: Verso.

Brophy, E. (2010) 'The Subterranean Stream: Communicative Capitalism and Call Centre Labour', *Ephemera*, Vol. 10, No. 3/4.

Burawoy, M. (1979) *Manufacturing Consent*, Chicago: University of Chicago Press.

Burawoy, M. (1985) *The Politics of Production*, London: Verso.

Burawoy, M. (1998) 'The Extended Case Method', *Sociological Theory*, Vol. 16, No. 1, pp. 4–33.

Carley, M. (2008) *Developments in Industrial Action 2003–2007*, European Foundation for the improvement of Living and Working Conditions.

Carley, M. (2012) *UK: Annual Review — 2011*, European Foundation for the Improvement of Living and Working Conditions.

Castoriadis, C. (1975) 'An Interview with Cornelius Castoriadis', *Telos*, Vol. 23.

Cavendish, R. (1982) *Women on the Line*, London: Routledge & Kegan Paul.

Cederström, C. and Fleming, P. (2012) *Dead Man Working*, Winchester: Zero Books.

Cleaver, H. (1979) *Reading* Capital *Politically*, Brighton: Harvester Press.

Davidson, N. (2013) 'The Neoliberal Era in Britain: Historical Developments and Current Perspectives', *International Socialism*, 139, pp. 171–233.

De Angelis, M. (2007) *The Beginning of History: Value Struggles and Global Capital*, London: Pluto.

Dehn, H. (1998) 'UK: Back to the Floor', *Management Today*, available at: www.managementtoday.co.uk/news/411264/UK-Back-floor

Denby, C. (1989) *Indignant Heart: A Black Worker's Journal*, Detroit: Wayne State University Press.

Department for Business Innovation & Skills (2015) *Trade Union Membership 2014 Statistical Bulletin*, London: Department for Business Innovation & Skills.

Dubois, P. (1979) *Sabotage in Industry*, London: Penguin Books.

Edwards, R. (1979) *Contested Terrain: The Transformation of the Workplace in the Twentieth Century*, New York: Basic Books.

Edwards, P. K. and Scullion, H. (1982) *The Social Organization of Industrial Conflict*, London: Basil Blackwell.

Egan, D. R. (2006) 'Eyeing the Scene: The Uses and (Re)Uses of Surveillance Cameras in an Exotic Dance Club', in *Culture, Power, and*

History: Studies in Critical Sociology, edited by S. Pfohl et al., Leiden: Brill.

Ellis, V. and Taylor, P. (2006) '"You Don't Know What You've Got till It's Gone": Re-Contextualising the Origins, Development and Impact of the Call Centre', *New Technology, Work and Employment*, Vol. 21, No. 2, pp. 107–22.

Faulkner, K., Bentley, P. and Osborne, L. (2015) 'Shame of the Charity Cold Call Sharks', *Daily Mail*, 7 July, available at: www.dailymail.co.uk/news/article-3151533/Shamed-charity-cold-call-sharks-Britain-s-biggest-charities-ruthlessly-hound-vulnerable-cash-try-opt-receiving-calls.html

Fernie, S. and Metcalf, D. (1997) *(Not) Hanging on the Telephone: Payment Systems in the New Sweatshops*, Centre for Economic Performance: London School of Economics.

Fischer, C. S. (1992) *America Calling: A Social History of the Telephone to 1940*, Berkeley: University of California Press.

Fisher, M. (2009) *Capitalist Realism: Is There No Alternative?*, Winchester: Zero Books.

Foucault, M. (1991) *Discipline and Punish: The Birth of the Prison*, London: Penguin.

Fredman, S. (2003) 'Women at Work: The Broken Promise of Flexicurity', *Industrial Law Journal*, Vol. 33, No. 4, pp. 219–399.

Friedman, A. L. (1977) *Industry and Labour: Class Struggle at Work and Monopoly Capitalism*, London: Macmillan.

Glaberman, M. (1952) *Punching Out*, Detroit: Correspondence Publishing Committee.

Glaberman, M. (1955) *Union Committeemen and Wildcat Strikes*, Detroit: Correspondence Publishing Committee.

Glengarry Glen Ross (1992) Zupnik Cinema Group [Indie film/Drama].

Glucksmann, M. (2004) 'Call Configurations: Varieties of Call Centre and Divisions of Labour', *Work, Employment & Society*, Vol. 18, No. 4, pp. 795–811.

Goodrich, C. L. (1975) *The Frontier of Control: A Study in British Workshop Politics*, London: Pluto Press.

Graeber, D. (2013) 'On the Phenomenon of Bullshit Jobs', *Strike Magazine*, 17 August, available at: http://strikemag.org/bullshit-jobs

Haider, A. and Mohandesi, S. (2013) 'Workers' Inquiry: A Genealogy', *Viewpoint Magazine*, Vol. 3, available at: http://viewpointmag.com/2013/09/27/workers-inquiry-a-genealogy

Hardt, M. and Negri, A. (2001) *Empire*, London: Harvard University Press.

Harper, E. B. (1968) 'Social Consequences of an Unsuccessful Low Caste Movement', in *Social Mobility in the Caste System in India: An Inter-disciplinary Symposium*, edited by J. Silverberg, Supplement no. 3, Comparative Studies in Society and History, The Hague: Mouton.

Harvey, D. (2003) *The New Imperialism*, Oxford: Oxford University Press.

Harvey, D. (2007) *A Brief History of Neoliberalism*, Oxford: Oxford University Press.

Harvey, D. (2010) *A Companion to Marx's Capital*, London: Verso.

Hastings-King, S. (2014) 'Looking for the Proletariat: Socialisme ou Barbarie and the Problem of Worker Writing', *Historical Materialism*, Vol. 71.

Hedges, N. and Beynon, H. (1982) *Born to Work: Images of Factory Life*, London: Pluto.

Hochschild, A. R. (2012) *The Managed Heart: Commercialization of Human Feeling*, Berkeley: University of California Press.

Hodson, R. (1995) 'Worker Resistance: An Underdeveloped Concept in the Sociology of Work', *Economic and Industrial Democracy*, Vol. 16, No. 1, pp. 79–111.

Holman, D., Batt, R. and Holtgrewe, U. (2007) 'The Global Call Centre Report: International Perspectives on Management and Employment (executive Summary)', www.ilr.cornell.edu/globalcallcenter/upload/GCC-Intl-Rept-UK-Version.pdf

Huffington Post Canada (2012) 'Cathay Pacific Smile Strike: Cabin Crews Threaten to Withhold Services Over Pay Dispute', *The Huffington Post*, 13 December, www.huffingtonpost.ca/2012/12/13/cathay-pacific-smile-strike_n_2292796.html

Huws, U., Jagger, N. and Bates, P. (2001) *Where the Butterfly Alights: The Global Location of eWork*, Institute for Employment Studies, Report 378.

Hyman, R. (1975) *Industrial Relations: A Marxist Introduction*, London: Macmillan.

Iles, A. (2005) 'The Insecurity Lasts a Long Time', *Mute*, Vol. 2.

Income Data Services (2012) *Pay and Conditions in Call and Contact Centres 2012/13*, London: IDS.

James, C. L. R., Dunayevskaya, R. and Lee, G. (1950) *State Capitalism and World Revolution*, Detroit: Facing Reality Publishing Committee.

James, C. L. R. (2001) *The Black Jacobins: Toussaint L'Ouverture and the San Domingo Revolution*, London: Penguin.

Jermier, J. M. (1988) 'Sabotage at Work', in *Research in the Sociology of Organizations,* edited by N. DiTomaso, vol. 6, Greenwich, CT: JAI Press.

Jones, S., Quinn, B. and Urquhart, C. (2013) 'Woolwich Attack Prompts Fears of Backlash against British Muslims', *The Guardian,* 23 May, available at: www.guardian.co.uk/uk/woolwich-attack

Kafka, F. (2000) *The Castle,* London: Penguin.

Kolinko (2002) *Hotlines – Call Centre | Inquiry | Communism,* Duisburg.

Korczynski, M. (2002) *Human Resource Management in Service Work,* Basingstoke: Palgrave Macmillan.

Lafargue, P. (1883) *The Right to Be Lazy,* Charles Kerr and Co. Co-operative, available at: www.marxists.org/archive/lafargue/1883/lazy

Lanzardo, D. (1965) 'Intervento Socialista nella Lotta Operaia: l'Inchiesta Operaia di Marx', *Quaderni Rossi,* Vol. 5.

Lebowitz, M. (2009) *Following Marx: Method, Critique and Crisis,* Boston: Brill.

Lefort, C. (1952) 'Proletarian Experience', *Socialisme ou Barbarie,* No. 11. trans. *Viewpoint Magazine,* available at: http://viewpointmag.com/2013/09/26/proletarian-experience

Lewig, K. A. and Dollard, M. F. (2003) 'Emotional Dissonance, Emotional Exhaustion and Job Satisfaction in Call Centre Workers', *European Journal of Work and Organizational Psychology,* Vol. 12, No. 4, pp. 366–92.

Lewis, J. S. (1948) *Partnership for All: A Thirty Four Year Old Experiment in Industrial Democracy,* London: Kerr-Cross Publishing.

Linhart, R. (1981) *The Assembly Line,* Amherst: University of Massachusetts Press.

Marshall, N. and Richardson, R. (1996) 'The Impact of "Telemediated" Services on Corporate Structures: The Example of "Branchless" Retail Banking in Britain', *Environment and Planning A,* Vol. 28, No. 10, pp. 1843–58.

Marazzi, C. (2011) *Capital and Affects: The Politics of the Language Economy,* Los Angeles: Semiotext(e).

Marx, K. (1844) *Economic and Philosophic Manuscripts of 1844,* www.marxists.org/archive/marx/works/1844/manuscripts/labour.htm

Marx, K. (1852) *The Eighteenth Brumaire of Louis Bonaparte,* www.marxists.org/archive/marx/works/1852/18th-brumaire/ch01.htm

Marx, K. [1857] 1973) *Grundrisse,* London: Penguin.

Marx, K. ([1867]1976) *Capital: A Critique of Political Economy Vol. 1,* London: Penguin Books.

Marx, K. (1880) *A Workers' Inquiry*, www.marxists.org/archive/marx/works/1880/04/20.htm

Marx, K. and Engels, F. (1848) *Manifesto of the Communist Party*, www.marxists.org/archive/marx/works/1848/communist-manifesto/index.htm

Matheron, F. (1999) 'Operaismo', *Generation Online*, available at: www.generation-online.org/t/toperaismo.htm

McKarthy, K. (2005) 'Is Precarity Enough?', *Mute*, Vol. 2, No. 0, Precarious Reader.

McKinlay, M. and Taylor, P. (1998) 'Foucault and the Politics of Production', in *Management and Organization Theory*, edited by A. McKinlay and L. Starkey, London: Sage.

Miliband, R. (1982) *Capitalist Democracy in Britain*, Oxford: Oxford University Press.

Miller, T. (2014) 'Foucault, Marx, Neoliberalism: Unveiling Undercover Boss', in *Foucault Now*, edited by J. D. Faubion, Cambridge: Polity Press.

Minority Report (2002) Twentieth Century Fox [Film].

Mitropoulos, A. (2005) 'Precari-Us', *Mute*, Vol. 2, No. 0, Precarious Reader.

Mulholland, K. (2004) 'Workplace Resistance in an Irish Call Centre: Slammin', Scammin', Smokin' an' Leavin'', *Work, Employment & Society*, Vol. 18, No. 4, pp. 709–24.

Murphy, R. (2010) 'Vodafone's Tax Case Leaves a Sour Taste', *The Guardian*, 22 October, www.theguardian.com/commentisfree/2010/oct/22/vodafone-tax-case-leaves-sour-taste

Negri, A. and Hardt, M. (2009) *Commonwealth*, Cambridge, MA: Harvard University Press.

Ness, I. (2011) 'Introduction', in *Ours to Master and to Own: Workers' Control from the Commune to the Present*, edited by I. Ness and D. Azzellini, Chicago: Haymarket Books.

Ness, I., and Azzellini, D. (eds) (2011) *Ours to Master and to Own: Workers' Control from the Commune to the Present*, Chicago: Haymarket Books.

Ness, I. (2014) 'Introduction', in *New Forms of Worker Organization: The Syndicalist and Autonomist Restoration of Class Struggle Unionism*, edited by I. Ness, Oakland: PM Press.

O'Connell Davidson, J. (1993) *Privatisation and Employment Relations: The Case of the Water Industry*, London: Mansell.

Office for National Statistics (2013a) *EMP04: All in Employment by Status, Occupation and Sex*, Labour Force Survey, Office of National

Statistics, www.ons.gov.uk/ons/rel/lms/labour-force-survey-employ-ment-status-by-occupation/index.html

Office for National Statistics (2013b) *Labour Disputes – Annual Article 2012*, www.ons.gov.uk/ons/rel/bus-register/labour-disputes/annual-article-2012/art---labour-disputes--annual-article-2012.html

Office Space (1999) Twentieth Century Fox [Film].

Ollman, B. (1977) *Alienation: Marx's Conception of Man in a Capitalist Society,* Cambridge: Cambridge University Press.

Osborne, H. (2013) 'Call Centres in BBC3 Programme Hit with £225,000 Fines', *The Guardian*, 18 June, www.theguardian.com/money/2013/jun/18/call-centres-bbc3-programme-fines

Peachey, P. (2013) 'The Real Minority Report? Kent Constabulary Tests Computer Program to Predict Crime', *The Independent*, 4 October, www.independent.co.uk/news/uk/crime/the-real-minority-report-kent-constabulary-tests-computer-program-to-predict-crime-8744940.html

Pollert, A. (1981) *Girls, Wives, Factory Lives,* London: Macmillan.

Pollert, A. and Charlwood, A. 'The Vulnerable Worker in Britain and Problems at Work', *Work, Employment & Society*, Vol. 23, No. 2, pp. 343–62.

Ramsay, H. (1980) 'Phantom Participation: Patterns of Power and Conflict', *Industrial Relations Journal*, Vol. 11, No. 3, pp. 46–59.

Rawick, G. (1969) 'Working Class Self-Activity', *Radical America*, Vol. 3, No. 2, pp. 23–31.

Rieser, V. (2001) *The Political, Cultural Development and Main Reference Points,* available at: www.generation-online.org/t/vittorio.htm

Roediger, D. R. and Esch, E. D. (2012) *The Production of Difference: Race and the Management of Labor in U.S. History,* New York: Oxford University Press.

Roggero, G. (2010) 'Romano Alquati — Militant Researcher, Operaist, Autonomist Marxist — Has Passed Away, Age 75', *Fuckyeahmilitantresearch,* http://fuckyeahmilitantresearch.tumblr.com/post/502186794/romano-alquati-militant-researcher-operaist

Roggero, G. (2011) *The Production of Living Knowledge,* Philadelphia: Temple University Press.

Roggero, G. (2014) 'Notes on Framing and Re-inventing Co-research', *Ephemera*, Vol. 14, No. 3.

Romano, P. and Stone, R. (1946) *The American Worker,* Detroit: Facing Reality Publishing Company.

Romano, P. (1947) 'Part 1: Life in the Factory', in *The American Worker,* www.prole.info/texts/americanworker1.html

References

Romano, P. (1949) 'L'Ouvrier Américain', *Socialisme ou Barbarie*, Vol. 1.

Romano, P. (1955) 'L'Operaio Americano', *Battaglia Comunista*.

Roscigno, V. J. and Hodson, R. (2004) 'The Organizational and Social Foundations of Worker Resistance', *American Sociological Review*, Vol. 69, No. 1, pp. 14–39.

Rowbotham, S. (1977) *Hidden from History: 300 Years of Women's Oppression and the Fight against It*, London: Pluto Press.

Russell, B. (2008) 'Call Centres: A Decade of Research', *International Journal of Management Reviews*, Vol. 10, No. 3, pp. 195–219.

Scott, J. C. (1987) *Weapons of the Weak: Everyday Forms of Peasant Resistance*, New Haven: Yale University Press.

Seymour, R. (2012) 'We Are All Precarious: On the Concept of the "Precariat" and Its Misuses', *New Left Project*, 2 October, www.newleftproject.org/index.php/site/article_comments/we_are_all_precarious_on_the_concept_of_the_precariat_and_its_misuses

Skeggs, B. and Wood, H. (2012) *Reacting to Reality Television: Performance, Audience and Value*, New York: Routledge.

Simms, M. and Holgate, J. (2010) 'Organising for What? Where Is the Debate on the Politics of Organising?', *Work, Employment & Society*, vol. 24 no. 1, pp. 157–68.

Spivak, G. C. (1988) 'Subaltern Studies: Deconstructing Historiography', in *Selected Subaltern Studies*, edited by R. Guha, New York: Oxford University Press.

Standing, G. (2011) *The Precariat: The New Dangerous Class*, London: Bloomsbury.

Strangleman, T. (2004) 'Ways of (Not) Seeing Work: The Visual as a Blind Spot in WES?', *Work, Employment & Society*, Vol. 18, No. 1, pp. 179–92.

Stone, R. (1947) 'Part 2: The Reconstruction of Society', In *The American Worker*, www.prole.info/texts/americanworker2.html

Tartanoğlu, Ş. (2014) 'The Conditions and Consequences of Informal Organisation in Turkish Call Centres', *International Labour Process Conference*, 13–15 April, London, available at: www.ilpc.org.uk/Default.aspx?tabid=6135&absid=921

Taylor, C. (2014) 'The Refusal of Work: From the Postemancipation Caribbean to Post-Fordist Empire', *Small Axe: A Caribbean Journal of Criticism*, Vol. 18, No. 2:44, pp. 1–17.

Taylor, F. (1967) *The Principles of Scientific Management*, New York: Norton.

Taylor, P. and Bain, P. (1999) '"An Assembly Line in the Head": Work and Employee Relations in the Call Centre', *Industrial Relations Journal*, Vol. 30, No. 2, pp. 101–17.

Taylor, P. and Bain, P. (2001) 'Trade Unions, Workers' Rights and the Frontier of Control in UK Call Centres' *Economic and Industrial Democracy*, Vol. 22, No. 1, pp. 39–66.

Taylor, P. and Bain, P. (2004) 'Call Centre Offshoring to India: The Revenge of History?', *Labour and Industry*, Vol. 14, No. 3, pp. 15–38.

Taylor, P., Warhurst, C., Thompson, P. and Scholarios, D. (2009) 'On the Front Line', *Work, Employment & Society*, Vol. 23, No. 1, pp. 5–9.

The Call Centre (2013) BBC, [Documentary, Reality-TV]

The Wolf of Wall Street (2014) Paramount Pictures [Biography, Comedy, Crime].

Thompson, E. P. (1966) 'History from Below', *Times Literary Supplement*, 7 April.

Thompson, P. (1989) *The Nature of Work: An Introduction to Debates on the Labour Process*, London: Macmillan.

Thompson, P. and Ackroyd, S. (1995) 'All Quiet on the Workplace Front? A Critique of Recent Trends in British Industrial Sociology', *Sociology*, Vol. 29, No. 4, pp. 615–33.

Tinwell, A., Grimshaw, M., Abdel Nabi, D. and Williams, A. (2010) 'Facial Expression of Emotion and Perception of the Uncanny Valley in Virtual Characters', *Computers in Human Behaviour*, Vol. 27, No. 2, pp. 741–9.

Tronti, M. (1966) 'The Strategy of Refusal', *Operai e capitale*, Turin: Einaudi, http://libcom.org/library/strategy-refusal-mario-tronti

Tronti, M. (1971) *Operai e capitale*, 2nd edition, Turin: Einaudi.

Tronti, M. (1972) 'The Struggle Against Labour', *Radical America*, Vol. 6, No. 3.

Turchetto, M. (2008) 'From "Mass Worker" to "Empire": The Disconcerting Trajectory of Italian Operaismo', in *Critical Companion to Contemporary Marxism*, edited by J. Bidet and S. Kouvelakis, Boston: Brill.

UCU (2012) 'Help Make UCU a Stronger Union', UCU, University and College Union, www.ucu.org.uk/index.cfm?articleid=6636

Undercover Boss (2010) Channel 4 [Documentary, Reality-TV], www.channel4.com/programmes/undercover-boss

UNISON (2014) 'Call Centres', www.unison.org.uk/at-work/energy/key-issues/call-centres/the-facts

van den Broek, D. and Dundon, T. (2012) '(Still) Up to No Good: Reconfiguring the Boundaries of Worker Resistance and Misbehaviour in an Increasingly Unorganised World', *Relations Industrielles/Industrial Relations,* Vol. 67, No. 1, pp. 97–121.

van der Linden, M. (1997) 'Socialisme ou Barbarie: A French Revolutionary Group (1949–65)', *Left History,* Vol. 5, No. 1.

van der Linden, M. (2008) *Workers of the World: Essays toward a Global Labor History,* Leiden: Brill.

Vivier, G. (1952) 'La Vie En Usine', *Socialisme ou Barbarie.*

Walker, P. (2010) 'BA Flights Disrupted despite End of Three-Day Strike', *The Guardian,* 23 March, www.theguardian.com/business/2010/mar/23/ba-flights-cancelled-strike

Walters, S. (2002) 'Female Part-Time Workers' Attitudes to Trade Unions in Britain', *British Journal of Industrial Relations,* Vol. 40, No. 1, pp. 49–68.

Weeks, K. (2011) *The Problem with Work: Feminism, Marxism, Antiwork Politics, and Postwork Imaginaries,* Durham: Duke University Press.

Williams, S. and Adam-Smith, D. (2009) 'Web Case: Trade Unions and the Prospects for Unionization in the Service Sector', In *Contemporary Employment Relations: A Critical Introduction,* edited by S. Williams and D. Adam-Smith, 2nd edition, Oxford: Oxford University Press.

Woodcock, J. (2013) 'Smile Down the Phone: An Attempt at a Workers' Inquiry in a Call Center', *Viewpoint Magazine,* No. 3.

Woodcock, J. (2014) 'The Workers' Inquiry from Trotskyism to Operaismo: A Political Methodology for Investigating the Workplace', *Ephemera,* Vol. 41, No. 3.

Worcester, K. (1995) *C. L. R. James: A Political Biography,* Albany: State University of New York Press.

Wright, S. (2002) *Storming Heaven: Class Composition and Struggle in Italian Autonomist Marxism,* London: Pluto Press.

Zerzan, J. (1976) 'Trade Unionism or Socialism: The Revolt against Work', *Solidarity,* No. 47, http://libcom.org/library/%EF%BB%BFtrade-unionism-or-socialism-revolt-against-work-john-zerzan

INDEX

absence 21
Ackroyd, Stephen 119, 139
activists, victimisation of 119, 126–7,
  131, 132–4, 143
affective dimension of work
  intensification of demands for
    55–6, 76, 89–92, 155
  as management challenge 8–9,
    52–9, 73–80, 89–92, 103, 154–5
  resistance opportunities of 102–3
agency
  of consumers 80
  of workers (see organisation;
    resistance)
alienation 53–9, 88, 137–8
American Worker, The (study) 25–6,
  27, 154
anti-work 145–7, 160
Automatic Call Distributors (ACD)
  13, 65–6, 67
autonomy 19
Azzellini, Dario 94

Babbage, Charles 66
Back to the Floor (TV show) 62
Bain, Peter, on call centres
  on control 13, 51, 59, 96, 156
  on growth of 50
  on job quality 112, 154
  on organisation 140–1
  on unions 118, 161
Benefits Street 153
Bentham, Jeremy 80–3
Berardi, Franco 'Bifo' 52, 53, 58, 137–8
Beynon, Huw 97, 118
Blackburn, Robert 141
Boltanski, Luc 88
Bolton, A. 97

bonuses 21, 37–8, 39, 69–70, 81, 93
Bourdieu, Pierre 136
Božovič, Miran 83
brain workers 56, 138, 155
Braverman, Harry
  on control and surveillance 29, 32,
    66, 67, 100–1
  on resistance 100–1, 117, 159
Brophy, Enda 32–3, 123–4
'bullshit jobs' 116, 117, 144–7, 155
Burawoy, Michael 66, 94–5, 111,
  119–20, 152, 159
Butlin's 62
buzz sessions 40, 69, 74–6, 105–6,
  149, 157
  worker-led 130–1

Call Centre, The (TV show) 1–3, 5–6,
  8–11, 51–2, 60, 152–3
call centres
  categories of 16
  development of 11–15, 18–19
  numbers employed at 20
  role in modern economy 32–3
  social value of 95
Call Centres for Dummies (book) 11,
  21–2
call recording 7, 37, 42–3, 59, 66,
  82–3, 90–1, 95
Capital see Marx, Karl
capitalism
  centrelessness of 6–7
  cold calls and 153
  neoliberalism and 86–7
  work types in 115–16
  see also neoliberalism
care work 115
case studies see inquiries

Index

Castle, The (Kafka) 6–7
casualisation *see* precarity
Cathay Pacific flight attendant strike
  102
Cederström, Carl 74, 130, 157
centrelessness 6–7
chain workers 56, 138, 155
charity-fundraising call centres 22,
  124–35
Charlwood, Andy 138
Chaulieu-Montal Tendency
  (Socialisme ou Barbarie) 25,
  26–7, 145, 151
Chiapello, Eve 88
Citroën 43
civil service 125
class composition 30–1, 113, 162–3
class struggle
  capitalists' success in 87, 117, 140
  inquiries and 30–2
  technology and 12
  in the workplace 101–2, 113–14
co-research and co-production 28, 32,
  152
collective acts of resistance 44, 48–9,
  106, 108, 158
Collettivo PrecariAtesia 123–4
computer technology and control
  aggressiveness of 17–18, 43–4, 51,
    64–7, 81–3, 155–6
  computerised Taylorism 49–52
  customers, control of 37
  impact on call centre development
    12–15, 17–18, 94–5
  intensification of labour, use of for
    67, 116
  resistance, role of in 48, 103, 107–9,
    127
conception vs execution 49–50, 66
consumers
  assumed lack of agency of 80
  negative experiences of 6–7, 21–2,
    45–6
  surveillance and enforcement of 37

control 49–52, 93–6
  see also computer technology and
    control; frontier of control;
    management

Davidson, Neil 141
De Angelis, Massimo 85, 87
de-regulation 14
Dehn, Hugh 62
direction (element of control) 93
discipline and punishment 36, 67–8,
  72–80, 82–3, 90–1, 93, 148–50
discretion at work 19
discrimination 9–10, 70–1
division of labour 54
Dollard, Maureen 53
dress codes 36, 149–50

Edwards, Richard 92–3
Ellis, Vaughan 14
emotional dissonance 53–9
emotional labour 2–5, 51–2, 102–3,
  154–5
  see also affective dimension
Engels, Friedrich 12
Esch, Elizabeth 146
ethnographies *see* inquiries
evaluation (element of control) 93
exchange, Marx on 15
execution vs conception 49–50, 66
exploitation 55–7

Fernie, Sue 83
FIAT car factory inquiry 28
films, call centres in 1, 2, 3–4, 9,
  10–11, 152–3
firing of workers 71–2, 82–3, 99, 132,
  135, 148–50
Fischer, Claude S. 12
Fisher, Mark 6–7, 7–8, 90
Fleming, Peter 74, 130, 157
flight attendants 102, 140
Fordism 24, 136, 137, 146
Foucault, Michel 67, 73, 76, 83–4, 137

freelancers, classification of workers
    as 124
frontier of control 2, 33, 72, 94, 101,
    113, 126, 155
    need to redefine 118, 161

general intellect 54–5
Glucksmann, Miriam 16, 18, 20
GoGen charity call centre 22
Goodrich, C. L. 94, 155
Graeber, David 116

Haider, Asad 24, 26
Hardt, Michael 114, 145
Harper, Edward B. 99–100
Harvey, David 86–7
Hayek, Friedrich von 86
Hedges, Nick 97
Hochschild, Arlie 51, 155
Hodson, Randy 101, 112
Holgate, Jane 142
Holman, D. 19
Hotlines call centre inquiry (Kolinko)
    31–2, 120, 124, 152
human resources (HR) 10
humiliation/infantilisation tactics 3,
    8–10, 40, 71, 75–6, 90–1, 125–6
Hyman, Richard 101

ICO (Information Commissioner's
    Office) 5–6
Iles, Anthony 137
indentured servants 99–100
India, call centres in 18, 19
information technology *see* computer
    technology and control
inquiries
    author's
        methodology 32–3, 150–2
        hiring process 34–9
        workday experiences 39–49,
            125–6
        resistance observed 103–12

organising activity experienced
    120–3, 152
    firing process 148–50
    Kolinko's (Germany) 31–2, 120,
        124, 152
    by managers 60–4
Marx and 22–4, 27, 30, 150, 164
    traditional 22–32, 154
International Socialists (Britain) 25
Italian Workerists 27–30, 32, 57–8,
    97–8, 113, 117

James, C. L. R. 145
job insecurity *see* firing of workers;
    precarity
job quality, measurement of 19
Johnson-Forest Tendency 25, 26, 27,
    145–6

Kafka, Franz 6–7
Keynes, John Maynard 116
Kolinko inquiry (Germany) 31–2,
    120, 124, 152

labour
    alienation of 53–9, 88, 137–8
    indeterminacy of 3, 68–9, 92–6
    intensification of 55, 58–9, 69,
        90–2, 116
    subsumption of 56, 93–4
    see also organisation; resistance
laziness 142–3
Lebowitz, Michael 23
Lewig, Kerry 53
liberation management 88
Linheart, Robert 43

management
    affective dimension as challenge for
        8–9, 52–9, 73–80, 89–92, 103,
        154–5
    computerised Taylorism 49–52
    control and 49–52, 93–6

discipline and punishment 36,
    67–8, 72–80, 82–3, 90–1, 93,
    148–50
humiliation/infantilisation tactics 3,
    8–10, 40, 71, 75–6, 90–1, 125–6
media portrayals of 1–11, 51–2, 60,
    152–3
panopticon analogy 80–8, 95–6,
    155–6
power abuses 9–11, 65, 70–2, 157
processes and methods 39–40,
    42–3, 49, 50, 59, 74–80, 154–7
supervisors, role of 67–72, 68,
    84–5, 96
undercover 60–4, 156–7
victimisation of activists 119,
    126–7, 131, 132–4, 143
wages of 20–1
see also surveillance
Marazzi, Christian 55
Marx, Karl
    on alienation 56–7
    on economic compulsion 100
    on exchange 15
    on labour and machines 54
    on technology 12
    workers' inquiries and 22–4, 27, 30,
        150, 164
Marxism
    anti-work and 145–7
    reclaiming of 25–6
    sociology and 28–9
Matheron, Francois 31
McKarthy, Kidd 138
McKinlay, Alan 85
media portrayals of call centres
    The Call Centre (TV show) 1–3,
        5–6, 8–11, 51–2, 60, 152–3
    Wolf of Wall Street, The (film) 1, 2,
        3–4, 9, 10–11, 152–3
meetings
    buzz sessions 40, 69, 74–6, 105–6,
        130–1, 149, 157
    '1-2-1' meetings 43, 77–80, 148,
        149, 157

mental labour 49–50, 52, 55–9, 155
Metcalf, David 83
migrant workers 138
Miliband, Ralph 143
Miller, Toby 63
Mirchandani, Kiran 19
Mitropoulos, Angela 137
Mohandesi, Salar 24, 26
monitoring *see* surveillance
Mulholland, Kate (framework of)
    98–113, 128, 157–60

Negri, Antonio 114, 145
neoliberalism 32–3, 86–8, 136–8, 140,
    161
Ness, Immanuel 94, 143
Nev (Wilshire) 1–3, 5–6, 8–11, 51–2,
    60, 152–3

Office Space (film) 89–90
Ollman, Bertell 54
'1-2-1' meetings 43, 77–80, 148, 149,
    157
Operaismo 145–6, 151, 160
organisation by workers 118–47, 160–2
    in author's inquiry 120–3, 152
    challenges for 118–19, 122–3,
        135–8, 143, 162
    concept of 142–3
    at other call centres 123–35, 161–2
    potential for 140–4, 160–2
    victimisation of activists 119,
        126–7, 131, 132–4, 143
    see also trade unions
outsourcing 17, 18–19

panopticon analogy 80–8, 95–6,
    155–6
part-time work 58
pay
    bonuses 21, 37–8, 39, 69–70, 81, 93
    disputes over 128–9
    for management 20–1
    rates of 37–8

peasants 100
Peter Lafargue, Paul 144–5
piecework pay structures 81
political composition of working class
   31, 113, 162–3
Pollert, Anna 138
post-Fordism 52, 55, 137–8, 155
power, abuses of 9–11, 65, 70 2, 157
precarity
   call centre work as 36, 64, 71–2,
      82–3, 124
   'chain workers' 56, 138, 155
   historical context 137, 163
   marketing of 139
   organisation and 114–15, 124,
      135–6, 143, 163–4
presenteeism 88–9
pressure 39–40, 43, 51, 65, 125, 148–9
privatisation 14, 87, 139
profits, drive for
   role of call centres in 14–15, 32–3
   value extraction and 17–18, 50,
      55–7, 58–9, 103
public *see* consumers
punishment *see* discipline and
   punishment

Rawick, George 98–9
reality shows
   Back to the Floor 62
   Benefits Street 153
   The Call Centre 1–3, 5–6, 8–11,
      51–2, 60, 152–3
   Undercover Boss 62–3
recipients of calls *see* consumers
recording of calls 7, 37, 42–3, 59, 66,
   82–3, 90–1, 95
recruitment
   on *The Call Centre* 9–10
   in inquiry 34–9
refusal of work 21, 110–11, 113–17,
   119, 144–7, 155, 157–60, 163–4
   continuation of after quitting 151,
      152
regulators 5–6

research *see* inquiries
resistance 97–117
   anti-work 145–7, 160
   in author's inquiry 103–12
   collective acts of 44, 48–9, 106, 108,
      158
   computer technology and 48, 103,
      107–9, 127
   concept and forms of 98–103, 163–4
   refusal of work 21, 110–11, 113–17,
      119, 144–7, 155, 157–60, 163–4
      continuation of after quitting
         151, 152
   soldiering 64, 66–7, 92, 158
   by supervisors 70
   trade unions and 161–2
   see also organisation by workers
retail sector 140
retention issues *see* turnover of staff
Rieser, Vittorio 28, 151
Roediger, David 146
Roggero, Gigi 98, 113
Roscigno, Vincent J. 112

scientific management *see* Taylorism
Scorsese, Martin *see* Wolf of Wall
   Street, The
Scott, James C. 100
scripts for calls
   job quality and 19
   role of 49, 59, 66, 93, 96, 103, 154
   use of in author's inquiry 38, 40–2,
      45–6, 48, 49, 73–4, 92, 103
service sectors
   call centres in 16–18
   organisation in 102, 125, 140
sexism 9–10, 70–1
Seymour, Richard 136
Simms, Melanie 142
Slammin' Scammin' Smokin' an' Leavin'
   98–112, 157–60
slavery 146, 160
smile strike 102
smoking areas 128

social value of call centres 95
Socialisme ou Barbarie
    (Chaulieu-Montal Tendency) 25,
    26–7, 145, 151
sociology 28–9
soldiering 64, 66–7, 92, 158
staff turnover *see* turnover of staff
Stalinism 25, 145–6
Standing, Guy 136
Strangleman, Tim 97
strikes 99, 102, 124–35, 139–40
subsumption of workers 56, 93–4
'subterranean stream of resistance'
    100–1, 117, 159
supervisors
  pay of 69–70
  role of 67–72, 68, 84–5, 96
  see also management
surveillance
  affective labour and 52–9
  call recording 7, 37, 42–3, 59, 66,
    82–3, 90–1, 95
  computer technology and 17–18,
    43–4, 49–52, 51, 64–7, 81–3,
    155–6
  continual monitoring 39–40, 42–3,
    50, 81–4, 155–6
  as counterproductive 51, 53
  of customers 37
  to maximise value extraction 17–18
  panopticon analogy 80–8, 95–6,
    155–6
  undercover managers 60–4, 156–7
  see also management

Tartanoğlu, Şafak 103
Taylor, Christopher 145, 146, 147, 160
Taylor, Frederick 29, 63–4, 154
Taylor, Phil, on call centres
  on control 13, 51, 59, 85, 96, 156
  on growth of 14, 50
  on job quality 112, 154
  on organisation 140–1
  on unions 118, 161

Taylorism 9, 27, 49–52, 58–9, 96, 146,
    154
technical composition of working
    class 31, 113
technological development 11–15
  see also computer technology and
    control
telephone, invention of 12–13
telephone preference service 5
temporary nature of jobs *see* firing of
    workers; precarity; turnover of
    staff
Thompson, Paul 93, 119, 139
Trade Union Congress (TUC)
    139–40, 143
trade unions
  inquiries on 26
  limitations of 112, 113, 118–19,
    127–8, 136, 161
  in other service sectors 102, 125,
    140
  potential for 140–4, 161–2
  successes and learnings 131–5
  unionisation attempts 47, 123,
    127–35
  victimisation of activists 119,
    126–7, 131, 132–4, 143
  see also organisation of workers
Tronti, Mario 30, 57, 113, 114
turnover of staff
  as challenge for worker
    organisation 119, 162
  as problem for call centres 21, 39,
    157
  as rejection of work 21, 110–11,
    114–15, 117, 158–60
TV reality shows
  Back to the Floor 62
  Benefits Street 153
  The Call Centre 1–3, 5–6, 8–11,
    51–2, 60, 152–3
  Undercover Boss 62–3

undercover managers 60–4, 156–7
unionateness 118, 141

UNISON, on numbers of call-centre workers 20

van der Linden, Marcel 110–11, 114, 135
victimisation of activists 119, 126–7, 131, 132–4, 143
VoIP (Voice over Internet Protocol) 66

wages *see* pay
Walter, Sally 140
Wilshire, Nev 1–3, 5–6, 8–11, 51–2, 60, 152–3
Wolf of Wall Street, The (film) 1, 2, 3–4, 9, 10–11, 152–3

women
    discrimination and sexism 9–10, 70–1
    precarity and 138
    work to rule 102
    workers' inquiries *see* inquiries
    working class composition 30–1, 113, 162–3
    working hours
        management manipulation of 58–9, 71–2, 105, 106–7, 157
        modern increase in 55, 116
        precarity and 137
        worker manipulation of 107–9, 158

Zerzan, John 144